W9-BMO-350

MORE PRAISE FOR STANDING TALL

"Thank goodness we have someone like Vivian Stringer, someone with the clarity and courage to stand up for what is right. With *Standing Tall,* she has answered the call again; when we most need a story to inspire us, she has given us this extraordinary book."

—MAGIC (EARVIN) JOHNSON

"Vivian Stringer has a great mind and heart and she isn't afraid to show it. She is a true champion and hero, in basketball and in life."

—BILLIE JEAN KING

"The people who most inspired me in the civil rights movement—from Martin Luther King Jr. to Sidney Poitier and Harry Belafonte—were each protégés of the scholar, artist, athlete, and civil rights activist Paul Robeson, and I have long believed that C. Vivian Stringer continues in the proud tradition of this inspiring leader. In *Standing Tall,* Stringer confirms beyond any doubt that she does indeed stand tall in the tradition of Robeson and King, and I am certain that readers will not simply be moved by her story, but that their lives will be touched and changed for the better for reading it."

—ANDREW YOUNG

"C. Vivian Stringer is a woman of amazing principle and strength. On or off the basketball court, and whether coping with the triumphs or the tragedies in life, she is always C. Vivian. I have always admired her genuineness and her unfailing optimism, and now readers can too. *Standing Tall* is a fascinating look into the life of this extraordinary woman.

—PAT HEAD SUMMITT

"In a time of darkness, C. Vivian Stringer stepped forward and led her team—and then the nation. Our country got to see what Coach Stringer's players have seen for more than thirty years: a model of grace and strength for a generation of young women. She has been an inspiration and a role model for me in coaching, and now *Standing Tall* gives us an uncommon glimpse of the woman behind the coach."

—TONY DUNGY

STANDING TALL

A MEMOIR OF TRAGEDY AND TRIUMPH

C. VIVIAN STRINGER

WITH LAURA TUCKER

CROWN PUBLISHERS NEW YORK

Published in the United States by Crown Publishers,
an imprint of the Crown Publishing Group,
a division of Random House, Inc., New York.
www.crownpublishing.com

Library of Congress Cataloging-in-Publication Data
Stringer, C. Vivian.
Standing tall : a memoir of tragedy and triumph /
C. Vivian Stringer with Laura Tucker.—1st ed.
p. cm.
1. Stringer, C. Vivian. 2. Basketball coaches—
United States—Biography. 3. Women basketball
coaches—United States—Biography. I. Tucker,
Laura, 1973– II. Title.
GV884.S765A3 2008
796.323092—dc22
[B] 2007044750

ISBN 978-0-307-40609-5

Printed in the United States of America

Design by Barbara Sturman

10 9 8 7 6 5 4 3 2 1

First Edition

For Bill, my bridge over troubled water, the backbone of our family, my rock.

Our time together was too short, but I thank God for each moment of it. I thank you for your love, devotion, and commitment to our family, and especially for the gift of our children. I see you in them every day—in strong, sensitive, hardworking David; in respectful, mild-mannered, outgoing Justin; and in beautiful Nina, whose smile lights up the whole room.

I know you're watching over them, and that you're as proud of them as I am. This book is dedicated to them and to you.

CONTENTS

Introduction 1

1 Team Together 7

2 The *C* Stands for—Cheerleader? 25

3 You Come in Through the Front Door 37

4 I've Got My Glove Too 57

5 Finding a Way 67

6 To Rise and Give Hope 87

7 A Mother Knows 107

8 Time to Leave 123

9 You Can't Go Home Again, but You Can Get Close 131

10 No Crumbs from the Table 145

11 Dig Deep 161

12 The Best of Times, the Worst of Times 171

13 Lost 183

14 Play Your Way Out 199

15 Do You Know Who We Are? 227

16 Team of Destiny 245

17 *This* Is Who We Are 265

Epilogue: We Stand 283

Acknowledgments 287

You may encounter many defeats, but you must not
be defeated. In fact, it may be necessary to
encounter the defeats, so you can
know who you are, what you
can rise from, how you
can still come
out of it.

MAYA ANGELOU

STANDING TALL

Introduction

Ten minutes.

Ten fouls.

Every time one of my girls moved, an official blew a whistle. Never mind that the players on the other team were much bigger and more aggressive—they had not a single call against them.

Those refs were seeing fouls because of who my girls were, not what they were doing, and my girls knew it. But they didn't say anything, and neither did I.

That might surprise you. But they were prepared. We'd spent countless hours in practice readying ourselves, mentally and physically, for whatever we might encounter, and none of us was willing to concede that the game was in anyone's hands but our own. We would not let them break our spirit.

The onslaught continued, and yet my team never stopped knocking at the door; their courage was magnificent. You see, my young ladies knew that in order to prevail, they needed to think like champions. That means stepping up, no matter what kind of obstacles life puts in front of you. It means digging deep within yourself and finding the will to fight, no matter how many times you get knocked down. Most of all, it means never taking the easy road out.

It means no excuses, no matter what.

I am the last stop before the young women I coach take their place in society, and it is a responsibility I take seriously. My goal is to give them the confidence to dream big and the skills to overcome any challenge they face, whether it's under the basket or in the boardroom. The drills we run in practice may be designed to condition my players' bodies and minds for competition, but for me, there's always a larger prize at stake than any individual win or season. By the time one of my players throws her cap in the air on graduation day, I want her to know that she is a true winner, in every sense of the word.

As much as I love basketball—and I do, as much as anything else in the world—it has always been a vehicle for me to instill values and self-respect in the girls I coach. For thirty years, my mission has been to create the next generation of leaders. As I always say to my teams, "It's more than a game; I'm teaching life lessons here." My hope is that they will come to share my fundamental and unshakable faith: that each and every one of us has the ability to triumph in the face of adversity, to lift ourselves up and succeed, no matter what trials we encounter.

It is a faith that has been tested many times in my own life. Too often, I have been called upon to be strong in the face of great personal tragedy. Ironically, these tragedies have always gone hand in hand with personal or professional triumphs. To have the best moments of my life so interwoven with the worst ones is a strange and painful symmetry.

I have prayed a great deal, and in those prayers, I have asked why these things have happened to me and my family. One answer came during my darkest hour. In 1981, my fourteen-month-old daughter, Nina, lay in the hospital, fighting for her life. A missed diagnosis of spinal meningitis left her brain hopelessly damaged; my happy, dancing baby girl would never walk or talk again.

In those early days, just after she was devastated, I looked to every quarter for comfort and counsel. A priest, passing me in the hospital chapel one night, suggested that perhaps this terrible thing had happened so that I could go on to inspire others, to give them hope.

It spoke to something I already believed. From childhood, I had believed that I had a purpose on this earth: to give hope to those without hope, strength to those whose strength had failed. At the time, the price seemed far too steep. It was not until more than twenty years later, when my own life was in danger, that I truly appreciated what that priest had said, when a woman I had never met reached out to comfort me.

To rise and give hope. Whether by bringing pride to a small, historically black school through basketball excellence or simply by believing in a young woman even after she has stopped believing in herself, I have been able to achieve that purpose in my life. But I believe that the time has come to widen the circle.

In 2007, my team came to the nation's attention when we responded to comments made by radio host Don Imus about us after our participation in the NCAA championship game. Many people were surprised by the intensity of feeling surrounding the debate. I was not. The overwhelming show of support for us in the aftermath of those comments showed me very clearly that Americans are ready for something better than the casual vulgarity and hurtfulness that characterize so much of our culture. My team stood up and spoke out, not just on our own behalf, or on behalf of all female athletes, but for all of us. And people all around the country saw, some for the first time, how—and whom—this kind of thoughtless prejudice hurts.

As Myles Brand, the head of the NCAA, pointed out, we became part of a great tradition of athletes who helped shake America out of its complacency, who set an example in the eyes of the world. When Jesse Owens sped past Hitler in the stands to take four gold medals at the 1936 Olympics in Berlin, he didn't just make America proud; he showed Hitler's ideas of racial superiority for the dangerous nonsense they were. When Joe Louis fought Max Schmeling in 1938, he was there as an American, not a black athlete. But he *was* a black man, and when President Roosevelt told him, "Joe, we need muscles like yours to beat Germany," he was putting the hopes of the whole country in the hands of a black man—and that sent a message to the world. When the Brown Bomber beat Schmeling, it felt like more than a fight; it felt like a country united against all the prejudice in the world.

They say that God never gives you a burden you can't bear, and maybe that's true, but I know that there have been plenty of days when I have not been able to see my way forward, days where I have thought, *I cannot lift my head and go on.* But I know that it has *always* been better for me to pick up that burden, no matter how heavy, and to carry it to the very best of my abilities.

You have to stay true to yourself and to what you believe. The minute you allow disappointment or tragedy to stop you in your tracks, you have stolen something from yourself, something more precious than you can even imagine: your dreams.

It is through overcoming that we understand what we are capable of; it is only after we have been tested that we can go on to offer comfort to others. My dream for the young ladies I coach is that they never measure themselves with someone else's yardstick, or simply by wins and losses. I would like them to know that real success is achieved when you set your own worth, fulfill your own destiny, and stand up for what you know to be right. And I want these young women, the leaders of tomorrow, to go forth and multiply: what we have learned, we now must teach.

1

Team Together

"Tell us something we don't know about you."

Every year, I give my teams the same icebreaker: at the end of every dinner, one player is chosen to stand up and share. The challenge comes when it's time for me to stand up. Like everything else, I see it as an opportunity to coach. If practices have been tough, I'll tell them something that will give them a good laugh. But during the 2005–2006 season, there was something else on my mind.

In the first days of 2006, the whole country stood by and waited for word on thirteen men trapped deep underground after an explosion in a coal mine in Sago, West Virginia. Prayers for those men came from all around the world, but I felt a special kinship with those families. You see, I grew up watching my father go down into the mines of Pennsylvania every day of his working life, and I prayed each and every night for his safe return. I know, as everyone who grew up in a mining town does, what it feels like to hear that siren rip through town. I know what it feels like to see my own panic reflected on every face I pass. I know what it feels like to run into the fire hall, asking, "What shift was down there?" And I know what it feels like to wait.

So one night, I stood up after dinner and said, "I ask a lot of you, especially in terms of discipline and hard work. You come out of practice banged up and sore, and if I don't feel that you're being as aggressive as you can be, I'll push you some more. But you know I never ask you for anything in the hard-work department that I don't give myself.

"My father loved music more than almost anything in the world. He was invited to record and tour with some of the best jazz musicians in the world at the time, but he didn't believe that a career in music could give our family a stable life. So he crouched in the wet, dark corridors of the mine, knowing that a metal bucket hitting a wall ten miles away could cause a spark, trapping him and the men he worked with. In the middle of August, he'd go to work dressed like it was twenty degrees below zero, because miles under the earth it felt like the dead of winter. And at the end of his eight-hour shift, he had nothing but a paycheck to show for it. No glory, no trophies, just a hacking cough that sent up black phlegm—and money to put food on our table.

"My father worked hard with his back bent over, miles underneath the ground. We get to stay in the light. When I fall asleep with *X*s and *O*s running through my brain, I feel like the luckiest woman alive, and I want you to know how lucky you are, too. Basketball may be the greatest game there is, but it's *more* than a game—it's a reflection of life's lessons. What you learn on the court will take you everywhere you need to go. That's why I don't mind the work we have to do to be the best, and why I push you so hard to show me the purest effort you've got."

I could tell by the looks on the faces around the table that I had told my team something they hadn't known about me. People often ask me where I get my drive, my work ethic, my discipline, and the ability to go on under circumstances that might stop someone else. When they ask, I see the faces of my parents—as I do whenever I am up against a challenge.

I'm the eldest of the six Stoner kids. We were an extremely close, tight-knit family, growing up in the extremely close, tight-knit community of Edenborn, Pennsylvania, a town so tiny that it's not on most maps. In the fifties, when I was growing up, there was one paved street in Edenborn, along with four side streets, three churches, two taverns, and about five hundred people. That's it. There wasn't even a stoplight. In rural Pennsylvania, they call places like Palmer and Gates and Leckron and Edenborn "patches."

I'll never know how my parents did such a great job of making us feel special. They never burdened us with the everyday problems of their lives—the bills they had to pay or the decisions they had to make. And because they did such a good job of pinching pennies, we were never hungry. We'd get day-old bread and packaged cakes and cookies from the thrift store, but it didn't matter to us; we just knew that the day my dad got paid, we'd have cookies with fresh milk from a nearby farm.

It might sound funny, but, growing up, I didn't know that we were poor. We had each other, and that was all that mattered. Of course, I heard my parents talking; I knew that we went to a certain store because a can of condensed milk was a few cents cheaper there than at another. I could tell that money was tight when the miners were on strike, because we ate powdered eggs, corned beef, and pork and gravy from a can. And sometimes, when the week was especially tight, my brothers and sisters and I would walk to the slate dump near the elementary school and dig for coal to fill the furnace. But I didn't really understand the economic situation we were in until I left the area and heard what people say about the coal-mining towns of Appalachia. Apparently, the rest of the world knew I was poor, but I didn't!

The truth is, we were rich in our souls, and we wouldn't have been happier if we'd lived in a palace. When I think of my childhood, I immediately think of the music. Every Sunday afternoon, my father, Buddy, would sit down at his organ and play for hours, lost in his own world. I loved seeing him getting ready to play jazz at the Crawford Grill in Pittsburgh on a Friday or Saturday night. Most miners have permanent black lines under their nails, but when it came time to play, my father would sit there with a hard wooden brush and 20 Mule Team Borax soap and work until his hands were immaculate.

Sometimes my mother would go to the club to see him play, and we were so happy to see them go off together! Everyone called her Bird. She was so young and beautiful; she liked pretty things, and they looked great on her. Everything always matched, and she wore high heels so gracefully. And my father was so handsome in his starched shirt and white pocket handkerchief, his shoes shined to a mirror finish, his suit with not a wrinkle in it. We thought they'd live forever.

My dad didn't go to church but once every three years; when he did, *everybody* understood that Buddy Stoner had been there. He'd give his own rendering of a church song and he'd bring the house down. I was always so proud. But everyone in the community would come around our house for the music, late on Sunday afternoons. We had an organ, a piano, a trombone, a flute, a xylophone, and a saxophone. The whole family participated in those Sunday-afternoon sessions; if you were too little to play an instrument, you'd use a stick to bang on a bucket or a jar full of marbles to help the rhythm section. We used a big soup pot as a bongo drum, and we'd beat out the bass on an old galvanized wash tub, the same one my mom scrubbed clothes in and where the little ones took their baths. People would come and sit on the porch—and on the neighbors' porches—to listen. If they could play, they'd bring their guitar or their sax and join in, and if they could sing, they sang.

Sometimes the professional musicians whom my dad played with at the club would stop by. He played the organ and loved the music of Richard "Groove" Holmes and Jimmy Smith. There would be food and cold sodas, and people would stay late into the night. Those nights were really special, and to this day, nothing soothes and transports me like music. Music is a gift my parents gave all of us, a gift that has lasted our whole lives. I can't think of a better way to spend an evening than in a jazz club with my sons, and when my brother Tim comes to visit, you'll often find us sitting up to all hours of the night, just listening to the sounds coming out of the speakers. And I never hear Ray Charles's "Drown in My Own Tears" without thinking about my dad.

Nothing was more important to my parents than family unity. We sat down and ate dinner together every single night of our lives. My brothers and sisters and I really enjoyed spending time together. There were six of us, so there was always someone to talk to. We had lots of friends, but we never slept over at their houses, and when we played with them, we always had one of our siblings by our side.

When we were a little older, we'd fill a shopping bag with popcorn, make a jug of Kool-Aid, and go to the outdoor drive-in. We loved the smell of the popcorn and the hot dogs from the concession stand, but we didn't have the money to pay for something we could bring from home. I saw *Guess Who's Coming to Dinner* and *The Graduate* from the hood of our car, as well as more monster movies than I could count. Sometimes we'd see a couple necking and we'd interrupt them by pretending to get into the wrong car; we thought that was just the funniest thing imaginable. Nobody could make me laugh like my sisters and brothers could, something that's true to this day.

My dad always told us, "The clothes don't make the man; it's the man that makes the clothes!" but my mom knew how important it was for us to look and feel good about ourselves, especially the girls. She understood about a purse matching a dress, and she always made sure we had nice new outfits each Easter and Christmas, even if she had to work an extra job to afford them. It was important to her that we were strong and that we understood the consequences of things, just as it was for my dad, but she would plead our case if she thought he was being too hard on us. And she'd usually find a way to slip a dollar or two into our pockets, because she felt that a young lady should always be in the position to make a phone call or buy herself her own soda.

My father's policy was to buy you what you needed—once. Tim and Verna were better at holding on to their personal belongings than I was; I never got through the winter without losing a mitten, so I'd put a sock over one hand to keep it warm, and hide that hand in my pocket until I got to school.

We always got together to buy something special to celebrate my parents' birthdays. We never talked about who had put in five cents or five dollars; those gifts came from all of us. After I started working after school, we could afford something a little better, and that year we all chipped in to get my dad a Helbros watch.

My sister Verna always slept late, but we were so excited to give him his present that we couldn't wait for her to wake up. As soon as Dad was sitting with his coffee at the kitchen table, the rest of us gathered around and gave him the box. He was so surprised and happy; he just loved it.

An hour later, we heard Verna getting dressed upstairs and decided to play a joke on her. We grabbed the gift, rewrapped it, and told Verna that she should be the one to give it to Dad. He had a nickname for everyone and often he'd call you the exact opposite of what you were. Sure enough, when she solemnly presented the watch to him, Dad just looked at her and said, "You're a little late, aren't you, Zip?"

She realized she'd been had, and the rest of us died laughing. After that, on birthdays, Verna would be the first one down.

My brothers and sisters are still the people I let in when I want to shut out the rest of the world, the ones who know what's behind my professional persona. They help connect my past to my present. No matter what hits I have taken in my life, my family has always been there to make sure that I wouldn't fall. I could never have been successful without their support, and sometimes I think that I couldn't have survived without it.

That closeness is something I've tried to replicate with my teams. I want them to play with and *for* one another; even if a girl doesn't have the self-respect or discipline to go that extra mile for herself, she'll do it out of respect for the girl next to her. Whether she's a starter or someone who plays half an hour all year, I'll make her feel like she's part of something important, and she'll look within to find whatever she can give to make it better.

My parents believed in hard work, and my mother was, and is, a meticulous housekeeper. Every one of us, no matter how young, had a list of chores, from washing the dishes to sweeping the floors to raking the yard. We banked the furnace every night, so it would be a little cooler when we slept. You had to shake the ashes down and then cover the fire without smothering it. You didn't want to do that halfway; if you were careless, everyone would wake up cold. Everything was always scrubbed spotless and in its place; we couldn't afford steel wool pads, so my father would gather ashes from our coal furnace for us to scour the pots and pans.

A master manipulator, my mother could get anyone to do anything. You can buy all the books you want about managing people, but my mom was born knowing everything there was to know about getting people excited to work for her. We used to tease her, asking her if she'd had six kids just to make sure she'd have a clean house. The only way you could get out of helping was by doing something cultural or educational; for instance, you didn't have to wash breakfast dishes if there was a play rehearsal before school. I hated housework so much, I was in every band, choir, and play at our school.

To make sure we were all toeing the line, my parents held a family meeting every Sunday, right after church. We went over our grades, our extracurricular activities, our chores, and the way we'd been treating one another. Although my father ran the meeting, we all had an opportunity to ask questions and clear the air about perceived injustices. If we were having problems with one another, my parents helped us to iron them out. If a punishment was in order, my father always asked what we thought would be appropriate. My parents made the final decisions about everything, but we always felt that we had a say.

Being the oldest, I always went first. My parents made it clear that I had a position of special responsibility. "Your brothers and sisters look to you to know what to do, and how to act," they'd tell me. That was the price you paid for the privilege of having everyone look up to you: you had to do the right thing.

After me, Verna would go, and then Tim, Madeline, Richelle (whom we have always called Ricky), and finally, Jack, the youngest. By the time we got to Jack, my dad would always say, "Well, Jackson, what do you have to say for yourself? 'Cause it looks to me like there's nobody for you to talk about except the dog." Poor Jack's eyes would be big, because by that point, everyone ahead of him had accused him of something.

The meetings I hold with my teams are very much like the

ones my father held when I was growing up. It's good to be able to talk frankly about what's going right and what could be better, and for the freshmen to feel as comfortable talking as the seniors do. "Team together," I always say, and I learned that from my family. Nobody felt more important than anyone else in my family, and I want everyone to understand that we're all equal in the family that is our team. Everyone is entitled to an opinion, if she has worked hard and done the best she can possibly do; you don't have to be the person who scores the most in order to speak. From the manager to the practice player to the all-star, everyone has a role to play and a responsibility to give what they can for the sake of the others. In order for us to rise to the highest level, to taste that rare air, each one of us must do our part.

We were sheltered from a lot of the pressures and injustices out there in the world, not just by my parents, but by the community we lived in. Coal miners are a breed apart, because they need to be. When your life and safety depend on the man next to you, the color of his skin or what church he goes to ends up mattering much less than what kind of a man he is. You aren't black or white, Christian or Jewish—you're a miner.

We had every nationality under the sun in Edenborn, and my father was respected by everyone, white or black. He would often go across the street on a Sunday evening to have a glass of homemade wine with Mr. Tiberi, who was Italian, and no one thought anything about it. Everyone in our community cared about one another so deeply that it didn't seem unusual for a black man to sit down with a white one for a drink and a neighborly chat.

My parents always taught my brothers and sisters and me never to think of ourselves as "less than." They told us that if we worked hard, didn't look for excuses, and never gave up, we could do whatever we wanted to do, and become whatever we wanted to be. We were always told to sit at the head of the table and accept no crumbs from the floor.

I believed them; I dreamt about faraway places. I could see myself playing Beethoven's "Moonlight Sonata" on the stage of a great concert hall in Vienna, taking a bow afterward to wild applause. I could see myself reading a jury's verdict in my judge's robes; all would stand as I changed the laws of the land and the social consciousness of the world. I imagined taking my victory lap at the Olympics, cameras flashing as I bowed my head to accept the gold medal. I'm not sure how many young girls were encouraged to hope and dream like I was, especially in the 1950s, and I credit that dreaming with a great deal.

As I was to learn, though, it's not enough to have a dream. You have to know the price of your dreams, and you have to pay that price. My piano teacher, Mrs. Everett, would come to our house every Saturday to teach me Mozart, Chopin, and Bach. I took the lessons, but my parents were wasting their money, because I was busy not practicing Monday through Friday. I loved the idea of playing jazz in a nightclub like my dad, but I didn't like running scales; I liked to improvise, to go where the music took me.

But when I was a junior in high school, I came to realize why my father had always emphasized the fundamentals. Mr. Tokish announced auditions for the cantata, our school's annual musical theater production. I wanted to play the piano music for that show more than anything in the world. Anyone could sing in the chorus, but the person selected to accompany the singers was going to feel pretty special, and I wanted to be that person.

Auditions for the cantata were held in the school auditorium. There were only two people auditioning for the part of accompanist: me and a friend, an excellent student by the name of Carla Daruda.

I went first. I sat down at the piano, which was in front of the stage, and Mr. Tokish opened an enormous book of music to the piece we'd be playing. I was not a good sight reader, and as soon as I took a look at the sheet of notes in front of me, I knew I was in real trouble. The sheet was black with sharps and flats, and I could see that the piece changed keys a number of times.

I didn't have time to panic. Mr. Tokish counted, "And a-one, and a-two, one-two-three-four," and I started playing. It was rough going, and I stumbled my way through; I could tell that it didn't sound great. But I still thought I had a chance; after all, I'd have lots of time to practice it before the show, and when the time came to perform, every note would be perfect.

But then my friend Carla sat down. She looked up at Mr. Tokish as he counted off the intro, and then she put her hands on the keys and started to play. She'd never seen the piece before either, but you'd never know that she hadn't been practicing it every day from the way the music sounded. The music just flowed from her fingers, pure and clean and clear, with such expressiveness and beauty that everybody stood still and listened. Carla played the entire piece through without a single mistake, and by the time she was finished, it was obvious to everyone in that room that Carla would be the pianist for that year's cantata.

I thought to myself, *Well, Vivian, that's pretty clear, isn't it? You can't, and she can. Why? You didn't practice; you didn't do what you needed to do.* I realized then that if I had paid attention to the lessons my parents had scrimped and saved for, I might have been up to the challenge.

I might have fantasized about the standing ovation I'd get on the concert stage, but you need *passion* to do the work it takes to succeed. I see the same thing in my players sometimes: they see the victory lap very clearly, but they're not willing to do the work it will take to get them there. Sometimes it takes a humiliating defeat—or a series of defeats—for them to get serious.

When you really want something, you're willing to pay the price. My parents stopped paying for my piano lessons, so I got a job selling clothes on the second floor of Moss's supermarket so that I could pay for lessons myself. (My mom got me that job. She went to see Mr. Moss and pointed out that although there were a lot of minorities shopping at Moss's, there weren't any minorities working there, and why did he think that was?)

I ended up accompanying the choir with a few songs at our senior graduation. I can feel, to this day, the pride I felt when they announced that the Germantownship senior choir would sing "Climb Every Mountain," accompanied on the piano by Vivian Stoner.

In a small community like Edenborn, your name meant something. Even if you were meeting someone for the first time, they knew something about you. "You're Buddy Stoner's kid? He was a smart boy; I remember when he was captain of the football team, and your aunt Stella was president of her class. You make them proud, you hear?" And so you did.

"Do you know who you are?" my father used to ask us. "Do you know what that means?" Our name was a badge of honor, and it went before us. "The Stoners do well in school. They pay attention, they work hard, and they bring home good grades, and this family is going to continue that tradition."

My parents didn't settle for anything less than excellence, so neither did we. Every child in the community memorized a poem or an essay to present at church during the holidays; it was called the Christmas speech. Some would get up there and freeze, or forget the words, or lose the rhythm, but not the Stoner kids. My father made sure that we went through those poems again and again. We practiced everything: our entrance, the bow or curtsy we'd make, making eye contact with the audience. We were so well rehearsed that we usually ended up knowing all of our brothers' and sisters' poems as well as our own. We'd try to fake out one another during the tricky passages, staring at our siblings and willing them to crack up or forget the words, but it never happened. The honor of our family name rested on the fact that we never stumbled.

This is going to sound funny, but when we learned that my sister needed to start wearing glasses, I felt embarrassed, as if she'd let us down. Isn't that something? Having poor eyesight seemed like a sign of weakness, an indication that the Stoners were less than perfect. It goes to show you how much pride we had in our family.

When you grow up in a place like Edenborn, where everybody knows everybody, you can pretty much forget about getting away with anything at all! One of our neighbors, Ms. Annette Poole, had grapevines in her yard, and one day on my way home from school, I found occasion to cut through and snag myself some of her good grapes. By the time I got home, Ms. Annette had already been on the phone with my mother. Another time, just after I got my driver's license, I passed a school bus at the top of the hill, down the street from my house. I don't know how in the world I thought I was going to get away with that, but I can tell you that I didn't. By the time I walked in the door, not five minutes later, our neighbor Mr. Ware had already been on the phone to my house. "You're done," my dad said, his palm out for my keys.

It went both ways: when you did something right, it seemed like the whole town was proud of you. One of the first awards I ever got was Pennsylvania State Conference Coach of the Year. I was twenty-four years old, and the ceremony was at the state capitol in Harrisburg, Pennsylvania. Mr. Ware organized a couple of vans, so when I walked out onto that floor, surrounded by all that granite, there was a row of people from my hometown, applauding: "There's our V.I.!" (My nickname, pronounced Vee-Eye.) Many of them had never traveled outside of a twenty-five- or fifty-mile radius of Edenborn before, but they came to clap for me. I felt as much pride in them as they did in me. Their only claim to fame was to have worked hard and protected one another, but I felt like people saw how special our little town was that day.

Today it's much harder to have a sense of your family's place in a community. In Edenborn, you knew who your neighbors were, and it was very important that they thought well of you. Not in a "keeping up with the Joneses" kind of way, because none of us had enough of anything to worry about fancy cars or stylish clothes or anything like that. (I remember being served Ritz crackers and cream cheese at someone's house and thinking it meant they were rich.) But it was important to represent our family honorably, and we knew that people were looking out to make sure that we did. We might have chafed under the scrutiny, but there was a comfort in knowing that people were looking out for us, too.

That's not to say that we were perfect. One New Year's Eve when I was about seventeen, my mom went with my dad to hear him play music, and my friends Randy, Raymond, Lionel, and Chuckie came over. We sat down with Verna to figure out what we could do. I was responsible for the younger kids, so we needed to find something we could do around our house. One of us came up with an idea: we'd cut down Mr. Metro's Christmas tree. Mr. Metro was our neighbor across the street, known in the community for the accordion polkas you could hear coming out of his house on Sunday mornings. He had a massive pine tree in his yard, almost as tall as the house itself.

We thought the whole thing would be hilarious. Every New Year's Eve, Mr. Metro would come outside and shoot off his rifle to ring in the New Year. Imagine the look on his face when he came out and saw that tree in the street! So we got our lanterns, flashlights, and the saw and got busy. As we started to saw, the lights went on in the Metro house and we could hear Mr. Metro yelling in his Polish accent: "Who there? Who go down there?" I think he'd gotten a little toasted, so he wasn't coming out. We stopped, putting our hands over our mouths to cover the laughter, but as soon as he left the window, we started sawing again.

That tree finally fell, right across the only street in and out of Edenborn. The noise was fearsome, even though it landed on a huge pile of snow. I don't think I've laughed that hard since. Lights went on in all the houses; Mr. Metro was hysterical, crying and yelling from his window, and Mrs. Tiberi could be heard yelling, "What the devil did they do?" in her heavy Italian accent. We scattered and ran, of course, but my brother Timmy, stuck inside with the little kids, turned the outdoor floodlight on so everyone could see which house we were running back to.

I remember sitting in our kitchen, laughing until our stomachs ached. Needless to say, I did not have any idea how much trouble we were in.

The next morning, we were all getting ready to go to church when my father called us into a line. "It took me about an hour to get into Edenborn last night; seems there's a tree lying right down the middle of Main Street, and I had to go all the way around. Any of you know anything about that tree?"

Nope, no sir. We didn't know anything about that tree. "You know, that tree, it took a couple of hundred years to grow," my dad said. I felt a little sick—I hadn't known anything about that—but, of course, I couldn't act like I felt anything at all.

He said, "Well, they'll get to the bottom of it soon enough. The police are getting involved. I was down at the firehouse and the Belkos saw who did it. They're sending the state police down to the school. You sure you kids don't know anything?" I couldn't tell if he was bluffing or not. My sisters and brothers always looked to me for direction, and I was shaking my head no. "No, Dad, we don't know anything about that."

"Well," he said, "I sure hope none of the kids involved wanted to go to college, because that won't be happening now. In the meantime, I'm going to have Mrs. Tiberi come over to do a lineup. She saw whoever it was running into this house, and I want to make sure she doesn't recognize any of you."

Trust me, I made sure my brothers and sisters knew to keep their mouths closed once we were called onto the carpet. "She can't prove anything," I told them.

My father lined us up against the wall, pointed to me, and asked Mrs. Tiberi: "Was V.I. one of the kids you saw running into our house from the street?" I looked at her while she answered in her heavy, singsong accent. "Oh, no. Vivian is a good girl, a polite girl. She always say hello to me on the street. She play the piano. No, Vivian is a good girl."

Was it Verna? "Verna! Oh, no. She's a good girl. She study hard."

My father pointed to Tim. "Tito. No, no, he's a good boy. He plays the horn; he takes the garbage out. He's a good boy—like you, Buddy."

By this point, she's down to Madeline and Ricky, who were clearly much too small to have had anything to do with it. She shook her head. "Madelina. I don't know about her. We talk about her. Maybe it was Madelina." Madeline started crying and carrying on. "I don't know anything about this!!! It wasn't me!" Then Mrs. Tiberi looked at Ricky, who wasn't more than seven or eight and hadn't even been there. She stopped and thought, and then began nodding her head. "Yes, Buddy. I think I recognize that-a one. Yes, I think it was Ricky; she was the one."

It didn't take a minute for Ricky to start jumping up and down, her voice high: "It wasn't me! It was V.I. and Verna! They did it! I didn't do anything!"

They pressured the little one, and the little one ended up caving.

It was funny the way they did it, but we were in trouble for months. I honestly thought my chance at a college education was ruined. Most of all, we had hurt Mr. Metro. My dad walked us over to apologize in person. We'd just been playing, but he genuinely loved that tree.

I think of that tree caper sometimes, when one of my children or one of my players has made a mistake. We were all good kids. We hadn't meant to hurt anybody, or to destroy something that had taken hundreds of years to grow. We were mischievous and thoughtless, not malicious; it never occurred to us that we were causing real harm. That's something that has been good for me to remember over the years.

Late one night, when I was in high school, my father was driving back from playing jazz at a club in Pittsburgh, hauling his organ behind the car in a trailer. We couldn't afford a new car, which meant he rarely got home without having to raise the hood. This one cold night, the gas can fell on my father's toe and cut it, but he didn't feel anything until he got home. I watched him and my mother bandage it and cut a hole in his shoe so that it would be more comfortable, but that toe never healed, and it soon became clear that it was a much bigger problem.

Eventually, the doctor had to amputate the toe, and then the foot on that side, and then the leg just below the kneecap. Ultimately, he lost both of his legs up to the knees. They never did figure out what was wrong with him; some of the doctors I talked to years later thought it might have been a circulatory disorder called Buerger's disease. The fact is, coal mining is hard on the body. One of my father's doctors said that he looked like a twenty-five-year-old outside, but his arteries were that of a ninety-year-old man.

Dad learned to walk again using his prosthetic legs at the Harmerville Rehabilitation Center, which was located about fifty miles north of Pittsburgh. Tim would travel after school to pick him up on Friday afternoons so Dad could spend the weekend at home, but Tim was the star quarterback on the football team, so they'd have to hurry back to make his games.

Even with all his health problems, my father didn't take the easy way out. Before he got sick, he'd had perfect attendance at his job in the mine. After he lost his legs, he could easily have sat back and collected disability. But he didn't take a day more than he needed. Instead, he had our beat-up car fitted with hand controls so he could drive himself to a job in the mine office.

I never once heard him complain, though many times I would wake up in the middle of the night to hear muffled moaning coming through the walls; my father lived with great pain. But he never talked about the hurt or the inconvenience in front of us kids. He never wanted us to think that he couldn't handle it. In the morning, he would slide down the stairs, sit at the table, and put on his prosthetic legs, cracking jokes as if he'd slept like a baby. When people in the community would ask him how he was, he'd always laugh and say, "I'm kicking, but not too high."

My father's example inspires me every day of my life, and I use it to inspire my players. He went back to work at the coal mine even after losing both of his legs, so you can imagine how I feel when I hear some gifted nineteen-year-old at the peak of her physical condition tell me that she "can't" do this or do that!

Can't wasn't a word in my father's vocabulary, and it's not one in mine. All things are possible as long as you've got breath in your body, as I tell my players. I would have done anything for my father to have had his legs back again; I would have been glad to sit up on a mountaintop and never mix with life again. That's why during practice, you'll often hear me say, "You have all these God-given talents, and the chance at a world-class education, and all you have to do is give everything you can to a sport you love. If this is what you want, how can you look me in the face and say 'I can't'?"

No, I don't have much tolerance for "I can't."

2

The *C* Stands for— Cheerleader?

When we weren't doing housework, the six Stoner kids were always outside, riding our bikes in the summer, sledding in the winter. To this day, I can't smell leaves burning without wanting a football in my hands. I would wake up every morning, eat a bowl of Wheaties, drink a glass of milk, and then run around the neighborhood, sure that I was the next Wilma Rudolph. I'm sure the neighbors thought I had lost my mind.

I loved using my body, and I loved every sport imaginable. Especially basketball.

I'd hear the kids outside, bouncing the ball and yelling for me, and I couldn't get down the stairs fast enough. Of course I couldn't leave until my chores were done, and my mother saw a golden opportunity to get some work done. The boys would help me out in order to get me onto the court faster; my mother, sweet as could be, treated them like her own personal army.

"Ronald, as long as you're here, would you use those big strong arms to clear these chairs out of here so we can really get this floor clean? Get lots of soapy water, too, sweetheart." She had the nicest way of correcting you, too. "Wait, wait, wait a minute, hon—let's lay that dishcloth out flat so it dries nice and evenly for Bird."

"Yes, Miz Stoner," they'd say, and these hulking teenage boys would meekly follow my tiny mother around, washing dishes and sweeping the porch. She was generous with her thanks and compliments, and, even though they'd look away and pretend not to hear, it pleased them. It's human nature to enjoy a kind word, and she always seemed to make you wonder what more you could do. It was from my mother that I learned how powerful a positive word can be.

By the time we were ready to play, the boys had dishpan hands, and my mother's whole house was sparkling. That night, their mothers would be on the phone with my mother in complete disbelief. "Doggone it! I can't make him lift a hand to help at home—how in the world did you get my Ronald to take out your trash?"

I was often the captain of the teams we put together, and always one of the first to be chosen when I wasn't. A girl named Arlene Gary lived down at the other end of Edenborn, site of the one little basketball court in town, and she was a very talented basketball player, too. Arlene was a much bigger girl than I was, and she could hit a softball so hard it was something to see. We picked who would play, and we called the shots; it was an unusual situation, now that I think of it.

There were terrible potholes on the court, and the balls we played with often had bubbles in them. You had to have *good* hand-eye coordination; between the holes and the bubbles, there was no predicting where that ball was going to come up. I'd squat and draw the play in the dirt: "Bobby, I need you to set a hard screen for Teapot, who's going to take the shot at the top of the key. Raymond, you need to rebound. This is our game-winner." Then they'd do it! I didn't know it at the time, but I was already coaching.

When we played football, we played this game called "Dare I," which boiled down to the person with the ball against everyone else on the field. We'd just drop the ball in the middle of a crowd, and someone had to have enough courage to grab it and run past everyone else to the goal line. If there were twenty of us, it was the one with the ball against the other nineteen! Trust me, you figure out some offensive moves fast when everyone else is trying to take what you have. It tested your willingness to get hurt, that was for sure.

When I was in charge of taking care of my younger sisters and brothers, we'd change the game to kickball so they could play. It always felt like Tim would wait until I was on second base to tell me he had to go to the bathroom. Nobody wanted my sister Verna to play because she was left-handed and kind of awkward—we always used to tell her she played like a girl—but the rule in our house was all for one and one for all. My parents would say, "Your sister can't play? Guess what? You can't play either." So I got her into all the games.

To be honest, we also wanted her ball. Verna, always smart and careful, saved her money, so she always had a new ball, while the rest of ours were busted up and worn. We had to be careful with Verna; if we got on her case too much, she'd threaten to take her good ball home.

The pickup games I played on that broken-down court behind the elementary school was some of the most enjoyable basketball I ever played in my life, and for a long time, it looked like they were as close as I was going to get to the game. There were no girls' teams in our school, and there were certainly no girls playing on any of the boys' teams. I just wanted to play, and Sunday through Thursday I did. But when Friday and Saturday came, the boys could put on their uniforms and represent their school, while I was stuck on the sidelines.

That still hurts me. I believe that each person should be given an opportunity to succeed or fail; every one of us has the right to pursue happiness and fulfillment in all that we do. When someone is denied that, it hurts all of us. Although the injustice of being forced to stay on the sidelines still rankles, I find comfort in knowing that while I may not have gotten a chance to play, I can now coach—and offer a scholarship—to someone who can.

It wasn't just at school where I felt the sting of being treated like a girl. Once I hit eleven or twelve, adults started talking to me about what girls do and what they don't do, and a lot of them thought girls didn't have any place playing sports. It didn't matter—I put my shorts into a paper bag so the neighbors wouldn't know that I was going to play basketball after church.

My friend Lorraine's grandmother told her she'd get knots in her legs from playing sports. Once we were playing badminton over a clothesline and her grandma chased her home with a switch. But Lorraine was incredibly talented; I think she could have turned into an Olympic-caliber track athlete. We'd walk back from church and the boys—boys who would later go on to become all-state football players—would bet her a box of vanilla wafers that they could beat her in a foot race. Lorraine would go behind the church and pull off her shoes and stockings, and then come back to leave those guys in the dust—in a dress and bare feet. She was so fast! We'd walk off with those cookies and laugh.

When a scout from West Virginia University came to our high school to ask Lorraine to consider a track scholarship, her grandmother wouldn't hear of it. In the end, she didn't attend university at all. It still makes me sad to think of it—what a waste of a great talent, and of an opportunity for an education.

I loved to play with the boys but hated it when my mom called me a tomboy. What did liking sports have to do with being a boy, or looking like one? I would get muddy like everyone else, but as soon as I was finished with the game, I would shower, change my clothes, and put on some jewelry. I didn't want to be a tomboy; I just wanted to be a girl who played sports.

When I was out there, it felt like there was nothing else in the world except the opportunity to play. I've seen plenty of parents who have to push their kids to participate in sports, but mine never did. With basketball, I was always willing to do the work I wasn't willing to do with music—the mastery of basic skills, the repetitive drills, the setting of new goals for myself when I'd conquered something. Once I heard the sound of the boys running to play ball, nothing could keep me inside practicing my scales, but I would practice shooting until there was no more light. Maybe it was easier to do the work because it never felt like work to me.

I wonder to this day why I feel so happy and right when I walk into a gym and hear the sound of sneakers. I love that sound more than anything in the world. I always say that I'll know it's time to quit the day I don't feel my heart race when I hear it; I'll know the light has burnt out and it's time to go. I'd have to—the kids you're coaching need to feel your enthusiasm, your passion, your drive. But I don't see that happening anytime soon.

I will tell you something about me that has stayed true since those days: I always just wanted to *play*. There were kids who would take twenty minutes to fight about whose foot the ball had touched before it went out of bounds. I hated that. The game is so pure and so beautiful to me; I've never understood why you have to make it ugly with a stupid argument. Playing for the sake of playing was enough for me.

To this day, it's just not in me to fight about possession. I know it sounds like a crazy position for a basketball coach to take, and it sometimes drives my kids and my assistant coaches crazy when we scrimmage in practice. It's not that I don't want to compete—

I *always* compete. And believe me, it's not that I don't want to win; I want to win. I just don't want to take twenty minutes to argue about possession. I'd rather give you five points and then make it my business to beat you anyway; I know I'm good enough to make them up.

The boys never cut me a break when we played, and I wasn't looking for one, but those days couldn't last forever.

Late one Sunday afternoon, we were playing tackle football. I was quick, so the guys would form a wedge and I'd dart in and out. It was our last play before going home, and I had the ball. The boys had blocked for me, and I was weaving and dancing, making those moves like I was on television. Then, out of nowhere, my next-door neighbor Bobby left his feet and took a flying dive at me, and I just went down—*bam*.

He caught me from my blind side; I never saw him. But I can still feel the sheer force of his body hitting mine; I had never felt anything so hard or so heavy. I saw lights and just lay there, the wind knocked out of me, gasping and trying to take a breath for what felt like an eternity. Everybody gathered around me, asking whether I was okay. They were stunned that I wasn't joking and bouncing back up, as I usually did. As hurt as I was, I looked up at those boys and almost cried for them, because I never saw people look so scared.

My mother had always worried about me; she used to tell my father, "Buddy, Vivian has got to stop playing with those boys. Their bones are bigger and heavier, and they're going to hurt her, even if they don't mean to." He always told her, "Don't worry about the girl, Thelma. When it's time to stop, she'll know."

He was right. That tackle was the defining moment; that day, I knew it had to end. I was quick and my reactions were there, but the boys were just too big. *This is harder than I can play,* I thought. *If I keep playing with them, I'll be holding them up.* It wasn't something I could laugh off or outsmart; it was just the way it was.

People always ask me what the *C.* in *C. Vivian Stringer* stands for. Sometimes I'll joke that it stands for "Cheerleader," and then I'll tell them why. When I was in high school, I heard that they were going to have an audition for the cheerleading squad at my school, Germantownship High. The tryout was high pressure: it was going to take place in front of the entire school. Cheerleading hadn't ever been a goal of mine, but I knew it would get me onto the courts, if only on the sidelines, so I learned the routines cold, and I could do back flips, cartwheels—tricks that most of the other girls couldn't touch.

The tryouts went beautifully. I nailed every single cheer and went into the weekend completely exhilarated. So imagine how I felt Monday morning, when the 1964 Germantownship High School cheerleading squad picks were announced and my name wasn't on that list.

To this day, I can remember that feeling of sickness and shame in the pit of my stomach. I cataloged everything that had gone wrong with my performance. Suddenly, all the small errors, things I had thought were inconsequential, loomed like mountains. "Did I move a little bit instead of completely sticking that landing?" I asked myself. "Was my voice too high during that cheer? Maybe I should have put more energy into my arm movements and kept my fingers together during that last one."

What I didn't notice was what every one of the girls who had made the squad had in common: they were white.

That night, there was a knock at the front door of my parents' house, and a friend of my father's, Mr. Sun Still, asked for a minute of his time. I hadn't told my parents about trying out for cheerleading, and I certainly hadn't told them about not making the cut, so it never occurred to me that I was the subject of discussion. But after a little while, my father called me in.

"Mr. Still is the head of the local chapter of the NAACP," he told me. "He was at the cheerleading tryout last week, and he says that you were the best one out there."

Suddenly all the pieces of the puzzle fell into place. We and the others in the mining community might have been raised colorblind, but the rest of the world hadn't been. I would have been more than happy to take responsibility if I'd fallen short, but even with all of my self-doubt, I hadn't been able to completely squelch what I knew to be true: I'd been damn good out there.

"There's never been a black cheerleader in the history of the high school. Mr. Still wants to bring you and Kathleen Morris [another talented black athlete who had not made the cut] before the school board to protest the decision," my father said. "You have the grades, the respect, and the talent. They need you to stand up, Vivian."

I felt even sicker than I had before. What was the best possible outcome? They'd posted the list already; if they let us on the squad now, the whole school would think that we'd been given special treatment just to avoid trouble. I'd never asked for anything, and I didn't make excuses; my father had taught me that. For the first time, I thought about how it would play out in the locker room if I were on the squad. The cheerleaders sometimes had pajama parties at one another's homes—how would I fit in?

"No," I told my father. "I don't want to make trouble for the squad."

My father knew that I was afraid. And before I went to sleep that night, he said something to me that I have thought about many times since.

He said, "This isn't just about you, V.I. Perhaps it's not even *for* you, but for future generations of young women who deserve to be given an opportunity. There comes a point in your life when you must stand, because if you don't stand for something, you'll fall for anything. I want you to think seriously about giving, because you are the one who can." With that, he turned out the light in my bedroom and left me to think.

My father was like that: he never told you what to do. He'd lay out your options, help you to see the consequences of each one, and then leave you to make your own decision. I didn't want to get involved in controversy, but my father made me see that the problem was bigger than me. No matter how intimidating it would be to be the school's first black cheerleader, no matter how scared I was of looking like someone had handed me something I didn't deserve, I couldn't back down now. When I thought about all those other little girls coming up against the sick feeling I'd had in my stomach that morning, listening to those names being read, I realized that I couldn't afford *not* to stand up for what was right.

That night, I realized that fear is just an excuse, and a poor one at that. There would be no shutting up that quiet voice inside me until I got past my dread and embarrassment and took a stand.

I went and appeared before the school board.

It was a weekend afternoon, and the school would normally have been empty, but the parking lot was filled with cars. I couldn't believe that all those people were there because of *me*. My dad went ahead into the meeting while I sat outside and waited in the hallway. I couldn't hear much, but voices were raised, and it went on for a long time.

Finally, someone poked his head out and called me in. The room was crowded. A lot of people from the black community were in the audience, while the members of the school board were sitting, with the principal and the school supervisor and a few politicians, behind a big table in front of the stage.

Thankfully, I didn't have to say anything. Mr. Still stood up and said, "This is Vivian Stoner. She's a great athlete and a good student, and I'm telling you here and now that she did you proud in those tryouts. I didn't have to be a cheerleader to see that she was clearly superior to the other girls who tried out; the entire student body saw it. And I was just appalled that she wasn't called to the squad."

The response from the audience let me know that this cheerleading tryout was just the tip of the iceberg; people from the black community were fed up with a lot of things. Then one of the white politicians stood up. "You know me. I serve the district well, and I believe in helping your people. I get the Redstone candy for the miners; I'm the one who gets you the turkeys at Christmas! You can vouch for me." Right in the middle of his speech, this ancient black man in the audience stood up and interrupted him in this deep, deep voice. "No, sir—you're a snake in the grass! You pretend that you're supporting the community, but you're doing anything but." And then he started enumerating every shady thing this politician had ever done, ticking them off on his fingers.

I could not believe what I had started. Eventually people calmed down, and they cleared the room and took the vote. And that was how Kathleen and I became part of the 1964 Germantownship High cheerleading squad.

It wasn't easy. I was in the bathroom changing for our first practice when a group of other girls came in to change after me. As I sat in the bathroom stall, my feet pulled up so nobody could see, I heard them talking about the pancake makeup they used to make their legs look uniform; I'd had no idea about anything like that. And as I peered through the crack of the stall, I wondered and worried, "What color are they going to use on me?"

The idea of a child, uncomfortable and ashamed, wondering if there's a makeup color to match her legs, hurts me to this day.

I never wanted to be a cheerleader for the sake of being a cheerleader; I wanted to be on the sidelines so I could encourage the boys to do what they needed to do. What I was really doing was taking another step closer to coaching.

I remember seeing the surprise on the faces of the coaches who played us—I guess they weren't used to hearing a cheerleader yell, "Put your head down and drive through that hole!" or "You're shooting too much, Teapot! Lift your body into the shot!" But I hated to see the boys making a mess out there.

Verna joined me on the squad the next year. When our school lost, I would go home and cry in my room. It would drive my mom crazy. "What's wrong with her?" she'd ask. My father understood the problem. "It's her passion, Thelma," he'd say. "She cares so much, but she can't affect the outcome of the game the way she could if she was out there."

I had occasion to think of that cheerleading incident only a few years ago. In 2004, I was assistant coach for the Olympic gold-medal-winning U.S. women's basketball team in Athens, Greece. Imagine my surprise when I found that my name was nowhere to be found on the official scoresheets. The officials claimed that three assistant coaches were too many to list, and my first instinct was to chide myself for being petty. *Let it go, V.I.,* I told myself. *Everyone who matters knows you were there.*

But the omission kept gnawing at me. So I prayed on it, trying to see if there was something more than wounded pride behind my irritation. And my father's words came rushing back to me, resounding with the same impact they'd had forty years before. Standing still while they write you out of the history books isn't selfless, but the exact opposite. Are you going to accept crumbs when you've spent a career telling young women never to do that same thing? I had a responsibility to ask that my name appear, not just because I had worked hard, but so that a young black woman in the future might think, *I can do that too.*

To this day, I don't know if my name was listed, but I did stand up before the Olympic Committee, just as I had in 1964, when Kathleen and I appeared before the school board.

And when I was going through boxes of old photographs as part of my research for this book, I ran across a shot of my nieces, Teonta and Keonte, wearing red-and-black Germantownship High cheerleading uniforms—the very uniform that I had argued for the right to wear. I'd known they were cheerleaders, of course; I'd seen them cheer. But it had not occurred to me that those "future generations of young women" whom my father had spoken to me about so many years ago were my own nieces until I saw that picture.

The *C.*, incidentally, stands for *Charlaine.* I'm named after my father, Charles, although everyone always called him Buddy. It's too much of a boy's name, which is why I never use it. Not that it matters—these days, pretty much everyone assumes that the *C* stands for *Coach.*

3

You Come in Through the Front Door

Education was priority number one in the Stoner household. My father never minded helping us with our schoolwork, and he could tell you a history lesson in a way that would have you hanging off the edge of your seat—even if the very same story had put you to sleep in class that day. Although he had been offered a number of football scholarships, my father had chosen to have a family and to work in the mines instead of going to college. I don't know whether he regretted that decision, but he made it clear, right from the start, that a life of manual labor was not what he wanted for us. As he always said, "If you don't use your head, you're going to end up using your back." By the time we could walk, we knew that our goal was to get an academic scholarship and go on to college so that we could make a living pushing a pencil, not carrying a bucket of coal.

In my senior year of high school, I was accepted at Slippery Rock University, a small school in Pennsylvania outside of Pittsburgh. I also applied for and received an academic scholarship from the state of Pennsylvania. And so I was off to college—the first person in my family to go.

In the very first semester of my first year at Slippery Rock, I met a young man called Bill Stringer. Actually, it wasn't the first time I'd seen him. When I was still in high school, my friend Joyce Royster and I had gone to College Day at Slippery Rock, where we saw a gymnastics exhibition. Bill was on the trampoline. At the time, there were probably ten black students in the whole student body at Slippery Rock, so we noticed him right away.

He was gorgeous! He had these cute freckles, and his body was so beautifully defined that a few years later my anatomy professor actually brought him into class and had him flex so that we could see the muscles we'd been studying. My father always teased him by calling him "Charles Atlas."

As soon as I laid eyes on him—and Joyce will back me up on this—I turned to her and said, "I'm going to marry that guy." We both laughed, but I was serious, and she never lets me forget that I told her I was going to marry Willy Stringer (that's what they called him then) the very first time I saw him.

We were introduced that day, when I was still in high school. He looked me in the eye and said, "Hi." I was just a kid, a country girl, and I thought, *Wow. That was so mature, so sophisticated, the way he looked me in the eye and said hi.* It's so funny what you think! But I was just a kid, and Bill *did* have a sophistication about him. Everyone who knew him would tell you that he had a way of carrying himself that was entirely his own.

Nothing got off the ground that day. Joyce was acting all cute and blinking at him in the cafeteria, and he was blinking back at her. But I knew I was going to Slippery Rock and she wasn't, so I thought nothing of it—or of the statement I'd made.

At the beginning of my freshman year, I was playing basketball with some guys I knew, and my friend Fred Lucas, one of the track stars at Slippery Rock, was watching our game with another guy from a balcony in the gym. I didn't look too closely—even the best-looking guy wasn't enough to distract me during a game. Afterward, Fred came over and introduced us: "V.I., I'd like you to meet a gentleman who's on the track team with me, my good friend Bill." And lo and behold if it wasn't that cute gymnast! He asked me if I'd like to get a bite to eat with him sometime.

Our first date took place at the hot-dog shop, which was the campus hangout. I ordered a lot of food, as I always do, and was about halfway through my chili-cheese dog with onions when I realized that Bill hadn't gotten anything for himself except a soda. "Why aren't you eating?" I asked him. He didn't say anything about not having enough money to feed both of us. What he said was, "I've watched you in the cafeteria, and you're wasteful. I'll eat what you leave."

I practically choked on that chili dog, but I had to laugh—he was right. When I was growing up, I wasn't allowed to leave anything on my plate; my father didn't tolerate wasting good food, so we ate everything we were given, whether we wanted to or not. That's probably why, ever since I was a little girl, I've wanted to leave a little something on my plate—the corner of a sandwich, a little pile of salad. Even now, no matter how delicious it is, or how small the portion, I won't finish it.

I told Bill what had made me laugh, which led to a conversation about our families. I learned that we had very similar backgrounds. We both came from big families; he was one of nine kids, I was one of six. We both grew up in the country; his parents had an eighty-seven-acre farm. We both loved sports and music more than anything else in the world. *This guy is just like me!* I thought. *He's from the country, he's got a whole bunch of sisters and brothers, and his parents are hardworking people, just like mine.*

Bill didn't act cute, and that was important. I couldn't have handled someone slick, but I didn't have to get all armored up to deal with Bill. "I'm just a country guy," he'd say, and he was. There was nothing pretentious or fake about him, and you'd never have known from the way he acted that he was so handsome. This was in the late sixties, when a lot of guys would primp to get their hair just so. That wasn't Bill, although he had great taste and real style. He was the kind of guy who'd smoke a pipe—not a cigar, and certainly not a cigarette. Bill was *Father Knows Best.*

We talked for hours that night, and by the time our first date was over, I felt as though I had known him my whole life. He was a senior, and I was only a freshman, but it didn't matter. I'd had boyfriends before, but I could tell right away that he was different. First of all, I knew that Bill liked me for *me.* I didn't have to transform myself for him or put lipstick on to get a compliment. He saw me on the basketball court—covered in sweat, bossing men twice my size—and it didn't bother him one bit. All he wanted to know was when I was going to play again.

Later, when we were going together and he was student teaching, he'd drive three or four hours to stand on the sidelines and watch me play field hockey. How many men do you see doing that, even in this day and age? He played field hockey, too, during the summers, and our teams would travel together. He was often the only boyfriend watching the women's games, but he loved to see me out on the field.

Although it's unfortunate, I've heard many female athletes deny who they are for the sake of the men in their lives. Now, there's nothing wrong with putting on a pretty dress and earrings; anyone who knows me knows that I don't feel good myself if my clothes and hair and jewelry aren't right, and I take a lot of pleasure from those things. But, as I tell the girls who come to my camps, there is a problem when you start to pretend you can't do the things you can do, when you act like you don't sweat and run after balls. I've seen a lot of very talented athletes drop out, especially in their teens, when dating and getting social acceptance are so important, and it's a shame. I always tell my girls to find someone who allows them to be who they are.

The big thing that stands out to me about that first date at the hot-dog shop is how well Bill knew me right off the bat—better than I knew myself! It annoyed me sometimes after we were married. He'd tell me I was going to do the thing I'd just said I wouldn't do, or what I was going to like or dislike, and sometimes I'd try something, just to prove him wrong. Eventually, I learned to trust him. About me, Bill was always right.

I did not distinguish myself academically in my freshman year, so I was asked to take summer classes. If it worked out, I could continue in September. Unfortunately, it didn't.

The problem was that I was playing sports all the time. I played softball, field hockey, and basketball. I'd run into my good friend Barb Yenchik—we called her Stumper because she was the smallest person you'd ever seen—heading out to play basketball. "Hey, V.I., we need another person," she'd say, and I would go play. Then, when I was walking back to the dorms, I'd see my friend Linda Argall and her group coming out: "V.I., you gonna come play with us?" So I'd turn right around and play another game with them. I'd head back to the dorms with the second shift, we'd clean up and have dinner, watch a game on television, and then it was time for bed.

I never saw my friends studying, so I assumed they weren't. I thought, *Hey, I'm as smart as everybody else.* What I didn't realize was that Linda had been studying all day and was blowing off a little steam on the courts before dinner, and that Barb was heading back to the dorms to catch a shower and hit the books. Everybody was doing what they were supposed to be doing, except me.

This is a story I tell the kids I coach all the time because it's one of the most important lessons we can learn in life: you cannot compare yourself to others. You cannot concern yourself with the girl next to you. As I always tell them, know thyself. I had to know what I had to do for *me* to be successful, but I didn't.

One of my physical-science classes that year was taught by a visiting professor. When he handed back our midterm papers, I looked down and saw that I'd gotten an F. That's one difference between sports and academics; in sports, everyone knows when you've messed up, but you can get an F on a paper and smile, and nobody will know the difference. After class, the professor asked to speak to me. He sat me down and said, "Vivian, I've seen you out there, and you are a beautiful athlete. But the truth of the matter is that you need to take care of yourself. Nobody's going to look out for you but *you*." He was dead right. It was too late, but I really appreciated that he'd taken the time. Too often in life, people don't tell you what you need to hear, and it's a shame.

Sure enough, at the end of the term, I got a notice telling me to see Dean Roberts, the academic dean of the school. I was sick at heart. It seemed like everybody in the world was sitting outside the dean's office that day, and he was throwing one student after the other right out of that school. I couldn't believe I was there.

As soon as I got into the dean's office, I broke down, crying like you've never seen anyone cry before. He handed me one tissue after another—I am sure that I went through the whole box just sitting there—and he tried to help me to see where I'd gone wrong.

"You know, Vivian, I used to watch you walking across campus, holding Bill's hand. He's a senior, and you're just a freshman. How could you have been doing what you needed to do?" What he meant was that Bill had one semester left before starting his student teaching; he'd earned the right to take it easy. I hadn't paid my dues yet; I was just starting out.

I felt such a deep sense of shame; there was nothing left to do but beg. Frantically, I tried to explain to the dean that the hopes of my family were resting on my shoulders. My dad and mom were counting on me to make good. I simply could not go home and tell my family, who had worked so hard and sacrificed so much for me, that I had blown the opportunity I'd been given.

You have to understand: people didn't leave Edenborn. Most of the people in the community had never been farther than Pittsburgh or Charleston, West Virginia, and those trips were a big deal. Going to college was practically unheard of. Even good students seldom went; their parents couldn't afford it. The boys went into the mines, and the girls got married to the boys who went into the mines, and that was all you could expect from life. But my father wanted better for us, and we wanted better for ourselves, and he told us from a very early age that education was our way out.

"Please, please. If you give me a chance to stay here at this school, I'll make you so proud. You'll never see me in this office again. I know what I need to do now, and I promise you that I'll do it." I don't know why he believed me, of all the kids he was kicking out that day, but he did. As long as I made up the coursework I'd failed, he told me, I could reapply for school in January.

Dean Roberts had granted me a reprieve, but my problems were just beginning. I'd lost my academic scholarship, and I didn't have any money or a job—how in the world was I going to pay for the classes I needed to take? And where was I going to stay while I was taking them? I certainly couldn't afford a spot in the dormitory.

I went to my sister Verna, who had come up early to start her freshman year at Slippery Rock. We had always been extremely close; in fact, people thought we were twins for most of our young lives. Verna had worked two jobs, as a waitress and at a funeral home. She told me she'd give me the money she earned at the funeral home to pay for my classes, and that I could stay with her in her dorm room while I was making up the credits. We did not say a thing to my parents, but my aunt found out and did not help;

she tried to divide us, saying, "Vivian's the one that messed up; I don't think you need to give her anything." Thank God Verna found it in her heart to reach into her pocket anyway—I'm grateful to her to this day.

So I started sleeping on a cot in Verna's dorm room. She hadn't been assigned a roommate yet, but they were superstrict about who was in the dormitories at that time; you couldn't just walk in to visit a friend. I had to wait outside at night until late, so late that no one would see me coming in. Dean Perrin, who was in charge of that dormitory, didn't fool around; she had the sternest look I'd ever seen. I'd creep in when she had her head turned and pray that nobody set off the fire alarm that night. Verna would slip me whatever extra food she'd managed to save from the cafeteria, and then we'd go straight to sleep, afraid to make any noise for fear that someone would find out and turn us in. Long before everyone else would get up, I'd wake up and sneak out.

I think that was the most humiliating experience of my life; it just devastated me. I was a fool: I'd had it all, and I'd thrown away every last bit of it. I was the first kid in my family to go to college, and the great state of Pennsylvania had offered to pay my way—I'd been on top of the world. Then all of a sudden, I was forced to sneak in the back door like a thief in the night, hoping that Verna had brought me a sandwich. The shame of that experience is something that I will never forget, and from that time on, I never wanted to back into anything again.

I never did tell my parents. I intercepted the letter home so they couldn't see that I was out of school, and I did not tell my mother what had really happened until I'd been coaching at a university for at least ten years. A couple of years after I graduated from Slippery Rock with my master's degree, Dean Roberts and I had a nice moment when I was being inducted into the Alumni Hall of Fame. He put a medal around my neck and we shared a big smile. I believe that he was an angel placed in my path when he gave me that chance.

Slippery Rock was full of lessons for me. When I was reinstated at school, I needed work because I didn't have as much money as some of the other students. The school gave me a job washing dishes in the cafeteria. I hated it. The dishwater splashed all over your clothes, and in the winter, the whole front of your shirt would turn into a stiff sheet of ice. I always tried to get home late because I didn't want anybody to see.

I applied for another job, and they told me I could sweep the floors in the dormitory as long as I did it at six o'clock in the morning. I hate waking up early, but I got up at four-thirty to do the chore because I didn't want anybody to see me holding a broom. If someone came into the lounge when I was sweeping, I'd throw the broom behind the couch and pretend that I'd just been watching television.

Those jobs were painful. At Slippery Rock, there were just two or three minority students in my graduating class, and only twenty or thirty in the whole school. I didn't want people to see me as a janitor, but I needed the money. Those feelings are still vivid for me, and they're part of the reason why I fight so hard to make sure that my girls always feel as though they can come in through the front door and take their places at the table as the first-class citizens they are.

As soon as I got my academics in order, sports once again became an enormous part of my time at Slippery Rock. I was good at basketball, to be sure, but anyone watching me would have seen that I was an even better field hockey player. My field hockey coach, Dr. Pat Zimmerman, was a woman of tremendous character and integrity, and she made a deep impression on me before I even started playing for her.

I met her when the class I was in played a game against the class Dr. Zimmerman was teaching. I scored a number of goals against them, but I was just learning and didn't know that if you were a front-line player, you couldn't be ahead of the ball. After the game was over, Dr. Zimmerman quietly complimented my playing; she also mentioned that some of the goals I had made hadn't been legal.

Alarmed, I asked my own professor if it was true. "She doesn't know what she's talking about," she told me. "She's just mad she lost. You were fine." But later that night, I read the rules closely and realized that Dr. Zimmerman had told the truth. It impressed me so much. She hadn't contested my illegal goals, so it hadn't been about winning or losing. She wanted *me* to know, for me.

It was an honor to play for her because it was clear that she had her eye on more than the game. One year we advanced to regional-level competition in Pittsburgh. We competed for a full day to find out who would be invited to the mideast regionals. To my surprise, I was chosen. I was good, but not as good as some of my teammates, one girl in particular. In the same way I had known at the bottom of my heart that I deserved to be on that cheerleading squad, I knew that I *didn't* deserve to be on that field hockey team.

Dr. Zimmerman was in my mind when I went to the mideast committee and told them I couldn't accept the spot. I didn't want to take anything I hadn't earned. I did something similar at a game when I was coaching at Cheyney. An official made a call in our favor, but it wasn't right—we didn't deserve it. So I told him, and he took it back. My players were astonished, but it felt right. I've never wanted anyone to hand anything to me; I just want everyone to do the right thing.

I couldn't help but notice that the administration at Slippery Rock didn't seem all that interested in women's sports. So one afternoon I made an appointment with the president of the school. When I got into his office, I very politely asked him why he hadn't been to any of our field hockey games and extended an invitation for him to attend one in the future.

He did, with several of his vice presidents. They stood on the hillside in the pouring rain and they watched the whole game, from start to finish. That day, our team was the happiest bunch of girls you could imagine—our school president was watching us play! After it was over, they complimented us on our play and thanked us graciously for the invitation. I felt so empowered.

"How'd you get him to come, V.I.?" my teammates asked. I told them the truth: "I just asked." Nobody ever had before. I learned something vital that day: Never be afraid to ask questions—you can't assume anything.

I also played basketball on a winning team; we didn't lose a single game in three years. My coach was Dr. Ann Griffith. She was in her twenties, and she compensated by being a little standoffish and very proper. We all respected her immensely. Every other woman on the team was scared to death of her and would cast her eyes down when Dr. Griffith spoke. I took a different approach; if it looked like she was in a bad mood, I'd tease her a little, or ask about her day. As an athlete, I was always the team clown, always laughing and entertaining everybody, but I don't honestly know why I felt comfortable enough to be more familiar with her—I just knew that she had a soft heart.

One time she asked me what I wanted to do after I graduated, and all I could talk about was how I was going to get my hands on the pink Cadillac you get for selling Avon products. She just looked at me and laughed. "V.I., you are out of your mind."

"Nope, I'm having a pink Cadillac," I told her. "When I roll into Edenborn, everybody's going to see my Cadillac." She never lets me forget that.

Dr. Griffith left before my senior year to get her doctorate at the University of Iowa. We were disoriented and heartbroken. It was very painful for me in particular; I felt like my whole world was coming to an end. Because of that experience, it was never difficult for me to understand why my players at Cheyney and at Iowa cried when I left them; I knew exactly how they felt.

I never had a good relationship with the coach who came in to replace her, Dr. Powell. She felt that my politics were militant, and that I played halfway for her. In truth, it was a difficult time for me. It was 1968, when slogans like "I'm Black and I'm Proud" and "Black Is Beautiful" were in the air. It was the time of Angela Davis and the Black Panthers. It was the time of the assassination of Dr. Martin Luther King, of Bobby Kennedy, and I felt the need to declare myself.

We seldom talked about race when I was growing up; you just knew that you were accountable for yourself and looked within to find what you needed. But the Civil Rights Movement had made it clear that things had to change, that people had to speak out for what was right. It was not a time to be gray; you had to take a stand.

It came naturally to me. My father had always worked for equal rights and opportunities for coal miners, and men like the union organizer Jock Yablonski were heroes in our home. When the miners in our community needed someone to stand up and speak out about safety issues, they came to my father. I know it cost him—he and my mother lost a house they really wanted because he was so outspoken, and we got more than one threatening phone call—but he never let that stop him.

That year at Slippery Rock, it seemed to me like the good had died young, and the hopes of our country with them. Dr. King and the Kennedys had stood up for social justice, and they had been cut down in their prime. The students at Kent State had been shot for standing up for what they believed in, just as I was standing up for what I believed in, and I couldn't see the United States of America in quite the same way.

The whole thing came to a head during a big game against our rivals, Mansfield. At that game, there was a big group of black students sitting together in the stands—more than fifty of them, probably, which was more than the entire black population at Slippery Rock. And when they played the national anthem, as they do at the beginning of every game, a group of those black students refused to stand up.

I looked at them, and I understood what they were doing and why they were doing it. We all felt that our generation was going to have to be the one to take a stand and fight. I saw those students sitting down, and I took strength from their numbers. Suddenly, I wanted to say something, too.

I didn't sit down, but I put my hands behind my back and lifted my chest instead of putting my hand over my heart, as I usually did. I wanted to show that the American flag no longer meant everything it was supposed to mean. And I didn't sing the national anthem, because my heart wasn't singing. It was all everyone could talk about after the game.

Around the same time, we played West Chester University, also of Pennsylvania. Now we didn't have rankings or ESPN to tell us who the national powers were, but there was no question that this was one of the best teams in the country. These girls were *big*, and they were great shooters. When we got out there on the court, our team looked just like gnats on a doggone wall.

It came as a total shock to us. You see, we'd been protected. We'd played schools in our area, and we thought our team was pretty good. We were, but we couldn't approach the caliber of a team like West Chester. Their team was also much more experienced with the five-on-five game. In my first years at college, we played what was called the "rover" game. There were six people on the floor at a time, and only two crossed the line; the rest of the team had to stay at half-court. Women's basketball was still in its infancy, and America did not yet believe that women could exert themselves in the way that was required to play a full-court game. I'd always played five-on-five with the guys, but this was only the team's second year competing at it.

The upshot was that the West Chester team ate us for breakfast, and Dr. Powell blamed me for our poor performance during that game. She was right. I was the point guard, and it was my job to run the offense, to make sure that everybody was where they were supposed to be. But I was totally overwhelmed by what I met out there; we didn't have anything for them. So she called Dr. Griffith and complained that I'd changed: Not only was I playing halfway, but I'd become politically strident as well. I spent a lot more time on the bench that year than I ever had before. (Ironically, that was the year my team voted me Most Valuable Player.)

That year was a difficult and introspective time for me, a time to figure out where I stood. I blamed Dr. Powell for my lack of success on the court, and felt that she was trying to diminish my role. I think now that she was right not to play me: I was immature, and I wasn't working as hard as I had been. I wish now, of course, that I had given more of myself; she deserved better from me.

But I remember very well how overwhelmed and confused I felt, and I try to keep those feelings in my mind when a young person lashes out and blames everyone around her for coming up short. It's too easy to forget what it feels like to be twenty-one.

My social life at Slippery Rock consisted mostly of Bill and sports. One year, there were some girls who wanted to join an off-campus sorority. The sorority's base was in Pittsburgh, but we could have a satellite group at Slippery Rock. In order to be considered, they needed ten girls, and they came to me because I was popular and had good grades. Now I wasn't ever the sorority type—basketball was my sorority—but I agreed to help them out by putting my name in.

The group from Pittsburgh held a luncheon; I guess it was to see if we passed muster, although at the time I thought it was a formality. These women were, to put it mildly, a little stuffy. At some point over the tea and cookies, I looked at my watch and said, "Excuse me, ladies. If you don't mind, I'm going to excuse myself because I've got to play in a basketball game today and we've got a training meal in about five minutes. It's been great meeting you, and I'm sure that we'll have a chance to get together later when we're sisters."

Those ladies just about choked on their spit. I remember this one girl Wanda, from Slippery Rock, looking at me; if eyes could speak, hers would have been saying, "Oh, no, *you did not just do that.*" Needless to say, we were not accepted as a chapter of the sorority. I'm sorry that I robbed the others of the chance to do it; I guess those Pittsburgh girls could see that the Slippery Rock group didn't really have ten people, because I was more concerned with getting to my game.

Nor did the course of true love run completely smoothly. Before Bill left Slippery Rock to teach, I started to feel a little smothered by him. I'd leave one of my classes, and he'd be there; I'd come out of the dorm, and he'd be there. He'd take me to the cafeteria; he'd walk me back to the dorms—every moment, he was there. So I decided I needed more space and broke up with him.

Do you know what he did? He went off to take the physical for the army—my friend Barb, who was very close friends with him, told me. They could never have taken him because he had a heart murmur and a bad back from an old gymnastics injury, and Bill knew that perfectly well, but I didn't know. I was so desperate to get in touch with him; I thought for sure that he was gone from my life forever—and worse, that he was going to end up in Vietnam. Barb just kept saying, "See what you caused Willy to do?"

Long story short, Bill had me fooled, and we got right back together. He went to teach at a high school a couple of hours away, but for the rest of my time at Slippery Rock, he'd drive up on weekends to see me.

Sometimes we'd stop by his parents' farm on the way back to Slippery Rock. As soon as we got there, Bill would say, "Come on,

Vivian, let's take a walk." I'd go, but I'd never go quite as deep into the woods as he wanted to. I'd grown up in the country, but this was *country* country. I wasn't about to get eaten by a bear for the sake of a stroll.

The Stringers lived on eighty-seven acres, in a white farmhouse with a pond right out in front, surrounded by giant apple and peach trees. It got dark there like no place I'd ever been, before or since. And it was so quiet! All you could hear were the crickets.

Mr. and Mrs. Stringer were quite a bit older than my parents. Mrs. Stringer spent the summers canning the food that they grew, and she loved to sew. She made quilt after quilt, each one more beautiful than the one before, and hundreds of gorgeous hats for herself. The food on the farm was fantastic. They grew their own beans and corn and butchered their own hogs, and Mrs. Stringer was a great cook. She'd put out lots of chicken and biscuits and potato salad, and she'd always set aside some of those biscuits for me before the boys ate them all up.

The Stringer house was different from mine in that it was always open; Bill never had to call to ask if it was okay to bring a guest. Sometimes he'd bring seven or eight guys from his track team down at a time. "Mom, we need five bedrooms," Bill would say. "Okay, hon! What time you all getting up?" she'd ask, and sure enough, you'd wake up to the smell of eggs and pork chops cooking.

The days on the farm seemed long to me sometimes. Bill's brothers and sisters were very smart and very quiet, and his parents could sit for hours on their front porch in their big rocking chairs, looking at the deer and the squirrels and rabbits playing on their land. You could go fishing or build a bonfire, but the rest of the time there wasn't that much to do except watch the dew come off the trees.

It was so different at my house! As soon as we walked in the door in Edenborn, I knew we'd find all my brothers and sisters and their girlfriends or boyfriends, talking and laughing together. The music would be loud, and people would be playing Monopoly or playing their instruments together, while the rest tried out the new dance steps. They used to make fun of me: Bill won dance contests, but I never did have any rhythm. My brothers and sisters always insisted on tutoring me in the steps so I wouldn't embarrass them.

The truth is that I didn't have enough sense to know how fortunate I was to have a place like the Stringers' farm. It was a place of peace. It's so ironic; you work so hard and run so fast that eventually you'll pay absolutely anything to do absolutely nothing. As I got older, I became convinced that Mr. Stringer really knew what life was all about. I told Bill once, "Your dad had the secret to life. He had the ability to stop, to stand still and reflect, and to take true enjoyment from every single moment." I pay serious money now to fly to some remote area and look at nature—exactly what Mr. Stringer did on his front porch every single day.

I had cause to think about my last year at Slippery Rock recently. The younger of my two sons, Justin, took a part-time job parking cars while he was finishing his coursework at Morehouse. About six months after he had graduated and moved back to New Jersey, I got a letter in the mail, informing me of a debt he'd incurred. Apparently, he'd gotten into an accident in one of the cars while he was parking it, and he owed the garage all of the money he'd made. He'd fallen behind in his payments, and they wanted me to do something about it.

It wasn't a lot of money, but I was concerned that he hadn't come to tell me about it before it had gotten serious. He came home that evening while I was writing up practice, my "lesson plan" for the next day, and I still had a thousand things to do—recruits to call, a speech to write, tapes to watch. "Okay, sweetheart, let's talk," I said when I saw him. But my tone was impatient, and when I looked down from his anxious face, I realized that I was still holding my pen.

Considering the amount he owed, I could have had a quick chat with him to make sure it wasn't a bigger problem, written him a check, and gotten the whole thing off my plate. But I said to myself, "No. I really care about what's going on in his mind. And if I don't find out, who will? Put the pen down, Vivian. You need to be here for this, really *here*. Practice will be okay; this is what you have to do right now."

So he sat down and we talked for a long time. He'd been carrying this burden for a while. "Why didn't you come to me with this?" I asked. He told me that he'd been too ashamed. "I wanted to take care of it myself," he said.

"But you don't have a job, and it's not good when you say you're going to do something and then you don't. Something like this can ruin your credit. That's what I'm here for, to help you out if you get into a bind."

"But I wanted to present myself to you as an adult, someone who can shoulder adult responsibilities," he said. "This isn't who I want you to think I am."

As a mother, I appreciated that he had wanted to handle this on his own, and I respected his decision to try. But I also know that it's difficult out there, and neither one of my boys has ever pointed at things and expected to get them. "I'm happy to see that you're trying to be upstanding, and I'm pleased about the young man you're turning out to be. But you've never been an irresponsible person, and I need you to know that if you get into a pinch, I'm here to help you," I said.

I told him a story then, a story that hurts me to this day, about a very similar patch of trouble that I got into when I was in my senior year at Slippery Rock. Like a lot of college kids, I had gotten a credit card in the mail, and I started using it, even though I had no job and just a little bit of scholarship money to spend on books and incidentals. It felt good to be able to put gas in my car and to buy myself little things.

Of course, when those bills started coming, the company didn't want to hear about how I'd pay them back when I got a job. I tried to handle it on my own, but the letters got more and more threatening, and finally they said they were going to contact the school to prevent me from graduating unless I sent them what I owed.

I was so scared! I had no choice but to go to my parents for help. It hurt me to ask because I knew they didn't have anything to spare. But they'd always told us that they'd be there for us, so I called them and told them the truth, and my father drove up and gave me the check in person.

After I graduated, I went home to apologize for my thoughtlessness and to thank them in person for bailing me out. That was the type of thing that was hard for me; if I was laughing and joking, I was fine, but expressing emotions in a real and meaningful way to my parents was difficult for me, especially then. Afterward, I asked my mom where they'd gotten the money. Her answer broke my heart: "You know we don't have it, Vivian, so your dad cashed in our life insurance policy."

When I was telling Justin this story, I started to cry. You see, I knew how important that insurance policy was to my parents. If they didn't pay anything else at the end of the month, they wrote a check for that policy; no matter how dire the financial situation was in our house, that was always the bill they paid. It represented something bigger to my parents than just life insurance; it was a savings account, proof that they could always provide for our family, no matter what happened. It was something they could turn to in an emergency.

But this hadn't been an emergency. I didn't need a car on campus; I didn't need to eat in the shops in town. If I'd just walked across campus and gone to the cafeteria, none of this would have happened. Later, I realized something else: they would never be able to get that insurance again. Dad had lost his legs by then; he had medical conditions he hadn't had when they'd applied the first time around. Nobody would ever insure him at that same rate.

I can't express how I felt when I learned how my carelessness had hurt the people I loved. In that moment, I thought, *I'll do anything and everything to make it up to them; I'll make it big and send them everywhere they've ever wanted to go.* And I am grateful for the opportunity I've had to make life a little simpler for my mom over the years. But I still feel the pain of that experience as if it had happened yesterday.

When Justin got up from the table, the tension was gone from his face. We'd made a deal: I'd pay the bills and get the creditors off his back, and he'd draw up a schedule and pay me back. To be honest, I think he was at least as relieved to be heard and understood as to have the debt taken care of. I appreciate the struggle, especially when you're just getting your independence; I know how hard it can be. And I know what it feels like to get into a bad situation. I'm just glad to be in a different position from my parents, so that a little mistake doesn't cost me what it cost them.

4

I've Got My Glove Too

I don't think I fully realized that my basketball career was over until after we played our last game in my senior year at Slippery Rock. It was wrenching. I wasn't ready for the way I felt; I'm not sure you can be, although I try to help my own athletes prepare. Once it sank in, all I knew was that I wanted to find a way to stay close to the sport.

But first I had to find a job. My father had always told me, "When you get that diploma, the gates to the world will open up." So when I graduated, I was stunned: I had that diploma, but those gates didn't move. My other classmates got jobs at nice schools where there were great facilities and gym equipment, but there were no job offers for me.

I was shattered. My grades were strong, and I had distinguished myself as a student-athlete—there should have been nothing standing in my way. But the only offer I got was from a high school in Pittsburgh's inner city; the administrators had told me I could have a job even before I graduated.

I spent the day there. There were bars on the windows, and I watched as the physical education teacher urged the students to come out of the locker room where they were playing cards. "I don't feel like it," one of the kids said, and he didn't even look up. *Nobody here is doing what they are supposed to be doing,* I kept thinking as I walked through the halls.

I'd never seen anything like it. In the Stoner household, teachers were revered; they were practically holy people. My father had always told us, "If you don't want to learn, that's your business. But if I ever find you disrupting the learning process for anyone else, I guarantee I will light you up." At that school, the disruptive forces were winning. I don't blame those teachers; they were overwhelmed. There were too many kids in their classes, and they didn't have enough help or resources to do better. But I wanted to teach students who wanted to learn, in a place that was conducive to learning. It wasn't the place for me.

So there I was, with nothing happening. I thought, *Well, if this isn't going to work, then I'd better go back to school and get my master's degree.* So I did, at Slippery Rock, with the intention of teaching at the collegiate level. Bill, who had been teaching phys ed and coaching volleyball at North Hills Junior High School in Harrisburg, quit and joined me in graduate school. We both got jobs at Slippery Rock, working in the Office of Student Affairs for the Recruitment of Minority Students. The idea was that we would serve as liaisons to bring minorities to the university, and help them through their adjustment period.

I also started working with Slippery Rock's basketball team as a graduate assistant. Even then, I liked the more complicated and technical aspects of the sport. Dr. Herman, who supervised my student-teaching at Slippery Rock, told me, "You'll make an excellent coach, but you shouldn't coach elementary and junior high school. You need to work with a higher level." I believe he was right.

I loved what I was learning. I still consider myself a student of the sport, and it gives me tremendous pleasure to pass along that knowledge. I'll always stop to explain something. I have never wanted my kids to follow what I'm telling them out of blind loyalty or obedience; I want them to understand what I'm asking them to do and why. Don't think that some of the kids on my teams over the years haven't taken advantage of my willingness to stop the clock to explain the *X*s and *O*s! I remember one player at Iowa always asking me very thoughtfully if I'd considered playing certain people together or running certain plays. It was nothing more than a stalling technique so the team could rest. Eventually, I'd just laugh and say, "Robin, I spent four or five hours considering the pros and cons, and I know exactly what we're going to do and why we're going to do it. Will you please get out there and run now?"

When Bill and I got our master's degrees, we interviewed for jobs at SUNY Cortland. The interviews went well, and we were promised that we would be hired, contingent on a few follow-up calls. We were thrilled; we were about to get married and we really wanted those jobs.

At the time, I was working in the student affairs office at Slippery Rock. As I've said, there were very few minorities at Slippery Rock, but those who were there were beginning to chafe under the administration's refusal to deal with their concerns, and there had been a number of protests on campus. As Bill and I were waiting to hear the final word from Cortland, Dean Marshall called me into his office.

"Did you know that the black students were going to march on the president's house?" he asked me. I told him I did. "Did you know about the protest in the cafeteria?" he asked. I told him I did. "Why didn't you tell the administration?" he asked me. I told him that I didn't know that it was part of my job to tell him anything. "As an administrator, your job is to be on the side of the administration. Here's a lesson for you: never bite the hand that feeds you," he told me.

We never did get those jobs.

A few weeks later, I was offered a job teaching health at Cheyney State College, a small, poor, historically black school near Philadelphia, and I accepted. But I am still shocked by that glimpse into how things work. Now that I think about it, I was lucky; some of those who marched lost their scholarships. Sometimes losing your future is the price you pay for standing up.

Bill and I got married in September 1971. We had waited a long time—five years—and had gotten to know each other really well. I always wanted to be out and doing something, and Bill was game for whatever I wanted to do. Interestingly, Bill was nothing like the stereotype of the black male athlete. He was an amazingly talented gymnast and a fantastic volleyball player, and, like me, he played field hockey in a league. He'd been awarded a dance scholarship to UCLA. But basketball? No. I think I was a better basketball player than he was; in fact, I know I was. We were pretty evenly matched otherwise, though. We'd put our tennis rackets on our bikes, pack a picnic, and go out to spend the day together—just a girl and a guy doing ordinary things.

He was my best friend.

Part of the reason we took so long to get married had to do with the way I was raised. My father preached independence for women long before it was fashionable to do so. There was no way any of the Stoner girls was going to marry a man because she was looking to be taken care of; my father would have found that revolting. We had to be in control of our own lives. He had a way of making fun of me or my sisters if we ever looked like we were too dependent on someone. You never wanted him to catch you waiting for a boy to call, for instance; he'd tease you until you cried.

My mother didn't get involved in the emotional ups and downs of being a young person, either. She just wasn't that way. We've all talked about that since then; I'm not sure it's a great idea to make your kids feel embarrassed for showing emotions or getting attached. I know that I never felt like I could share real disappointment with my parents, and neither did my siblings; we had to be strong and act like everything was fine. I'm sorry to say that I got a little of that from them. I sometimes wish that I'd been more affectionate with Bill. We held hands all the time, and there's no question that Bill knew that I loved him, but I probably could have been more expressive. In later years, I think sometimes I hugged and kissed our boys all the time as a substitute for how much I wanted to hug and kiss Bill.

To this day, I'm not sure whether Bill proposed, or whether I did. I wouldn't be surprised if at some point I just said to him, "Why don't we get married?" Since the early days of our relationship, he'd talked about what our lives would be like when we were married, so making the decision was nothing dramatic. But once we had decided, he visited my father to ask for my hand. Bill knew that when you got engaged to one of the Stoners, you weren't just marrying one of us; you were marrying the whole clan. Everyone had to be in agreement.

Everybody in my family got along with Bill; they respected him. As anybody would tell you, "Bill Stringer is about truth." If you wanted to get the whole, unvarnished truth about something, you could ask him, and he would tell you. He would be gentle, but he would be honest.

Bill was very different from my father, but there were some things that they had in common. Both of them were very solid and dependable, and both shared a real ease with people and a real interest in them. I used to say that either of them could be equally comfortable sitting down with the winos on the corner or having dinner with heads of state. They just had that kind of touch.

After Bill had spoken with my father, he surprised me during Christmas with a little star sapphire ring with two itty-bitty diamonds on the side. When he gave it to me, he told me, "I want to spend the rest of my life with you. I don't have any money or anything to demonstrate that I can take care of you, but I promise you that I will." He wanted me to know that he was just starting out, and that this little tiny stone wasn't going to be it! I didn't care about the ring; it was what it meant that mattered.

Our usual church in Edenborn was too small, so we had the ceremony at a church in Uniontown. My cousin Marian Stith Lowe planned the wedding. We were surrounded by people we loved, and my sisters and my two best friends were in my wedding party. It made me so proud to see my college coaches and colleagues there. We had always loved the way our friends Thelma and Otis sang "Bridge Over Troubled Water," so we asked them to sing it during the ceremony. I remember standing at the back of the church, looking at Bill, and thinking that I couldn't believe this handsome, stately man at the end of the aisle was going to be my husband.

My dad was back there with me. Even with his prosthetic legs, he still managed to walk me down the aisle. He was a jokester; he never stopped teasing us, and my wedding day was no exception. We were standing at the back of the church, looking down the aisle at all those people waiting for me to start walking, and my dad says, "Okay, now. You don't have to get married; we raised you young ladies to take care of yourselves. If the ship starts sinking, the rats start running. Which way are you going? Last chance, what are you gonna do?"

I looked at him and said, "Let's go."

"If you're happy, I'm with you one hundred percent," he said, and we started down the aisle. My mom and my family sat to my left, and everyone—me included—was crying so loud you would have thought it was a funeral. It was only then that I really understood the significance of what I was doing. It's strange, but I almost felt like I was breaking up our family. We had always been together, and now we wouldn't be, not in the same way. There was someone else now.

After the reception, which was held in Uniontown, Bill and I went back to my parents' house. It was the oddest thing: I didn't want to go inside. It felt like an ending to me. I kept thinking, *This is the last time. I won't ever be able to return here in the same way.*

My father was not an affectionate man. You always knew that he loved you; none of us ever doubted that for a minute. But you knew he loved you because he did things that showed that he loved you, not because he told you he did or because he hugged you. If there was crying or kissing on television, he'd always joke about it: "Oh, geez, here we go with all that soft stuff."

On my wedding day, I found myself standing at the top of the stairs, thinking about how badly I wanted to hug my father. I wanted to tell him how much I loved him, and it felt like this was my last chance. So I said to myself, "I'm going to count to twenty, and when I get to twenty, I am going to walk down these steps and run right up to him and give him a hug and tell him that I love him. That is what I am going to do."

I will tell you, I was shaking as I walked down those stairs, but I didn't give myself enough time to think. I just went right over to him, put my arms around him, hugged and kissed him hard, and said, "Dad, I love you."

He was so shocked! There was genuine surprise on his face, and tears in his eyes. He had four daughters, and we all idolized him, but he always had to be the strong, John Wayne kind of guy. I thought, *All this time, all I wanted to do is hug you. Why didn't you just let us love you?* I wished I'd done it before, but I was grateful to have been able to tell him that I loved him on my wedding day.

That night Bill and I left on our honeymoon. He didn't tell me where we were going. That wasn't unusual for the times, when it was pretty common for the honeymoon location to be the groom's surprise. It was definitely not unusual for us; Bill was always in charge of things like that in our relationship. And he had a surprise in store for me.

At the time that we got married, I was playing in a pretty serious amateur softball league. Bill and I both played in a field hockey club as well; it was a way to continue to play even after our collegiate careers were over. It happened that this particular year, my softball team, the Pittsburgh Orioles, had made it to what was called the World Championships, and wouldn't you know it, the championship game was being played in Williamsburg, Virginia, the day after our wedding.

I never mentioned this to Bill. Who would have guessed, when we were choosing our wedding date, that my team would be playing for the championship? There was no way of knowing; it was just the way it worked out. And once I found out, there was no way I was going to say anything. What was I supposed to say? "I know we've got this whole wedding thing planned, but there's this softball game I want to go to?"

At the same time, I couldn't help it: I really, really wanted to go.

Stop it, I told myself. *A championship softball game might be a once-in-a-lifetime opportunity, but guess what—so is getting married. And you're getting married, Vivian, you're not playing softball.* So I never breathed a word of it to Bill.

To this day, I don't know how he knew. But he knew that as soon as the car started moving down the highway, I'd be out like a light. We got to the hotel in the middle of the night and checked in; I never asked where we were, and I barely opened my eyes.

The next morning, our first as husband and wife, we got up to go out for breakfast. Again, I was in the passenger seat and not paying much attention until suddenly I realized that we'd stopped in a parking lot. I turned to him in confusion. He just smiled and said, "Are you kidding me? I know how much this game means to you."

At that point, I still didn't really understand what was going on. I turned around and saw my softball uniform, all clean and laid out in the backseat. I looked back at the field, and sure enough, I saw our team banners. I was speechless.

Bill saw how stunned I was and tried to loosen me up. "Hey, I got your uniform and everything. I think you need to get out there to get some practice, don't you?" So I got out of the car, but it still felt as though I were dreaming. The whole thing, even now, is a blur. I felt embarrassed; I had no business in the world being on a softball field that day—it felt like the most selfish thing in the world.

I was wearing a white blouse and I still had my wedding hairdo—all these little curls all over my head. I couldn't walk out onto the field. I just stood there, looking at Bill, unable to move. He saw the look on my face, and I knew that he understood. Then he did something that I will never forget as long as I live. Very gently, he said to me, "Come on. I've got my glove too." *I've got my glove too.* And so the two of us stood there on the sidelines, throwing the ball to each other, while I got warmed up.

So that's how, the day after I got married, I played in a championship softball game. This is why I say that I know what it means to be supported at the ultimate level. There aren't a lot of guys who would have made that sacrifice on that particular day, but Bill drove all night—on our wedding night—to get me to a game I cared about.

That day it seemed like every single thing was right in the world. When I finally got out onto the field, my team was surprised and happy to see me, although my coach, Mr. Johnson, claimed he knew I'd be there. You better believe they teased me about that hairdo, too. And no, we didn't win.

That was just the kind of thing Bill did. He wasn't the type to scatter rose petals on your bed, but he had a way of making a gesture that showed he *knew* you, the kind of gesture that would blow the guy who was sending you ten dozen roses right out of the water. I remember once, when we were in Iowa, he bought me a pair of footie pajamas. "What were you thinking, getting me those ugly flannel things?" I asked him. Very calmly, he said, "Vivian, you know your feet are always cold, and now they won't be."

He was a good man.

5

Finding a Way

In the fall of 1972, I started teaching at Cheyney. In truth, I felt a little guilty about my new job, like I'd gotten away with something. I'd never done hard physical labor like my father, and I felt that I needed to know what that was like. My Cheyney salary was barely enough to cover expenses, so when I saw an ad in the newspaper for a job at a box factory, I decided that was the answer.

The factory was really a giant warehouse, filled to the top with cardboard. Giant saws made the cuts; other machines creased the pieces so they could be folded into boxes. The guy who interviewed me in this tiny hole-in-the-wall office took one look at my polished nails and told me, "I'm not sure that you can do this kind of physical work, and I'm not inclined to hire you." But I convinced him that I knew what hard work was and that I came from people who worked hard. Eventually he relented and gave me the job.

I went home and told Bill that I was going to work at the box factory. "I want to know what hard work feels like," I told him. "I want to know what it's like to work with my hands and my back."

He just looked at me like I'd gone crazy. "I am telling you right now that you won't last one week, Vivian. Not one week, and I'll bet my last dime on it."

I was on the night shift, which meant that I had to give up my weekends. The machine perforated the cardboard, and I traced the perforations with a single-bladed box cutter. It *was* hard work, but that wasn't what I minded; it was the boredom.

I've never been so bored in all my life. You were never done. Every two and a half hours, you were allowed to take a fifteen-minute break, and I lived for those breaks, even though I spent them in a bathroom stall, trying to get a few minutes' sleep. I had always been a little impatient with the pace of baseball, but at the factory I listened to every single game on the radio as though I were a lifelong fan. The voices of the announcers were the only thing that lessened the boredom a little bit for me.

If I didn't handle the boxes correctly, they'd hit me hard in the chest. My hands were ripped up with cuts, and my lungs were coated with cardboard dust. But the worst part was that my mind was crying out, just begging to be used. I can't tell you how many times I thought, *The boredom must have killed my father.* He was such a brilliant man to be trapped doing the same thing over and over, which is what it is to pick coal. My factory job gave me a real appreciation for the workers of the world.

"How was the box-cutting business today?" Bill would ask. "Fine," I'd tell him. "Just doing what needs to be done for the family." I lasted two weeks. I would have quit sooner, but I couldn't let Bill win that bet.

I think I needed to do it so that I'd know what I *didn't* want to do. Before he got his law degree, my brother Tim went down and worked in the mine for the same reason. And I've said it a thousand times since: I'd rather coach basketball for free than go back and make a good living at the box factory, doing something repetitive that doesn't use my mind. And wouldn't you know it—coaching for free was just what I ended up doing.

One day, soon after I'd started teaching, all the teachers at Cheyney were called into a meeting. The school needed volunteers to coach the women's teams. I was so excited, my heart skipped a beat. It never occurred to me that I'd be leading a team, but I hoped to be someone's assistant. I was so excited that I didn't even care what sport I ended up with.

The dean looked around the room and asked who wanted to coach women's volleyball. I raised my hand, sure that I'd have to fight for it, but nobody else in the room even stirred. "Softball?" he asked. Once again, I raised my hand, positive that someone with more experience would snatch it out from underneath me. But my colleagues were all studiously avoiding eye contact with the dean, and I ended up with another team.

When he said "Basketball," I hardly dared to look around. For me, this was the Holy Grail, the pot of gold at the end of the rainbow, a dream I hadn't even allowed myself to dream. But when I looked around, mine was the only hand raised.

And that's how I ended up coaching women's basketball.

Of course, back then coaching the women's teams wasn't paid work. All I asked for, in exchange for taking on those three teams, on top of my full teaching schedule, was a slightly later start: no classes before eight-thirty. I can tell you, I think about that every time I negotiate a new contract—it still doesn't seem like a bad provision to me.

I coached for *eleven years* without receiving a single paycheck for it. There's no question in my mind that the influx of money has changed the sport. Most of the people coaching women's basketball when I started at Cheyney were women, and they did it for nothing except the chance to build the sport. When the shoe companies came in and television rights were at stake, the numbers of female coaches—and of minority coaches, both men and women—declined, especially at the higher-level schools. Now I don't think that there's a secret clubhouse filled with white male athletic directors and college presidents plotting about how they can keep jobs away from women and people of color. But I do know that if I'm smoking a cigar and you're smoking a cigar, neither of us is going to mind the smoke.

For there to be real equity, we have to look not just at the high-visibility positions, but at who's doing the hiring and firing. I'm not just an African-American woman in a prominent position; I make decisions that affect six or seven other positions. I hire assistant coaches, trainers, team managers, sports information directors, and so on. The more women like me there are working as head coaches, athletic directors, and university presidents, the more chances other women like me will have. There are many women toiling in the corners of the sport who would do a great job running an athletic department if they were just given a chance.

But I wasn't worried about any of that in those early days at Cheyney; I was just thrilled and honored to have the opportunity to coach women's basketball.

At twenty-two, I was the youngest coach in the country—younger than some of my players. I had never coached before; I'd never even been an assistant (in fact, I wasn't an assistant until I coached for United States Basketball).

Personally, I kept a little bit of a distance from the girls; I was young, and I'm not a very big person. I was worried that if I let the kids get too close, they wouldn't have the right degree of respect, and I knew they needed to accept my authority without question. I admired the way my own coach Dr. Griffith had commanded our respect, so I mimicked her reserved style. Despite that, some of the closest relationships in my life now are with the women I coached at Cheyney. In some ways, we grew up together.

The transition from player to coach was interesting. If you're on the floor playing, you have a very direct sense of how you're affecting the outcome of the game. You can point to what you've done: I scored three points there, or I prevented my opponent from scoring there. Coaching is more like chess; it's about outthinking and outsmarting the other team. I've always been the kind of person who likes to know that she's had a measurable, quantifiable effect on the outcome of a situation, and it's harder to get that feeling from the sidelines—especially when you're telling the players what to do and they're not getting it done! Still, I found a real satisfaction in coaching, right from the beginning.

The situation I walked into at Cheyney was less than ideal. The Lady Wolves, to put it bluntly, stank. Teams would come and beat us at will and by huge margins. We were known as "a sure win," a doormat team, barely more than a recreational club.

Many of the same girls were on both the volleyball and the basketball teams. During one volleyball game, the opposing team was getting ready to take a kill shot. Their girl went up in the air, but instead of hitting her ball to the floor, I saw her make a decision to take aim at one of the girls on our team. She slammed that ball so hard into my kid's face that it lifted her off the ground and knocked her off the floor. The rest of her team laughed. It was incredible to me: they didn't just want to see us lose; they wanted to *hurt* us.

I turned to the players sitting on the bench and said, "Look at them. They're not satisfied with just beating us; they have to humiliate us. And there's nothing you can do except earn their respect. We're going to get back in that gym, and we're going to work on all the things that we need to do. The next time that ball is set up, you will get up and strike it. You'll dig and go after every loose ball. We will make them understand that they will not have us to laugh at again."

What's more, the women's basketball program had no budget. Zero dollars a year. We had two leather balls and eight rubber ones. But what we did have was the support of the administration, and in particular, of the president of the university, Dr. Wade Wilson. He was a true visionary, and I got a lot more support from him than my colleagues at much bigger schools, even if he didn't have a lot to give. Knowing that he'd do what he could for us meant everything in the world.

To get it done, we did everything ourselves. If we were hosting a game, the girls swept the floor and wiped off the backboard before the other team got there. I got the team's lunches myself, usually scrounging up something in a paper bag from the cafeteria. We didn't have the money for a trainer, so I taped the girls myself. I drove the van to the games.

It sounds funny, considering how hard I was working—coaching three teams on top of my regular job—but I've never had so much fun. In those days, I felt that I could go forever. As long as one of the girls swung by the cafeteria and picked up a peanut-butter sandwich for me to eat between volleyball and basketball practices, I was good to go.

I might have been demanding on the court, but I always told my players *why* I was asking them to do certain things, and I encouraged them to ask questions. I never wanted them to follow my instructions blindly. I demanded, as I have demanded from every team since, that they think for themselves. I believe that had a lot to do with building their confidence. They weren't just robots out there, doing what they'd been told, but full participants in the process. They took it as it was intended, as a sign of respect—and this wasn't a team that had been shown a lot of respect by anyone before.

Basically, it was the way my mom and dad had raised us. They never told us what to do. Instead, they'd tell us, "This is your decision, but you have to understand the potential consequences," and they'd help us to see what those were. In that way, we learned to make the right decisions. And so did the girls on my teams.

My brother-in-law Greg Threatte was a medical student, and he had spent a lot of time talking to Bill, who was the assistant director of financial aid at nearby Lincoln University. One day, about three years into my stint at Cheyney, he said, "Bill, I know you'd be a brilliant doctor. Why don't you take the MCATs and consider going to medical school?" And Bill ended up going to medical school at Syracuse in upstate New York.

So there we were, newly married and living hundreds of miles apart. We would have loved to have been together, but we knew the separation was temporary, and it was a sacrifice we made with a very particular goal in mind. We knew that, as two young professionals, we'd be able to give much more to our children than our parents had ever dreamed of giving us, and we felt that was the most important thing we could do.

We couldn't afford two apartments, so I lived in the dorm with the Cheyney kids for about a year. Then I moved to a maintenance house on campus, where the janitor lived. Upstairs, there was a room with nothing in it but a bed and a metal hot-water heater. I didn't cook anyway, so I ate most of my meals out, or I'd get food and set it on the heater until it got hot. Then I'd watch my little television for a while and go straight to sleep. A lot of times in the three years that we were apart, I'd sleep in my office; I'd stay there, reading books and writing up practices until it got so late that I'd just close my eyes.

When I wasn't coaching, I'd spend time with my good friend Janice Fitzgerald, who was getting an advanced degree in journalism. Janice, who would later become godmother to my children, didn't know a soccer ball from a basketball, but she is one of the rare friends you're lucky to find in life. It doesn't matter how long it's been since we've last talked; we can always pick up where we were, as if we'd just been interrupted for a minute. We had a blast together; I love to dress, and so does she. We'd go to the mall and do some shopping, catch a movie or lunch, and then do more shopping. Janice and I shopped so long that we got locked in that mall on more than one occasion.

It was tough sometimes for Bill and me to be apart, but we never complained because we really did feel as though we were on top of the world. I was doing something I loved to do, and he was studying to be a doctor. We were living the American dream. I've got a much bigger house now, but I can't tell you that I'm happier than I was then.

We might have had to do everything ourselves in those early days at Cheyney, but we were surrounded by angels. A volunteer from the local high school, Bill Morton, did our stats. A volunteer trainer from West Chester University came by once a week to look at our injuries, and every once in a while one of them would volunteer to go to some of our games.

My dear friend Ann Hill was another angel. She worked in the admissions office, but she'd been a huge basketball fan—she'd say "junkie"—her whole life, and had played herself when she was in college. She started coming to our games, and I guess she was interested in the team I was putting out there because she eventually started coming to practices, too. Then one day, she came with us on the bus to an away game. I was busy thinking about the game we'd just played, while one of my players was in the back crying and wailing with a terrible toothache and someone else was asking me questions about something I'd taught them in practice. And the whole time, I was trying to back out into traffic. Ann saw my face and said, "You know what? You need some help." Eventually, she became my assistant coach. I was so grateful; I don't know what I would have done without her.

Not only did she work as hard as the rest of us, she *believed.* I never stopped dreaming, and Ann was kind enough to listen, even when the stuff I was talking about was just crazy. I would tell her, "Ann, this team is going to make history. We are going to play in the great arenas, on the East and the West Coasts, in front of thousands of fans. You will see us up on billboards, and people will pay to see us play."

She would laugh. "Vivian, you know we barely have enough money to get these girls back to the dorms tonight. Girl, we don't even have leather balls!" I would tell her, "It doesn't matter. We're going to be so good, the world is going to come to us. I promise you our time will come." And she'd say, "You know what? Because you said it, I believe you."

And she did. I'd hear her telling people, "If Vivian says she's going to put a band on the moon, you'd better get out your telescopes, because she's going to make it happen." And sure enough, in her time, we did play in Madison Square Garden and at the Los Angeles Forum. Our team was up on those billboards, and people paid to see my girls play.

There are always going to be people who tell you why you can't. Some don't want to see you succeed because your success will make them worth less in their own eyes; some don't want to see you hurt by pursuing something that you may not be able to achieve. But to my mind, it is far, far better to have worked hard and tried hard—even if you come up short—than to count yourself out and spend the rest of your life wondering what might have been. Ann believed that I could do what I set out to do, and it meant the world to me that she did.

Another one of our angels was my friend and teacher Coach John Chaney. He came from being the best coach in the Philadelphia high school system to take the position of coach of the men's team at Cheyney. He'd go on to distinguish himself with a national championship there and then, of course, a Hall of Fame career at Temple University.

I was hungry for all the knowledge I could get and spent all my free time watching other teams and reading books. As soon as I met Coach Chaney, I immediately understood that he was a tremendous source of information, truly one of the great minds of the game, and I was so grateful that he accepted me as a disciple. I loved the intellectual aspect of coaching—the strategizing—and so did John. Of course, we didn't have any technology, so nobody was breaking tapes down the way we do now, but we spent hours talking and fussing at each other about the finer points.

I learned so much from him, and I continue to. Would you believe that we pushed aside our lunches and set up sugar packets for an argument about matching zone defense as recently as this past summer? It's true. Thirty-odd years later, and I'm still driving the man crazy with questions.

As they say, necessity is the mother of invention, and we were without question the first men's team and women's team in the country to practice together. The gym at Cheyney was not a large space to begin with, and it was divided down the center by this flimsy partition, so that neither of us had a proper-sized gym. Scheduling practices around one another was a huge hassle, so we finally came up with the idea of doing practices together. I used to joke that it wasn't much different; all my girls could ever hear was John yelling at his players anyway.

In truth, I think both of us saw an opportunity. There's nothing male or female about learning basketball. We were playing the same game, after all—why shouldn't men and women practice the fundamentals together? The men on John's teams followed his lead: they showed us nothing but respect and treated us as equals.

John and I would meet before practice, coming up with themes and designing the best session we knew how. We spent hours talking basketball philosophy, and when we met with our teams, we'd alternate: he'd lecture one day, I'd do the next.

Those practices were something to see: we weren't playing women's basketball or men's basketball—just plain *basketball.* We'd set up a circuit of drills, doing defensive slides or practicing shooting skills or rebounding. When the timer buzzed, the whole room would rotate to the next station. At the end of practice, we'd separate and put the partition up again in order to develop our teams separately and to scrimmage. The only thing the men and the women didn't do together was get into heavy play.

We practiced and drilled and learned and practiced. And wouldn't you know it, slowly, that team started to get better.

What we were doing in practice gave the team confidence. You see, they had gotten used to losing. They expected to go home empty-handed; the teams that played us had beaten us before tip-off. I tried to instill a sense of pride in those young women. Even when they didn't believe in themselves, I maintained a high level of expectation and enforced a serious work ethic.

They understood that they shouldn't dare come out onto the court with less than their best. I remember coming back to the school after one particularly horrendous away game. They had played very poorly, and I was furious. We got back at about three o'clock in the morning, but I didn't care. I gave them twenty minutes to change their clothes and get back into the gym. If I couldn't sleep, nobody was going to sleep—those girls were going to run. They knew I wasn't fooling, and I was proud of them that night; they were exhausted but they wouldn't give up. They understood that if one of them broke, the entire team broke. They'd heard what I told them: we are only as strong as our weakest link.

As the team improved, I wanted to continue to challenge them. We could have stayed where we were, mopping the floor with teams less disciplined than we were, but my goal was to get into the NCAA, and the NCAA stipulated that you had to play at a certain level of competition in order to be invited. You couldn't just play Sisters of the Poor ten times and then ask for consideration. I wanted my girls to have the chance to participate, to compete, to sit at the table. So I started looking for better teams to play. "You have to play the best in order to be the best," I told them.

At that time, the NCAA didn't care what you did. They didn't want the big dogs to jump all over the little dogs, but if the little dog was dumb enough to jump up on the big one, then they weren't going to stop you. And those big schools were happy to play us in the very early days when playing Cheyney meant an easy win.

We took each game to play as well as we could, and to overcome whatever challenges were put in front of us. When we lost, which wasn't that often (I had a heck of a record at Cheyney: 251–51), we accepted that it was our fault. Maybe we'd let somebody get within ten points of us or we'd lost control in the last two minutes of the game, but we always knew that the outcome had been in our hands.

I think back now with some amazement to what we did to make our success happen. The elevators in the dorms never worked; I called that conditioning. We couldn't always get into our own gyms for practice: the roof on the little gym leaked all the time, and the floor would come up in an enormous bubble; it happened so often that John and I used to wonder if the floor guys had a deal worked out with the roofers. And during the winter breaks, the school would turn the heat off to save money. Trust me, in rural Pennsylvania, an unheated gym in the wintertime is no joke.

When the gyms were out of commission, we'd have to find somewhere else to practice—and then we'd have to get the team there, since we had no bus of our own. In order to get a van from the school, you had to fill out a requisition form a month in advance. So I used to borrow this old green bus from the university's maintenance crew. It was the sorriest vehicle I ever saw in my whole life. They used it to carry stuff back and forth across campus, and it was barely up to that job; it wasn't even registered for the road. The players called it the Prison Bus—appropriately, because one of the places we used to practice was an all-male home for juvenile delinquents called Glen Mills.

We'd all get into that green bus and onto Route One. Ann would follow behind us in her own car, flashers going the whole way, and a good thing too because we never got above 25 or 30 miles an hour, even on a four-lane highway. She always says that she died a thousand deaths driving behind us, and that she could never decide which terrified her more: the idea that the police would stop us or that they wouldn't—and that I'd insist on taking that bus out again the next week.

The thing had no brakes that you could rely on. So we'd be going down the hill, heading for the railroad tracks, and one of my players would be hanging out the window looking for trains, trying to hear the whistle. There were no springs, so the rest of the team would be bouncing around like popcorn behind me. Whoever had her head out the window would yell, "Clear," and I'd shift up and gun it and we'd careen down the hill over those tracks.

When we used to stay over at the school during the winter break to practice, they'd lock the cafeteria and there'd be no one there to cook, so we had to do all kinds of crazy things to get the team fed. John and I cooked for both teams on the two little burners in the concession stand, where they'd make popcorn and burgers for the games. The players still talk about the time I made scrambled eggs in aluminum pans. They turned the most terrible blue-green color, a color no food should ever be. The whole team was silent, just looking at their plates, until one brave soul picked up her fork and took a mouthful. Those girls were hungry; they ate those eggs.

One time, John broke into the pantry to get us some dishes. He had loaded all these plates and cups onto a cart and was wheeling it over to Cope Hall when a school security guard pulled up next to him: "How's it going, Coach? What're you up to?"

The answer was classic John: "Oh, I'm just stealing these dishes here so our teams have something to eat off of," he told the guy cheerfully. And the guard waved him on.

John got me in trouble, too. He came up with the idea of going around to some of the big companies in the area and asking them for small contributions to help our teams. They gave us a hundred dollars here, fifty dollars there, two hundred dollars. That was a lot of money to us then, and we were just thrilled. It was like Christmas.

Then one day we got a call from the university's development office. They'd written a formal letter to one of those big corporations, asking for a significant endowment—big money—and they'd been told, "Oh, no. We already gave to Cheyney. We gave a hundred dollars to that basketball coach!" So we were prohibited from going out and asking anymore, but we laughed pretty hard about what the look on that development officer's face must have been when they told him we'd gotten there first.

There are defining moments in every person's life. One of those moments happened for me at Cheyney—and it had nothing whatsoever to do with basketball.

As part of my teaching responsibilities, which included health, organization, and administration, I had to teach swimming. Now, I am not a strong swimmer. I have always had a terror of the water. Passing a basic swimming test was a prerequisite for graduation at Slippery Rock, and I tell you, it was almost the thing that stopped me from getting my degree. I audited that class three times. Every day, I'd get to the pool and I'd count to fifty thousand before getting in. Once I got in, I'd just sink. I'd find my feet, struggling and sputtering and spitting, and start over. It was just terrible.

With Bill's help, I got proficient enough to pass the test, but I hated every minute of it and was never comfortable in the pool. Then I got to Cheyney to teach health and they gave me a swimming class!

In spite of my discomfort in the water—or maybe because of it—I was an excellent swimming instructor. I really studied the strokes and broke them down, so that I could visualize what every part of the body was supposed to be doing at a given time. And, of course, I was very compassionate toward people who weren't confident in the water, because no one was as fearful as me. But I always kept my students in shallow water.

One afternoon, I was teaching the dead man's float, and one of my beginner students started to drift out of the shallow area. I saw that she was moving toward the deep end, but I didn't feel confident enough in my ability to support both of us to go in after her. So instead, using my most soothing voice to reassure her, I caught her under the arm with the shepherd's crook and pulled her back into the shallow area. Disaster averted; she never even knew there had been a problem.

But after the class, I was shaking and furious with myself. What if she'd been in real danger?

So that Saturday, early in the morning, without telling anyone—not even Bill—I drove over to the aquatic center. I used my keys to let myself in and locked the door behind me. If I had died in there, the headlines would have read, SWIMMING INSTRUCTOR COMMITS SUICIDE—and as I made my way up the ladder to the highest diving board, I wondered if that wasn't what I was doing. I kept thinking to myself, *Vivian, you fool, you're going to die here today.*

But I knew that my fear was holding me back, and that is something I have never been able to accept. I knew that the only way I'd be able to conquer that fear would be to face it head on, and so I kept climbing.

I have never felt quite as scared as I did at the top of that diving board. I was shaking so hard the whole board was moving. I got to the edge and I looked down—way down—at all that blue water, and I said, "It's either me or you; that's a fact. And you are not going to beat me." I held my breath, closed my eyes, and jumped.

It felt like I was falling forever, and when I hit the water, I thought my head had exploded. I went deep—so deep, my lungs felt like they were on fire. I couldn't tell which way was up. Air has never felt as good as it did when I finally broke through. I got myself to the side of the pool somehow, pulled myself out, and lay down on the deck.

I knew, in my rational mind, that what I had just done was plumb crazy. It was the kind of asinine thing I would have killed one of my girls for doing. Even strong swimmers shouldn't swim alone; I could have broken my neck and drowned, all alone in that pool. And yet I couldn't really regret it. Lying on the deck of that pool, with just the sound of my heart beating and the water lapping up against the side, I realized that this is just the way I'm built. I can't live knowing that there's some challenge out there that I'm backing down from, and I won't accept my fear as an excuse not to do something.

I got up and went home, knowing something more about myself than I did when I went in. I'm still not a strong swimmer, but I'm not afraid either.

It was also in those early days at Cheyney that my father passed away, Thanksgiving Day of 1972. He was in his forties, still a young man.

Even though he'd been unwell for years, his death took us by surprise. He'd been so strong about everything he'd gone through in his life, it was almost as if we thought he was indestructible; I really thought he'd live forever.

During the last stages of his illness, our family pulled even closer together. I could never stand to hear the news about his condition directly from the doctors. Verna was studying physical therapy, and her husband, Greg, was a medical student, so they'd talk to the doctor and then come around the corner to talk to me. They never told me exactly what he'd said; instead, they gave me an interpretation that left me with a glimmer of hope. To the world, it always seemed that I was the brave one in our family, but I always knew that I wasn't.

As my father was dying, I came to realize just how much I loved music, how great a musician my father was, and what he had tried to give me when I was young. Music is about mathematical formulas. My dad tried so hard to teach me chord progressions, but I was the kid who thought she knew and I learned just enough from him to be entertaining to people. When he'd try to teach me how to play a song, I'd always ask him to teach me in the key of C. There are no sharps or flats in the key of C; it's very simple to play music that way. He'd always tell me, "Vivian, you need to learn how to play these songs in all of the different keys." I'd get so upset if we were playing together and he changed the key on me. "Dad, why are you trying to show me up?" I'd ask. But he was just trying to show me what I needed to know.

He'd tell me stories about the musicians he played with in the club. In music, good goes with good, and great goes with great, just as it does in athletics. A lot of the really great musicians would stick around after the second set and do what they called a late-night gig, playing music at a much more complicated level than they'd done earlier. There was this one guitar player who would always try to trip up my father, but my father had perfect pitch, and he'd hear the change and just roll with it. "You need to play it however you've got to play it," he'd tell me.

I didn't understand. He was telling me that everything lies in an understanding of the fundamentals. You have to have a deep knowledge—not just of how to play something so that it sounds good in the key of C, but how to modulate the key if something changes. If you've mastered the basics, if you know the formulas, you can go anywhere and play anything.

So when he was lying in bed at Presbyterian Hospital after his first stroke, when he could still speak, I tried to make up for lost time. I sat beside him and asked him question after question about music and what he had tried all those years to teach me. But it was really too late. That experience taught me not to put things off. You can't wait for the appropriate time to do what you need to do—that time is always now.

A couple of days later, he had the stroke that led to his death. I stood by his bedside in the intensive care unit and prayed so hard that he would live, that he would just be able to open his eyes and speak to me. But I eventually understood that loving him meant letting him go. That, to me, is the deepest kind of love. There comes a time when you have to be at peace with someone passing, especially someone who had suffered as much as my father had. I stood at his bedside with Verna and Tim and Greg and Bill, and we looked at each other, and we let him go.

I loved my father more than anyone on earth and when he died, it was like the world had come to a stop. He taught me so many things. He died too young, but I'm glad that he saw me married to a good man and starting out in a job I loved; I know that he knew I was all right.

His death at such a young age hit all of us hard, but it was devastating for my mother. They had been everything to each other, and when he was gone, she had nothing. In 2005, I was honored to be asked to write a piece for a book called *My Hero: Extraordinary People on the Heroes Who Inspire Them*. Many of my heroes were in that book, including Elie Wiesel, Billie Jean King, Magic Johnson, and Congressman John Lewis. In my piece, I wrote about how my mother always held up my father as an example to us children. All she talked about was how brilliant he was, how brave and strong he'd always been, with all he'd had to go through. And he was. But after he died, she went out and got two jobs to support the kids still at home. She figured out how to run a household on one quarter of the income she'd had before. And, although she must have been scared and lonely every day, she never let us see her cry.

I feel so grateful that I've been able to spend so much time with my mother, to express the love and admiration I feel for her—no one deserves it more. I know that I have gotten through many things in my life because I knew she was there. If I ever felt like falling, all I had to do was look at her courage and bravery to know why I couldn't.

When my dad died, I was twenty-two years old, old enough to know better, but I am ashamed to admit that I didn't have a clue what my mother was going through. It wasn't until I lost my own husband that I understood. In fact, part of my grief when I lost Bill was finally comprehending what it must have been like for her. She must have felt very frightened and alone, but she carried that weight so gracefully that we never knew.

6

To Rise and Give Hope

At Cheyney we were the underdogs, and I liked that.

Once we got some momentum, I didn't have to push those girls; they pushed me. They wouldn't let me leave the gym until they'd mastered whatever I was trying to teach them that day. I saw how they looked out for one another; if a player didn't quite understand something but was too embarrassed to ask about it, someone else on the team would do it for her, and nobody would leave that gym until everyone was straight. They were always asking one more question, and I would stay as long as they were willing to learn.

At first, the announcers at games would pronounce Cheyney's name wrong. It got to be a little bit of a joke with us, because they did it every time. *Cheyenne, Shawnee, Chiney*—you name it and we'd been called it. Nobody ever got it right. When we started to win, I heard the girls gloat among themselves: "What's our name? How d'you say it? That's right. Next time, you'll remember how to say *Cheyney.*"

We didn't care who you were or how nice your gym was; we were Jack taking on the giant. "They might have more money, but we have more heart," I'd tell the team. "They may be more talented, but we're going to work harder." No matter who we were playing, we took it one game at a time; together, the ants will eat the elephant, I told them. "No one stops us when our minds are strong," I told the team, "and we will let no one control our minds. Forget about who they are; do they know who *we* are?"

Our reward was the tremendous sense of pride we felt in what we were doing, and the knowledge that we were playing for everyone at that tiny university. We saw how much hope we gave to the people on our campus, and it motivated us powerfully; their faith in us was an inspiration. Our victories felt like more than just basketball.

You could see the change in the girls, too. Nobody had ever believed in them before, but all that changed as we began to gain respect and win.

For me, the key to success on the courts was preparation. I never wanted to stop learning. If there was a book I thought would help me, I would get it. If there was a clinic I thought I'd learn from, I found a way to go. If I had a question and was in the presence of someone who could answer it—mostly Coach John Chaney, who I think is the most brilliant coach on planet Earth—I'd ask it. Basketball is made up of moves and countermoves, and I never wanted to be surprised. I always wanted to know what my opponents were likely to do and to have a response planned out.

One of the biggest obstacles to building a powerhouse program was that I had no scholarship money to attract recruits. So I burnt out a couple of my own cars driving to the playgrounds in New

York and Delaware to see promising players. My early attempts were not successful, so I asked myself, *Why on earth would someone whose child has been offered a scholarship from another school send them to play for you, Vivian?* I found the answer by thinking of my own parents and of what they wanted for their children.

In my house growing up, two things were held above all others: education and family. Get your education, my parents told us, and you can do anything. Once it's in your head, you've got it, and nobody can take that away from you. It was also understood that everyone in the family, even the littlest one, was working toward the strength of the whole unit. You did what was best for everyone, not just for yourself, and when those things were in conflict, you tended the needs of the family before your own.

So the next time I went on the road to recruit, this is what I told the mothers of the girls I wanted to bring to Cheyney: "I will take care of your daughter with the devotion of a loving mother. I will treat her just as you would. I will hold her hand when she needs help, and I will get on her case when she needs shaking up. I'll make sure she graduates, and do everything else in my power to make sure that she turns into the young woman you want her to be. Please trust me to guide her for the next four years, and I guarantee that I will be a part of her life for the next forty."

The faith that people had in me still astonishes me. I got the players I needed, and I made sure to follow through on the promises I'd made to their mothers. One of the first players to come was Yolanda Laney, who was from Philadelphia. I was so honored; her mom brought her to a game and she said to Yolanda, "I'm a pretty good judge of character, and this woman is the one I want you to be with."

Laney and I struggled mightily along the way, believe me. The first week of practice, I couldn't count how many times I told her to get out of my face and get off my floor if she didn't want to work; I even sent her back to Philadelphia a couple of times. At one early practice when she was just jacking shots up, I snapped on her: "Who gave you the green light to shoot? You don't shoot unless I tell you to shoot."

She just stopped and looked at me, and I thought, *Oh, no. Now we're in for it.* I told her not to shoot? Fine, now she's not going to shoot. Sure enough, in our next game, she's got an easy layup right in front of her and she doesn't take it—and it went on like that for the whole game. Anytime she had a shot, she pretended it wasn't there and passed the ball out to someone else. I had to laugh—it was always a battle with her. Ann Hill said she was the most stubborn person she'd ever met, except me. But she turned out to be one of the most powerful forces on that championship team, and although her mom died before she graduated, she went to law school just like she had promised her she would, and is now an attorney for the state of New Jersey.

I had one more card up my sleeve: I didn't automatically turn away the girls with difficult histories, girls whom other coaches, with their big budgets, would not even consider. Over the years, many of the girls on my teams have come from backgrounds ranging from the simply underprivileged to the seriously troubled. Some of them have had run-ins with the law; many of them have developed the kind of attitude that protects a young girl in a bad neighborhood, but can make her difficult to play with, and to coach.

Now, I resist the notion that the girls I work with are always poor, or from troubled backgrounds. I don't think it's fair to girls like Chelsea Newton, who was homecoming queen and the president and valedictorian of her class, or Tangela Smith, who was valedictorian of hers, or Laney, who was a straight-A student—or any of the many girls like them I've coached. But I've never shied away from the kids who weren't A students from middle-class backgrounds, either.

Who can say when you lose a kid? I've coached kids from the worst projects, kids from families so broken you can't even call them families. I always tell them, "You can look at your past and you can see it as a burden, keeping you down. Or you can draw strength from what has happened to you, and you can use that strength to make your own path." It doesn't matter if they've grown up with fewer advantages than the girl next to them; their God-given talent has given them a chance at something better, and all they have to do is say yes to the opportunity. And with very few exceptions, those kids have made me—and themselves—proud.

I remember recruiting Debra Walker to Cheyney. When she graduated from high school, she had an 0.7 grade point average. It wasn't that she couldn't do better, it was that she wouldn't; she wanted to hang out, play ball, and skip class. And there had been some sort of fight on the court when she was in high school, so many coaches thought she was a powder keg.

When I talked to her, the first thing I told her was that if she came to play for me, I'd make sure she'd graduate. I could tell by the pause on the other end of the line that she didn't believe me. She now says I was the only coach she talked to who mentioned education; in fact, she says I told her that she would graduate from college when most people didn't think she would live.

When she arrived, I told her, "I don't care what happened in the past; I care only about what you do now. I'm going to take you the way you come to me." But everything with Debra was a test, even the small stuff. I remember the first one. Before one of our early practices, I had been playing with some guys before the girls came in. I was sweating and hot, and Debra was drinking some water. She offered me some, so I took the bottle and drank it. Later I learned that she was waiting to see whether I'd wipe it off.

Although she was good, I didn't play her much that first semester because she just wanted to go out there and do what *she* wanted to do, not what I wanted her to do. I explained to her that I didn't need someone taking crazy, ambitious shots and turning the ball over. It was hard for her. She was talented, and she wasn't used to warming the bench; my assistants were actually starting to worry that she was going to cause problems with the rest of the team.

One day, we were playing West Chester University, and I went into the bathroom before the game. Debra followed me in and slipped a note under the stall door.

"Coach," the note said, "I sure would like some PT." I didn't have any idea what she was talking about. PT? What was PT?

"Playing time," she explained.

"Well, when you address the things that I need, you'll get it. I don't need a scorer, I need someone who can play defense and rebound." Understand that this whole thing is taking place in the bathroom, me in one stall, Debra in the next.

She said, "I can rebound. How many you want?"

"Ten is a good average," I told her.

"Well, if I can get ten minutes, you've got those ten rebounds," she said—just like that. You know what? That girl went in that day and gave me about sixteen rebounds. From that moment on, she led that team. She never looked back. And she graduated with a 3.6 in her major, by the way.

Another essential player for us was Val Walker. I remember meeting her for the first time. She was the best player in the country, and there must have been twenty or thirty coaches from various schools watching her play. After the game, all these coaches went up to her. They're telling her all about their schools and what she can do for their programs, but I'm watching from the back, and I can see that Val's still in her uniform, exhausted, cold and wet from the game. So when it was my turn, I simply said, "I'm not going to take your time right now; I'm sure that you'd love to take a hot shower. But I'd welcome the opportunity to talk to you; just remember my name, Coach Stringer from Cheyney State College in Pennsylvania, okay?" And I gave her my card.

It made an impression on her, the idea that I cared more about what *she* needed than what she could do for me. She came to visit and then she came to Cheyney. Val was very quiet; she had a giant Doberman pinscher and she loved jazz. I always used to say that she was a young person with an old mind because she had a real maturity to her, even as a freshman, that you don't often see. She went on to play professionally in Italy for many years.

More than anyone, Val was responsible for the rise of that team at Cheyney. Great players wanted to play with her. When one of the Cheyney guys was drafted to play for the 76ers, they asked him where he learned to shoot. He told them, "I learned from the great Val Walker." She was an amazing athlete, a player ahead of her time.

The transformation I saw in the girls on that Cheyney team was powerful, and it confirmed to me that basketball could be a way for me to teach bigger life lessons. Many of the fundamentals I developed at Cheyney are still in place today. In a way, it was clearer then, since there was no professional league for women to play in after college, and I didn't have any scholarships to give—all I had was basketball.

At Cheyney—as with all the teams I've coached since—community service was mandatory for the young women who played for me. Nobody asked me whether I wanted to wheel my grandmother around the grocery store after her stroke; it was my job, and I did it and took pride in doing it well. Giving back teaches you things about yourself that nobody can tell you.

Academics were another essential. My father used to go over our report cards, grade by grade, in front of the whole family. To this day, I'm not sure whether my parents' disappointment was worse than the teasing of my siblings, but I know one thing: the process made you accountable. If you hadn't tried your best, you would the next time around. To this day I make sure that my girls understand that when you play for a university, you are representing an academic institution first and foremost. So you have no other alternative than to do your schoolwork and keep up your grade point average.

I'm a realist: there aren't that many opportunities in basketball for a girl who has played in college. A few, like Tammy Sutton-Brown and Cappie Pondexter, will have the chance to play in the WNBA; some will go on to play overseas; and some, like Tasha Pointer, whom I hired in 2007 as my assistant coach, will get on a coaching track. But the majority of the girls who play college ball will find their way in careers outside of the sport.

I take pride in giving them the skills they'll need when they go out beyond the hardwood to make a life for themselves. I know that the qualities that we are working to instill in these girls in order to turn them into great athletes—endurance, discipline, integrity, and the confidence to stand up to any challenge and slap it down—will also make them great women, winners on and off the court. When I look at the players I've coached, I'm proud to say that while there are a number of WNBA players and even a few all-stars in there, there are also doctors, lawyers, psychologists, journalists, teachers, and successful business owners. One of my former players owns a seafood restaurant; another teaches French; another is a reverend. In many cases, these are girls who, without basketball, might have ended up in a much different place, a place with fewer choices and much less freedom.

Aimee Mullins, the president of the Women's Sports Foundation, told me recently that 84 percent of women business leaders in this country say that they were athletes. I'm not surprised: athletics breeds a level of confidence and leadership that can be hard for girls to find elsewhere. Parents act like they want their daughters to be as strong as their sons, but they're much tougher on the boys. Sports, on the other hand, doesn't discriminate. There's no opportunity to cover up anything on the court: you either get it done, or you don't.

I don't make excuses for my girls, and I have only the highest expectations for them. I tell the girls in my basketball camps—ten- and eleven-year-olds, sometimes—that there's no goal they should consider beyond their reach. "I expect to get a call from you when you're nominated to be a Supreme Court Justice, or tapped to be the next CEO of a Fortune 500 company," I tell them. "If you never shoot for those stars, you're never going to be quite at peace with yourself. You'll live in a kind of twilight, where you know neither success nor failure. That's a gray place, and it's not possible in my mind to be gray. You're either moving forward, or you're moving back."

And I tell my teams the truth. I don't try to butter it up and I don't apologize for it. I had an assistant once by the name of Tom Lewis, a young man who had played at the University of Kentucky and in the pros. He said he had never heard truth spoken so plainly as it was in our meetings. The truth may hurt, but I will always give you the tools you need to overcome and become what you want to be.

For me, that's what being part of a family means. You might have issues with one another, but you work through them together. You love each other and take care of each other, but most of all, you tell each other the truth.

I was at a recruiting event earlier this summer. These events are specifically designed so that college coaches can get a look at talented high school players. They're like auditions or college interviews—a time to put your very best foot forward.

I was watching one team closely because it had a number of players I was interested in. But here's what I saw: one girl wearing a raggedy long-sleeved shirt under her team jersey, another wearing two different-colored socks. A bunch of the kids were listening to their iPods while they warmed up; one of them was dancing. In other words, not one of them was focused or concentrating on what they were there to do: warm up for a game that would significantly contribute to deciding their future.

I was appalled. When I'm recruiting, I'm not just looking at how a young lady handles the ball, how athletic she is, or how big.

No, I'm looking at what she does *the whole time she's in the gym.* How much attention does she pay to the pregame drills? What are her off-court interactions like with her teammates and with her coach? When she's sitting on the bench, does she high-five her teammates, stay engaged in what's happening, and cheer for the players still on the court, or does she think that she's "off-duty" as soon as she leaves the floor? How does she react to a foul call? What's her response to the outcome of the game? All these things tell me about what kind of a teammate she'll be, and about what kind of a person she is. And each one of them goes into my decision to offer her a scholarship.

I don't blame the kids—kids will do what kids will do. A lot of them don't have anybody in their lives to tell them differently. But if these kids don't know any better, then it's their coach's job to show them the way. We're not just schooling them so that they don't show up to a job interview at the *New York Times* or Deutsche Bank wearing an iPod and chewing gum, which is essentially what those girls were doing. It's our job to help them to understand the principles behind the behaviors, the reasons we ask them for the things we do.

Many of those principles were firmly in place for me, even in those early days at Cheyney. Success at the elite level in basketball requires that you be mentally strong. It requires that you warm up with the same intensity that you will play, and that you give as much when it doesn't count as when it does. You don't argue with an official, even when the calls are excessive or unfair, because you understand that you don't ever look to anyone besides yourself to dictate the outcome of the game. You accept your losses as graciously as your wins. And you support the other players on your team, even if you play only ten minutes all year, because you will only ever be able to go as far as your total team unity will take you. You show that unity by dressing like a team, cheering together like a team, by winning and losing together like a team.

Of course I'm looking for talent. I'm looking for how a girl shoots, how she passes, how quick she is, and how strong her body is. But I'm looking for all these other things too, because they tell me what kind of a person she is, and whether she has the heart to give of herself.

Many of the girls on the Cheyney team had come from broken homes; this team was their first experience of a family. That's all a team is, a family that plays together; I go so far as to call my teams "basketball families."

Like my own family, the Cheyney team ate every meal together—just as my teams do now. Then, as now, I always select someone to say the blessing. The blessing is never simply gratitude for the food we're about to eat; it always contains a more personal prayer as well, whether it's "Help us to run," or "Help us to be confident," or "You've given us these blessings, please help us to deliver on our promise." I always listen closely to the blessing; it puts me in tune with how the team is feeling. If the blessing is "Help us to understand that we have to play as a team and be there for one another," I know that there's something going on between team members.

One day, the girl giving the blessing used the words "I hope." So I went into our team meeting looking to wipe away any trace of doubt that might have been in anyone's head. "Let me help you understand something," I told the team. "We hope *nothing*. We are fully prepared and we will deliver, I promise you that. The only time Muhammad Ali lost was the day he used the word 'if.' We didn't practice all those hours and prepare this hard just to have hope."

And when the meal is over, no one person can get up and go; someone from the table has to ask me if the whole table can be excused. If someone's a really slow eater, one of her teammates has to stay back with her while she finishes; nobody is ever left by herself. It's just one example, but as I am known for saying, I want everyone walking in the same direction at the same time.

Everybody looks for an identity; that's human nature—and it's especially true about young people. But that's why the ultimate sacrifice is to give up your individuality for the sake of the team. We can only be successful when everyone understands that the whole is bigger than the sum of its parts, but we will never get there if everyone is looking to carve out a little place for themselves, to steal her own identity at the expense of everyone else.

Yolanda Laney and I locked heads over this at Cheyney, big time. Laney had hair halfway down her back; it was the most beautiful hair you'd ever seen, and it must have taken her years to grow. At the time, it was very popular for black women to braid their hair. That didn't go with my understanding of a unified team. I want everyone wearing the same color socks, the same headbands—and I certainly didn't want someone on my team making a big statement with her hair.

So when Laney came in to our meeting with those braids, I told her to take them out. "I am not interested in any departure from what is uniform. If you intend to play in this week's game, you will not show up again with braids." The next day, she walks in with a baseball hat on. I was spitting mad; I figured that she'd kept the braids and tucked them up underneath the cap.

I told her to take it off, and she did, never taking her eyes off me—defiant to the last. Would you believe she had cut all that beautiful long hair off, right up to her ears? It was horrible. I felt sick to my stomach. Honestly, my first thought was of her mother, and how this was just going to break her heart. Laney's hair had been so long and so pretty, and now it was gone, all in order to prove a point: "Okay, fine, Coach, you don't want braids—how do you like this?"

Everyone just sat there, silent and perfectly still, with their eyes big, and Ann Hill made a little noise and turned to look at me. Everyone was wondering what I was going to do, but what could I do except tell her how sad I was? In that moment, if we could have rewound the clock, I probably would have let her wear the braids. But I know now that I was right to want everyone to be walking in the same direction: I have learned over the years that it is not good for anyone on the team when someone wishes to draw attention to herself.

Another one of the ways I emphasized unity was by asking the players to dress a certain way when they were traveling with the team. No jeans, no sneakers, no T-shirts, no big boots. Clothing had to fit properly; no XXXLs or shirts too tight to button. These were not wealthy kids, and I know that sometimes they had to beg, borrow, and trade in the dorms to scare up an outfit that was good enough to wear on the bus. It hurt me that it was hard for them, but I believed then, as I do now, that it was important. I wanted to show them how to be ladies, how to carry and present themselves so that they would command the respect I knew they deserved.

I used to call myself the Holiday Inn, because their slogan was "The Best Surprise Is No Surprise." With me, you always knew what you were going to get. To have structure is to have security. That's why you put a child to bed at the same time every night. Even if he throws a tantrum about it, some part of him is reassured by the fact that you're enforcing the rule.

If there's one thing I know after thirty-odd years of coaching, it's that kids will always press you. Debra Walker tells a funny story about finally getting a pair of Gloria Vanderbilt jeans; I think she'd gotten them in black to try to sneak them past me. I took one look at her and said, "You can't travel in those; go dress." She was devastated. They were the nicest thing she owned by far, and she had wanted them for months. To this day, kids are always trying me with some spin on the rules. "Look at these cute shoes, Coach. They have a rubber sole, but they also have a little bow—are they sneakers?"

Yes, they are. Go change.

One year at Cheyney, I had two very talented point guards on the team, which meant that at the beginning of the season, I had to choose who would start. Karen Draughn—we called her Pie—was the natural choice. She had everything I was looking for in a guard. She was quick, she was talented, but most of all, she was unselfish. Unfortunately, the other guard disagreed with my decision, and she let everyone on that team know what she thought. So I decided that I would let her see the truth for herself, and arranged for a game of one-on-one. Pie proved clearly that she was the superior player, but this other girl still wouldn't stop, and everyone could see the issue was soon going to cause problems for the team.

The next afternoon, I walked into my office and found Pie waiting for me. "Coach," she said, "I just want what's best for the team. I know you know what's going to make us successful, and if it means I don't start, that's okay. It doesn't matter, as long as we win."

In that moment, I knew that Pie was my true point guard. She was so selfless, she was prepared to throw away her own hopes and dreams in order to do what was best for the team. I've worked with many girls since then, and I'm not sure how many of them would have the maturity and the grace to sacrifice for the sake of the greater good the way she did. But if there was one thing that characterized that Cheyney team, it was heart, and I know that it was one of the reasons we began to see the kind of success that we did.

Right before the championship game against Louisiana Tech, that other player knocked at the door of my hotel room. Her family would be watching, the game would be televised, and she wanted to know how many minutes she was going to play. I was stunned. When I ask a player to come to play for me, I'm asking them to make a commitment to trust me to do what's right for the team. But there we were, minutes before the championship game, and once again, this girl was looking out only for herself.

She knew that I never promised anyone anything, because I have to be free to make decisions based on what's best for the team. "I can't promise you thirty seconds or thirty minutes," I told her. "That's the way it's always been, and that's the way it has to be." Her coming to me in that way and at that time really shook me. At the same time, I do deeply care that everyone who plays for me feels good about themselves and their contribution. And that, I think, led me to make a mistake during that game.

It was clear right away that Louisiana Tech had much more depth than we did, and never clearer than when they put in Debra Rodman, the sister of the great NBA player Dennis Rodman. She was a rebounding machine, much more powerful and threatening to us than the people they'd started. Our team shot and played badly the whole game, and when our biggest girl got into foul trouble, I looked down the bench and made a decision from the heart, as opposed to one from the mind—one of the few times I've done so in my career. In a move I now regret, I went against my better coaching judgment and put that other guard in.

I never ever hold a single individual responsible for the success or failure of our game. In my mind, there's never one moment that defines the outcome; you can always be sure that some other things were happening along the way that caused us to come to our moment of truth. We all win and we all lose, but we all do those things *together.*

But I believe to this day that my decision to put that player in was one of the things that delivered us to a loss. It was just as my father had always said: Even one dissenting voice weakens the structure.

Those were great times. Bill came down from Syracuse for almost every game; when I looked, he was always there, holding up a "Wolves" sign and jumping up and down. I swear, when we started winning, he was as proud of those girls as I was. Recently, one of the girls who was on the Cheyney team told me what he'd meant to them: "Everybody wanted to find someone just like Mr. Stringer."

Once we started to succeed, it was always important to me that we win as graciously as we lose. There were times when we could have scored more than a hundred points. We could have had break after fast break, but I would never allow my girls to run up the score like that; I always forced them to pull back, to run patterns and to execute, using four or five passes to take time off the clock instead of scoring. Not only that, I wouldn't let my kids show the other team what we were doing. It was important to me that the other team be able to save face, even if my girls wanted to show what they could do.

One time, after a win with a large margin, the opposing team refused to shake our hands after the game. They thought we'd taken advantage; they couldn't have guessed that we'd been holding back. Later, their coach came to see us play against a national power, and it was only then that he realized what we *could* have done. "Oh my God, you really spared us," he said, giving me a hug.

There was only one problem with our new success. As we got progressively better, it got harder to find good schools who would play us. We needed to earn credibility by playing teams of note, so that we'd have the strength of schedule that would make the selection committee consider us for postseason competition. But the big powers couldn't see the point of it, and to be honest, after coaching at some bigger schools, I know what they were thinking. It's humiliating for a powerhouse school, one that offers all kinds of sports, with 30,000 students and scholarships and a big coaching staff, to lose to a Cheyney, with 1,500 students and no money at all.

If they played us, they did it on their terms. If we wanted to play Maryland, Pitt, Temple, Rutgers, or Penn State, we had to go to them. Now, if you're on your home court, you have the advantage; you sleep in your own beds, warm up in your own gym, and have the support of your fans in the stands. But there was one year we were home for only four or five games of the twenty-six that we played.

Because we couldn't afford to stay over, we always had to drive straight home after the games, and those were some long nights because often the games would be scheduled back-to-back. They'd offer us a game, take it or leave it. If we were playing Maryland on Saturday and playing Penn State on Sunday, we'd just have to run to catch up.

We would go wherever and whenever someone would play us, glad and grateful for the opportunity. We were mentally prepared for the hardships, and we understood that our business was to play, not to make excuses. I called the girls my road warriors. "This is the price we pay because we want to play," we told one another. Some of my best memories of that time are late nights in the van; I loved those girls as if they were my own daughters.

The sport was young, too—we were all excited. It was very common to go to another coach's game because you admired their work; Ann would often pick me up to grab a quick dinner before going to see Immaculata or another school play. We're no longer allowed to do that by the NCAA—it's considered an unfair advantage—but I feel sorry that we can't support one another the way we used to. Jim Foster at Ohio State; Harry Perretta at Villanova; Tara VanDerveer at Stanford; Pat Summitt at Tennessee; Leon Barmore, who was at Louisiana Tech then; Rene Portland, who was at Penn State; Kay Yow at North Carolina State—we were all friends. We gave each other wonderful, warm compliments, we learned from one another, and we could always sit down to have dinner together after a game.

The late Sue Gunter and I would stand and laugh and socialize together when she was at LSU—and then we'd give each other a hug, go back to our respective teams, and go out on the floor to play as hard as we possibly could. Afterward, we'd give each other another hug, saying, "Hey, you really got me there, and there."

The Women's Basketball Coaches Association came about as a result of some of those friendships, during the Olympic Festival in Syracuse in 1981. There were a lot of coaches there, including Jill Hutchison, Pat Summitt, Kay Yow, Theresa Grentz, and Colleen Matsuhara. We wanted to have more control over how women's basketball was promoted and developed, and the right to determine our own direction. We had to dip into our own pockets, because someone had to quit a "real" job to run the thing. But we had a vision, and we believed that in time there would be enough memberships to support it.

At the time, my brother Tim had already graduated from Colgate University and was about to finish his law degree at the University of Pittsburgh. He was always looking out for the disenfranchised of the world, passionately advocating against injustice—something he continues to do to this day. That's why I didn't think twice before volunteering him to be the organization's lawyer, something he did pro bono for ten years simply because he loved our cause. He was one of the people who hung in there and believed, right from the inception, and we owe him a tremendous debt.

I remember laughing into the night with Betty Jaynes, the former coach at James Madison University who quit her job to be our first executive director. We were picking the site for our first convention and the two of us hoped and prayed that at least a hundred women would show up to justify what we were spending on the room. Everything great starts with a vision; the organization currently has more than four thousand members.

Maybe I just don't socialize now the way I used to, but I don't think the younger coaches today have the same opportunities to bond. I wish they did. The fast pace, the travel, the pressure of worrying about the security of your job, and the scrutiny of the public—it can all be very lonesome without the camaraderie and support of our fellow coaches. At the end of the day, we're all people who love the sport and care deeply about the young women in our care.

And as serious as the contests between us are, we always have to remember that basketball is just basketball. In our darkest moments of despair, we look to family, to God, and to our friends—not to an orange ball. Nobody knows that better than me.

After a few years, it got really difficult for me and Bill to be apart. He was approaching his junior year at medical school, and his courses were becoming more challenging; I missed not having him by my side and wanted us to feel more like a true family. So I applied for a position coaching at Syracuse University. My sister Verna was studying physical therapy there, and her husband was up there, too. I thought a coaching job at that school would be the greatest thing in the world.

I felt pretty good walking into the interview. After all, I had been making noise at a national level at this little school, and I thought the woman interviewing me would be impressed: "She's done such great things with nothing! I wonder what she'd be able to do with some real resources at a bigger school." But what she thought was that I was the cleaning lady.

No, I'm not kidding. I walked into that office wearing a cream-colored suit, and the lady behind the desk told me where I could find my "equipment." I didn't have the slightest idea what she was talking about, not a clue—until she pointed over behind me, to the broom closet. She thought I was the maid.

Polite as I could be, I said, "Excuse me, I have an appointment with the women's athletic administrator." And she says, "Oh, you came for the basketball job?" She comes out from behind the desk with a paper in her hand, and I can see that it's my résumé and that she's reading it for the first time.

We go back to her office, and I explain at great length about my success at Cheyney—the different tournaments we've won and the types of schools we've beaten, even without scholarships.

After all this, she asks me, "So, what makes you think you can coach at Syracuse?"

It was as if I hadn't spoken. What ran through my head is, *Excuse me, but are you an idiot?* But I took a deep breath and once again explained that I had taken this tiny, drastically underfunded school to some of the most elite competitions in the country, and that my team had beaten the real powerhouses of the day: Pitt, Temple, Maryland, West Chester, Penn State. I explained again that my husband is in medical school and that I'd love the opportunity to coach at Syracuse. In response, she asked me if I knew how much pressure a job like this comes with, and then, without waiting for my answer, she suggested that I try the high schools in the area, to see if they need some help.

At that point, I realized that I wasn't getting the job no matter what I said. I was so furious and so hurt, I was practically in tears.

I left and told Bill what had happened. True to form, he wouldn't hear a word of me coaching in a high school. "Vivian, don't they know who you are? Don't they know what you've accomplished? You've beaten them all. You don't have to put up with that. I can handle this. You don't need to come here. They'll be sorry one day that they didn't even give you a chance."

Eventually, Bill moved back to Pennsylvania so we could be together. He transferred his medical school credits to Temple University, where he worked on his doctorate in exercise physiology. I put the incident behind me and used my anger and humiliation as fuel. To this day, I don't have a problem with people doubting my team, or me; in fact, it's a much more familiar position for me than anything else. Go ahead and doubt us; we welcome the challenge.

7

A Mother Knows

I heard that one reporter called our rise at Cheyney "*Hoosiers,* with an all-female cast." I don't know about that, but it was a powerful thing we were doing out there. Suddenly, this scrappy team from a Division III–sized school was commanding respect from "money" schools with some of the best-established women's programs in the country, and it meant a lot to me to be carrying the hope of so many people. I felt I had the best of both worlds: we could compete at the highest levels and play in the greatest arenas, and yet I knew that my players were getting a first-class education and that we were graduating nine out of ten of them.

As our reputation grew, so did the support we got from our fans.

Coach John Chaney tells a story about those early days at Cheyney State. Since he tells it on himself, I guess I can repeat it.

One night, both the men's and the women's teams were scheduled to play Immaculata, the reigning national champions at the time. The women were playing the first game, with the men to follow. John arrived at the stadium and found it *packed.*

I remember the game. The parking lot was overflowing with buses and cars. Inside, people were standing in doorways and hanging off the bleachers, sitting on top of one another, and screaming their heads off. They'd spray-painted the school colors and the blue Cheyney *C* on bed sheets, which they hung from the rafters. The press was there in force, taking pictures and tapping out stories on portable typewriters balanced on their laps, and the fire marshal was trying to get some of those people out of there. The energy and enthusiasm in that gym were electrifying.

During our halftime, John went down to get his team dressed, and he riled those boys right up. He told them the fans were going crazy. "We've got the biggest crowd you've ever seen in your lives," he told them. "This is a tough team to beat, but I am *inspired* by those fans. They came out to see you, to cheer you on, to see you do what you do. So you better get up there and play your heart out."

All fired up, the men's team charged out of the locker room and into the gym. I just wish you could hear Coach Chaney tell this story, because he always ends it by throwing his head back and roaring with laughter: "By the time we got up there, there was no one there! The stands were empty; they'd taken their typewriters home! They'd come to see *Vivian's* team!"

Our fan base was growing, and so was my family. Bill and I were married for eight years before we had kids. We were just busy enjoying each other. He appreciated me, and I appreciated him. When we'd walk down the street, he'd grab my hand and say with real satisfaction, "My wife. My wife!" You could tell he just liked the way it sounded coming out of his mouth, and I loved hearing it.

We were thrilled to welcome our first child, David, on August 1, 1979. Bill took what it meant to be a man seriously and was very excited to have a son. "That boy needs to learn how to walk before he can learn to open doors for a lady," I used to tease him, but I knew he was going to be a great dad.

Right after David, our daughter Janine was born. We called her Nina. She was truly a beautiful little girl. People would stop us on the street, she was so pretty—just like a little doll, with a head full of hair, the prettiest dimples, the cutest eyes, and the longest eyelashes. I loved dressing her up.

She was the happiest baby you can imagine. She had such a giving personality. David was a little older, of course; when she was just learning to pull herself up to walk, he'd whiz by, bump her, and knock her over, and she'd start to cry. But as soon as I'd threaten to tear him up for not being careful, she would look up at him and start smiling. He couldn't help himself; he'd lean over and give her a big kiss. It would melt my heart. She was just that way.

After the kids were born, Bill really took charge of our family life, allowing me to stay dedicated to my work. He was so secure in himself; we didn't compete, and we didn't need to. It didn't matter who did what; we worked as a team. Sometimes I think that he grew up so that I wouldn't have to.

In November of 1981, it looked like everything was right with the world. I had a brand-new family, a winning team, and the support and love of the school community.

And then, everything went terribly, terribly wrong.

When Nina was fourteen months old, she got sick. Our pediatrician said it was just a routine childhood illness—a cold, teething problems, or one of the ear infections that babies get so often—but it wouldn't resolve. On our second or third visit, I told the doctor that Nina seemed different to me—she'd always been such a cheerful child, and now we couldn't get her to eat or to laugh—but she patted my shoulder and told me we'd all feel better with a little sleep.

I was putting Nina's coat on when the doctor saw something out of the corner of her eye. Instead of turning her head toward the source of a noise, Nina had turned her whole body. Without saying a word to me, the doctor picked up the phone and called an ambulance. Just like that, I went from putting on her coat to a Code Blue. Our lives changed forever.

She had spinal meningitis. It was a mistake, a missed diagnosis, and we were lucky that she survived at all, but by the time they caught it, the bacteria had completely devastated her brain. She had her first seizure that night.

"Your expectations for your daughter are going to have to change," the doctors told us. What they meant was that our beautiful little girl, who had loved to run and spin and tumble, who had loved to say "chick-en," would never walk or talk again.

The next two days were a nightmare. Nina was paralyzed by that point, and in terrible pain. But there was something else wrong with her—I was sure of it. Even after they assured us that she'd been stabilized, I was convinced that she was in imminent danger. Something *else* was wrong.

But it was like a nightmare; I couldn't persuade anyone to listen to me. "I'm a teacher; I have the best insurance in the world. I understand that she won't ever be the same, but even in this altered state she's in, I know that she's not right. Something's off; something's wrong. A mother knows," I said.

The doctors pushed aside my concerns. They thought I was still struggling with what they called the "new reality." And of course, I was. "She's not going to smile and move and talk; she's never going to be the way she used to be," they kept saying. That truth was horrifying enough, but it wasn't why I kept begging anyone who would listen to do another MRI. I knew in my heart that something else was wrong and that it was serious.

For two days, I begged, and for two days, they told me it wasn't necessary. Late that Saturday night, they came to me with a sheaf of papers to sign, giving them rush permission for an emergency surgery to put a shunt into the back of Nina's head, a device that would relieve the tremendous pressure on her brain. They'd finally done the MRI I'd begged them for, and they'd seen not only that I was right but also that there was no time to waste.

"If we don't operate immediately, she's going to die," they said.

That Sunday, after the operation, I walked into Nina's hospital room alone. Most of the time, at least in those early days, someone was with me—either Bill or one of my sisters, or my best friend, Janice. But that morning, I had no one with me. The doctor was in Nina's room, and I asked her what they'd found when they were putting in the shunt. I was thinking, *I will do anything, I will lay my life down, if you will tell me something I can bear.*

She just looked at me, as cold as you can imagine, and said to me, "Her brain's done. It's just dead. Didn't they tell you?"

I will never forget those words, or the matter-of-fact way she spoke them. I was so desperate, so hopeful, and it was like being hit in the chest with a cannonball. I just wanted to start walking, walking in any direction, to get away from her, from what had happened, from myself.

When my father was dying, I was always trying to squeeze just a little bit of hope out of what the doctors said. *Just tell me a little bit,* I wanted to say to them, *so I can look for the positive.* Where there's life, there's hope—I always believed that. But this doctor was telling me, flat out, that there was none, no hope at all for my baby girl. To this day, I wish I'd had someone with me who could have helped to shield me.

I've thought about it a lot in the years that have followed and now I think I understand why that doctor said what she said, the way she said it. I know that she saw the desperation in my eyes. I think she loved Nina and was so hurt by what had happened to her that she needed to say it as bluntly as possible in order to get it out. That's what I believe, anyway.

Well-meaning people said to us that they could imagine what it felt like, but I was pretty sure they couldn't. The only people I could open up to were people who had been in my shoes. You can't explain it to someone who hasn't been there. So Bill and I clung to each other. No matter how bad it got, I knew we would get through it because we were together. In the months that followed, when the doctors spoke to us about Nina's condition, I would turn to Bill for a "translation," and not just because he'd been in medical school. Even if I understood intellectually what they were telling us, I needed him to protect me, to turn what they were saying into something I could hear. The doctors seemed like gods, with the power to give life or take it away, and I would have given anything for them to tell us one thing that wouldn't break my heart.

We spent the next six months in the hospital, literally fighting for Nina's life. I moved in; I think I went home three or four times, total. In the intensive care unit, there are no windows, and the lights are on all the time; it's like there's no day or night. Janice brought soup to me every day, and she would stand there until I had drunk it down. "Drink the soup, Vivian. It doesn't matter if you like it or not. Drink the soup," she'd say. John Chaney physically carried me down to the cafeteria one time because I was losing so much weight that it looked like I was just wasting away. The only thing anyone could tell me to make me eat was that Nina needed me to be strong.

At first, we didn't tell the Cheyney team anything at all. They were so young, and this was such a heavy thing to put on their shoulders! Coach Chaney took over my practices, and Ann Hill helped out by reminding the girls what I had told them to focus on and running them through those drills. But I had never before missed practice—ever—so when I missed so many, they knew something serious was going on. Eventually, they called a meeting in one of the classrooms with the assistants and demanded to know what was happening.

When they found out, they immediately came to the hospital to see me. I was called downstairs to a large, open area in the lobby, and there I saw the team. The looks on their faces just broke my heart; I could see how sad and hurt they were for me. They asked me if I was going to come back, and I told them that I would, and they said that they would keep going if I kept my promise.

Meanwhile, Nina slept for days at a time. The doctors told us that all her energy was going to her brain as it tried to wake itself up, but sometimes she looked dead to me. When she woke, she'd cry and cry, and nothing we did could comfort her.

I spent many hours sitting on a small bench outside the chapel at the Children's Hospital of Philadelphia, struggling with the question of why this had happened to her—why this had happened to *us*. I'd always believed in a higher power, and I'd gone to church as a child, but I'd never really taken it seriously. My brothers and sisters and I spent more time at church laughing at the ladies' hats and the off-key singing than learning scripture. More than once my mom had to hit me on the head for being a distraction. The Reverend Hobie Green would stand up there and ask for prayers, and Ms. Cooper would raise her hand to interrupt him. "I need everyone to pray now, because I don't have the two hundred dollars I need to get my chimney fixed." As a kid, I would just die laughing.

Still, I must have picked up some things in that pew in Edenborn, because those Bible stories had stayed with me. And when Nina got sick, I felt a need to have a deeper understanding of my own faith. It was like I was clinging to the idea of a higher power as if it were a life raft. If I understood nothing else, I did understand that the Lord makes miracles happen. God was the one with the answers, when all hope was gone.

I spent many late nights on that bench, reading the Bible and searching for insight, searching for something to ease the pain.

There were always clergy of all types moving through the hospital at night, and I'd ask if they had a minute to sit and talk. We had been so perfectly contented. Had I done something so unforgivable that this had happened to my baby girl? I searched and searched, and I came to believe that God really does love all of us, no matter how sinful we might be. One night, a priest said something that made a little bit of sense to me. He said that God uses those of us who have endured a great deal as comforters. We are examples to other people who are suffering, so they know that, yes, you can make it, with the help of one another.

I do believe that we have God beside us, even in those terrible, dark moments, and that every one of us has an equal audience before Him. But I would be lying if I said I understood completely why bad things happen. I could say, "Hey, what will be will be, because that is the Lord's choice and because the devil walks on this Earth and because we sin," but I wouldn't be telling the truth. Sitting in that hospital, I did not want to be a comforter, an example of hope and courage to other people. I wanted my little girl back.

To this day, I struggle. I admire people who have suffered deeply yet are unshakable in their faith. As for me, I have had many bouts of doubt, and I have been very angry with the Lord. I do understand that I am truly blessed, and I am grateful for those blessings; I always know that things could be far worse. I know that I need to have continued trust in the Lord; honestly, for me to have come this far, I know that He has carried me. But I also know that I will need to have a far greater spiritual understanding before I can come to terms with some of the things that have happened to me in my life. All I can do is approach that struggle with faith.

It was while Nina was in the hospital that I came to believe in the power of the mind over the body. I'm someone who has always been prone to colds and the flu; Bill used to say that if there was a bug in the room, I'd bring it home. But not when Nina was in the hospital. For six long months, I was the healthiest I've ever been—

even though I was living in the hospital, showering there, surrounded by sick people and their bacteria, and barely sleeping or eating. You see, if you have the slightest sniffle or a cough, they won't let you visit the intensive care unit—a minor cold can kill someone with a compromised immune system. And I needed to see my baby every day.

After Nina had been stabilized, the basketball court became a place of refuge for me. My family and friends had stepped in to make sure I could keep working, and I was grateful for the opportunity to throw myself back into basketball. There have been times in my life where I have thought, *I don't even know how I am still standing right now, because the hurt is so real.* But the mind is powerful. It helps you accept the things you can, and shields you from what you can't. You move and keep busy and you don't give yourself the chance to let it all in.

And so I shuttled back and forth, from the hospital to the gym and back again. Trouble was, even on the court, my mind never really left Nina's side. I was there and not there at the same time. But those young women forced me to pay attention to them. They had decided among themselves, "Okay, it's time to take it to another level," and I could see the resolve in their eyes.

They played as if they were on a mission—in a sense, I think they were. They wanted to do everything they could so that I never had to get upset or question anything they did. It was something to see. Opponents fell before them and it was like they hardly noticed; they just moved on to the next game. The feeling you had, watching them, was that they *could not be beaten.*

Not everyone was thrilled to see us succeed, and one incident in particular really hurt me. One night, Rene Portland, the coach at Penn State, tipped me off with a phone call. "There's a new ruling: in order to be eligible for the NCAA championships, you can't play more than twenty-nine games, and that tournament you played back in the winter counts as two games." The issue had come up at a meeting she'd attended; the consensus had been to say nothing to me, and to let the Lady Wolves play the game we were scheduled to play at West Chester University that weekend, even though it would put us over the twenty-nine-game limit.

In short, these other schools had agreed to stand by and let us hang ourselves on a technicality without even realizing it. My athletic director, Ed Lawrence, was so shocked that he called Rene himself. Rene told him it was true. "My conscience wouldn't let me stop the best team in America from playing," she said. I've always had a special place in my heart for her as a result, and I am thankful to her to this day.

We went into the regionals with 24 wins and 2 losses for the season. We beat Auburn 75–64. We beat North Carolina State 76–68. And then we beat Kansas State 93–71, to take the regional title. At that game, the last game before the Final Four, I heard the NCAA officials at the scoring table, calling the NCAA headquarters and saying, "Oh my God, she's going to win. Shaney, Chenae—I don't even know how you say it. Where did they even come from?" They were alarmed—it was going to be one of the very first televised games, and I guess they wanted to make sure that big-time schools were playing. I just looked at Ann and laughed. They didn't know anything about us—this school, this coach, this team—and they sure weren't counting on us to be there. The game was set to be played at Old Dominion, one of the blue-chip programs in the sport, but Old Dominion wasn't playing—we were.

Even the Cheyney administrators were privately hoping we weren't going to make it. Do you know what it takes to feed and sleep a team—not to mention transporting them? The NCAA wasn't financing the women like they do now. We hadn't sunk the winning basket in the game that qualified us before my athletic director was on the floor, sweating and hollering, "Jesus Christ, Stringer, what have you done? Now what the hell are we gonna

Mom and Dad on their wedding day, July 30, 1947.

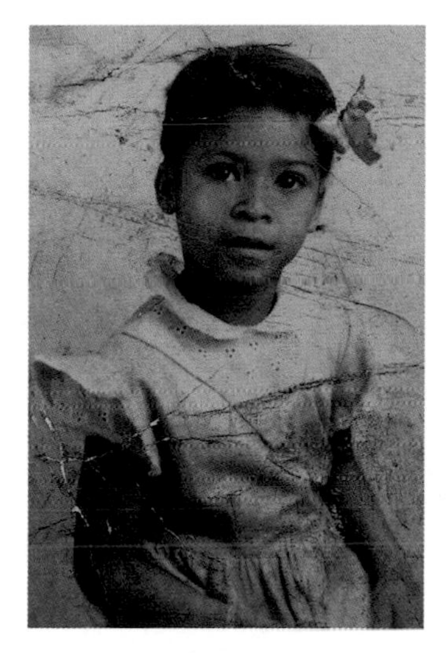

I must have been about five here. There aren't a lot of photos of us from childhood. We didn't have a camera until I was in high school and started working at Moss's Supermarket.

Here I am with my sister Verna, in a neighbor's yard in the tiny town of Edenborn, Pennsylvania. Verna and I were so alike as children, people often thought we were twins.

I had to fight to wear the red-and-black Germantownship cheerleading squad uniform. Verna's in the back row, on the left; I'm on the right. Kathleen Morris is seated.

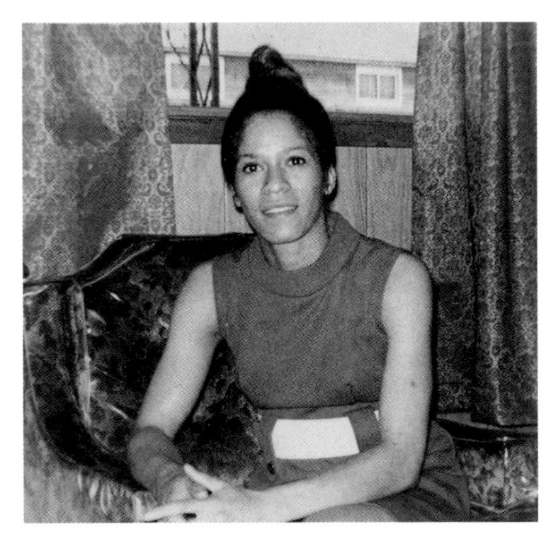

This was taken in 1966, my senior year of high school. Tell me that girl isn't going to change the world!

In 1967, my sister Ricky *(left)* was in seventh grade, Madeline *(center)* was a freshman in high school, and I was in my sophomore year in Slippery Rock.

My dad was a great musician. Losing his legs didn't stop him from performing. In this one, he's sitting in on piano with the Harold Betters Quartet. That's my brother Tim on the sax!

This was taken my first year at Slippery Rock. I had just met a handsome gymnast named Bill Stringer. He gave me that rose.

September 1971. My dad walked me down the aisle. It was a new beginning, but it also felt like I was breaking up my family.

When we got engaged, Bill promised me he'd take care of me, and he always did.

Bill and I waited eight years to have kids after we got married. We were busy having a great time together.

Nina just idolized her big brother, David. She was the happiest baby you could imagine.

Bill, with baby Justin, in the kitchen in Iowa. He loved being a dad.

The Stringer family, 1985. Bill is holding Nina, Justin is on my lap, and David is on the right. We were always there for one another.

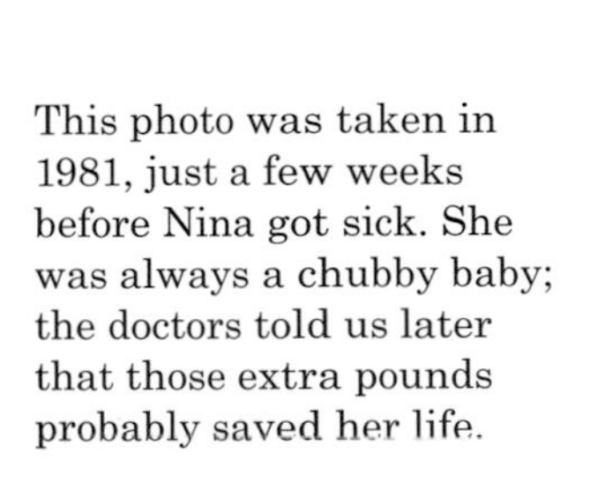

This photo was taken in 1981, just a few weeks before Nina got sick. She was always a chubby baby; the doctors told us later that those extra pounds probably saved her life.

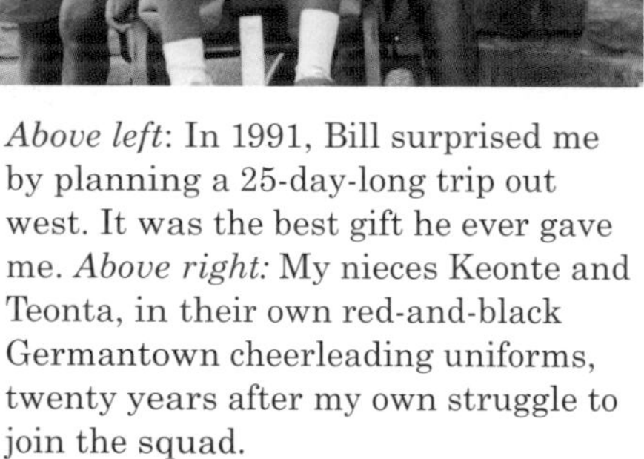

Above left: In 1991, Bill surprised me by planning a 25-day-long trip out west. It was the best gift he ever gave me. *Above right:* My nieces Keonte and Teonta, in their own red-and-black Germantown cheerleading uniforms, twenty years after my own struggle to join the squad.

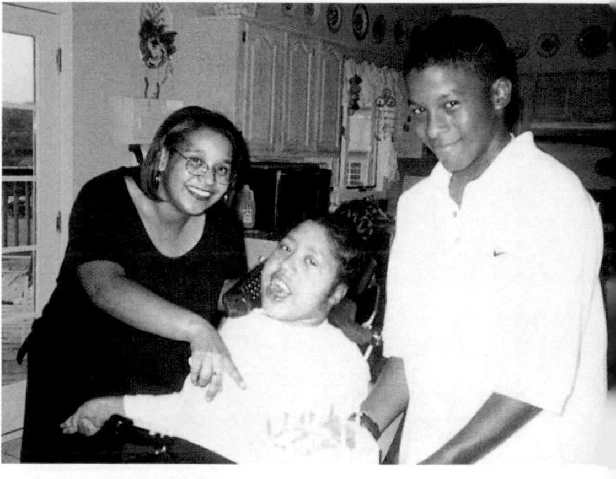

Above: Keonte with Nina and Justin. Keonte, my eldest niece, moved with us from Iowa to New Jersey when I took the job at Rutgers. She's been like a sister to Nina, and a daughter and a best friend to me.

Left: David at eighteen, in his North Carolina State uniform, with me and my dear friend Janice Fitzgerald, the godmother to all three of my children.

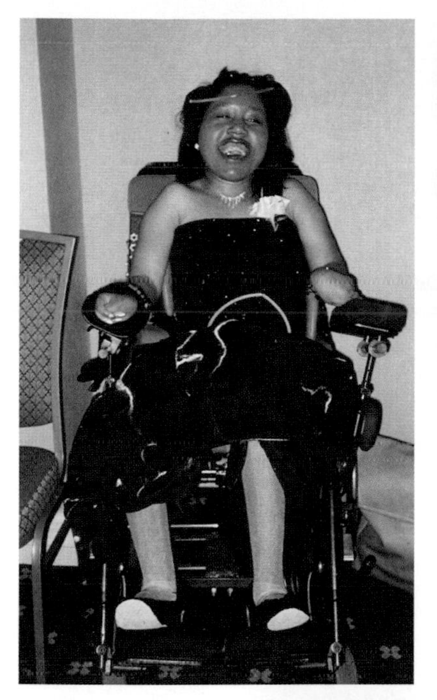

Imagine my pride as my sons walked me down the aisle to be inducted into the Women's Basketball Hall of Fame in 2001. Bill would have been so proud of all of us.

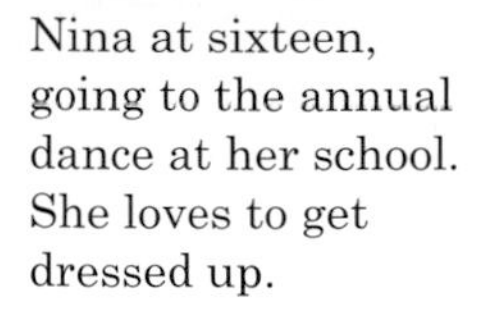

Nina at sixteen, going to the annual dance at her school. She loves to get dressed up.

Above: The Stoner girls, 1991. From left to right, Ricky, me, my mother, Madeline, and Verna. My mom is often mistaken for one of us; you can see why.

Left: My brother Jack with our sister Madeline's daughter, Teonta, at her law school graduation.

Top: Here I am with my siblings, their spouses, and many of my nieces and nephews in New York City on New Year's Eve 1996. I often think that I could never have succeeded without my family; sometimes I think I couldn't have survived without them.

Center: Here I am with my mom in 2003. There's nobody on earth I'd rather talk and shop and laugh and dance with.

Bottom: Nobody could ever have asked for a better advocate or a more devoted friend than my brother Tim.

do? We can't do it! We don't have any money! We can't even afford to get you down there!"

Ann Hill, bless her heart, stepped between the two of us, and said, "You just get out of her face, right now. We'll find a way."

Ann was right: we were going to make it happen. But Ed was right, too; we didn't have the money. So we all sat down and figured out where we could get some. The president of the university, Dr. Wilson, went to some of the big businesses in the area and asked them for contributions. I put up a chunk of my own money; Coach Chaney dipped into his pockets, too.

I went to the First Baptist Church of Philadelphia to ask for donations. I'm sure that some of the congregation had never seen a basketball in their lives, but I tried to make them see the larger significance of this team. I told them we had a lot to be proud of, but that we needed a little help. "I sure would like to see them look nice when they get on the plane," I said. The people in that congregation didn't have much either, but they dug deep into their pockets when they passed the plate. Mrs. Kelly at Kelly's Sporting Goods in West Chester, Pennsylvania, generously made up the shortfall, and when my Lady Wolves boarded the plane, every single one of them was wearing a brand-new white sweater, with a big blue Cheyney *C* sewn onto it.

You talk about a proud moment; I thought my heart would burst. I don't think any one of us will ever forget it.

It was the very first NCAA Final Four in women's college basketball history, and the Lady Wolves from little Cheyney State were there. It was the biggest game of my career and, if things had been different, I might have been focused on nothing but that, but I had my daughter to think about, too. In fact, right before the start of the tournament, I was in Nina's room at Children's Hospital, talking to one of her doctors, when I got a call from Ann Hill. "What size underwear do you wear?"

The NCAA had announced a press conference, scheduled for 6 p.m. that night. Ann had explained the situation with Nina to the officials, but they would not make an exception: the head coaches had to be present to take questions from the media. So Ann, knowing that I would be wearing whatever I had slept in at the hospital, had gotten into her car, bought me some fresh clothes, and was on her way over to take me to the airport. I made the press conference by the skin of my teeth and then flew right back to Nina's bedside.

Like my 2007 team, the Cheyney team of 1982 was a young team, mostly sophomores. We might not have had many seasoned players, but we had one another. The commitment that those girls showed to one another and to me was truly fierce—and it had staying power. There were eleven players on the Final Four team, and I bet that Debra Walker and Yolanda Laney could give you ten of those girls' phone numbers today without even having to look them up. And do you know that almost every single one of them was in the stands cheering when I went to the Final Four in 2007 with Rutgers?

We didn't have a band in Norfolk; we could barely afford to get ourselves there! Norfolk State was kind enough to lend us theirs. They let us eat in their cafeteria, too. We were the underdog team, and people wanted to help where they could. I guess I thought their colors were blue and white like ours, but they were green and white—and remember, the game was televised. I had visions of people adjusting their sets, trying to make the band's colors match the team's. I can still hear John Chaney laughing about that: "Life on a shoestring, Vivian. We're living life on a shoestring."

The four teams were Maryland, Tennessee, Louisiana Tech, and Cheyney. Amazingly, we won our first game against Maryland. When the buzzer sounded, one of our deans came running out of the stands and picked me up off my feet. I thought she was excited about our victory; I didn't know that Bell Telephone had pledged $10,000 to whichever team won that game. We'd be able to pay for our hotel rooms after all!

Later that day, we were having practice, and there was no transportation back to the hotel. The girls, sweaty and exhausted, were standing in the parking lot. Ann Hill and I had to ask Mr. Whittaker, one of the teachers at the school, if he would take the girls back so that they could shower, have a meal, and get some rest before the biggest game of their lives.

As I'd told my players a hundred times, it doesn't matter where you come from, but where you're going; it doesn't matter where you start, but where you finish. And where we finished was at the NCAA championship game, the very first in women's basketball history.

We fell to Louisiana Tech, 76 to 62. The most powerful women's basketball program of the decade, they went on to dominate the rest of the 1980s. But I couldn't have been prouder, or more grateful, for the effort and heart my team gave me. We didn't need scholarships; we had our minds and the willingness to work hard. It didn't matter that we were poor; we had a cause. We had loved overcoming impossible odds and proving all the doubters wrong. We represented the disenfranchised, the dismissed, the forgotten, and we had made them proud.

Those girls were the believers. They had played their hearts out, and I knew that they had done it for me and for my family.

The loss to Louisiana Tech was emotional. There's no greater high than victory—and no more total silence than the one that comes from a loss. It's like life and death; in the blink of an eye, you can be on the other side. Oftentimes, I've said to the team at the end of the season that nothing is ever as good—or as bad—as it seems. The reality rests somewhere in between, and I know that better than anyone.

The night of that game, the team was tired and feeling bad about their day, but the guy who was holding our airline tickets was nowhere to be found. Bill kept asking me, "Where are the tickets? Do you want me to go find him?" It made him crazy to see our girls waiting to leave after the day they'd had. I asked him to please sit tight. Now Bill knew never to interfere with my profession, but this must have been too much for him to bear.

Apparently—and I didn't find this out until recently—Bill excused himself to go to the restroom and went into the lounge, where the guy who had our tickets was drinking and carousing. Ann Hill followed him, worried about an altercation. She saw him lean over, right into this guy's face, and say, "Don't you ever disrespect my wife and this team. You get yourself downstairs and give those tickets to those girls right now."

Bill never said one word about it to me. He came back, sat down, and the man holding the tickets got them to me. It's good that I didn't know. I would have been furious at the time, but it's the most wonderful story in the world to me now.

After seven or eight months, Nina was finally stable enough to come home. Those days were hard. Nina required round-the-clock care, and the house was filled with medical equipment. She was in a lot of pain, and she would cry so long and so hard it was like someone was torturing her. Sometimes it would last all night long, and Bill and I would take turns rocking and holding her. We thought she was blind, so for months we traveled three days a week to a school for the blind in Delaware. We were so completely immersed in caring for her that I almost felt like I'd become a licensed doctor. Feeding her meant sending a flexible rubber tube down her nose and throat, waiting for the pop that told you that it had entered her stomach. It's amazing what a person can learn to do if you have to—if you want to.

It was rough on the whole family. David was just fourteen months older than Nina, old enough to understand that everything had changed, but not old enough to understand why. In one fell swoop, he had lost his best friend and playmate, and his mom, for months, to the hospital. My mother and Janice took good care of him, and together we did whatever we could to make his life seem as ordinary as possible, but we were a far cry from a normal family in those days. Most of our attention was focused on Nina.

I sometimes wonder how David felt during that time. When he got a little older, David appeared while Bill and I were giving Nina a bath and asked a question that must have been on his mind for a long time: would Nina ever walk and talk like other kids? He remembered, of course, that at one time, she *had* been like other kids, running and playing and getting into mischief. When Bill told him, as gently and as lovingly as he could, that his sister wouldn't ever be like other kids, that she wouldn't ever be the way she had been, David ran out of the room and disappeared for a little while, to his own quiet spot. He never asked the question again.

Nina was still partly comatose—it took her about three years to fully come out of it—which meant she slept between fifteen and twenty hours a day. The sad thing was that when she slept, she looked just as she had before she'd gotten sick. Standing in the doorway of her bedroom, I could almost trick myself into believing that this whole thing was just a terrible dream that we would soon wake up from.

I believed with every bone in my body that we were lucky for Nina's life. I know it probably isn't true, but they say that you should pray for exactly what you want. In those days, I prayed so hard, "Lord, let me just see her smile again, and let her know that we love her." To this day, I wonder if I should have prayed for something more for her.

8

Time to Leave

The year after we went to the Final Four, we were playing a game at Louisiana Tech. An English professor from Grambling State University, which was just down the road, was sitting in the audience watching practice. Afterward, she came down to shake my hand and to tell me that someone wanted to meet me. That someone was Coach Eddie Robinson, one of the greatest coaches of all time.

I was so honored that one of my heroes, the winningest football coach in all of America, wanted to speak to *me.* I went to his house, which sat up on a hill overlooking the football area, and we talked for a long time. Coach Robinson was so kind to me, so complimentary about the things he'd seen me do and my passion for the game; and he asked me many questions about my plans for the future.

I told him how much I loved Cheyney. I told him how it felt to go out onto the court against a Penn State or a Maryland, knowing that my little old school of 1,500 kids, with barely a nickel and dime to rub together, was their equal on the court. Their big names and bigger budgets didn't matter; on the court, it was just two referees, ten kids, and a ball. I told him how glad it made me to see the stands full for every game, our students and faculty chanting and cheering, jumping out of their seats. I told him how indebted I felt to our president, Dr. Wilson, who had always told me that he wanted me to fly as high as I could go.

I had always felt that it was my calling to rise and give hope to the have-nots of the world, and for me Cheyney was as good as it could get. No, we didn't have scholarship money, but that was why our program made people feel so good: we were the underdogs, the giant-killers.

But there was a problem. People were developing conferences, where schools of similar sizes and finances were banding together and playing each other. It didn't matter what your record was or how good you were; if you had fewer than 3,000 students, you had to play Division III. I wanted to test myself against the best, but no longer were they going to allow the little dogs to jump up on the big dogs. Our name was synonymous with an outstanding basketball program, and yet they were trying to squeeze us out.

I told Coach Robinson that over the course of my career, I had gotten calls from USC, and Old Dominion, and Kansas State, and Duke, and Kentucky. Dean Smith of the University of North Carolina had called me, as had Joe Paterno at Penn State. "Vivian, come up to Happy Valley," Joe had said. And I had told all of them, "No, no, no. I'm not leaving Cheyney."

Coach Robinson listened and then he said: "Vivian, when the time comes, you must go. You have to consider what it means for you to assume a greater stage, and to give America the opportunity to see a black female in a head coaching position, calling the shots at a major school."

I said that I couldn't imagine coaching anywhere else, that I'd rather quit basketball than leave Cheyney. He said, "I've got more players in the NFL than the coach of any other university in this entire country. I've been asked to coach in the pros by the Green Bay Packers, by Chicago . . ." and he named a couple more teams. "But as I sit here in my house and look down at that field, I know that my purpose in life is to be here. The young people here need to learn basic things, like how to handle a fork and a knife, and the importance of getting an education, so they can have an impact in their turn, and I'm like a pop to them.

"You, on the other hand, need to open up and consider your options. Don't worry about how successful the basketball program has been in the past. You may have to take a step or two back in order to move forward; you're a winner, and you will be a winner. But you can affect far more people if you understand your destiny, and I don't know how much further Cheyney can take you."

I heard what he said with tears in my eyes. "Cheyney is my heart, and that's where I want to be," I said. But his words must have stayed in the back of my mind, because it was the next year that I started talking to Iowa.

Ann Hill knew about the opportunities I had been offered over the years, and I often talked things through with her. One afternoon on the golf course, Ann turned to me and said, "Vivian, the track team has qualified for the state track competition, and we don't even have enough money to put gas in the vans to get them there. You know I'm the last one that wants you to go; I love you like a sister, and I've been with you since the beginning. But I'm going to tell you something: you have stretched this rubber band as far as it can go."

Ann, as usual, was right. You give me a challenge, and I will meet it. If the administration at Cheyney had been reluctant to give us what we needed, I would have fought it until they gave in. But that was the heartbreak: there wasn't anyone to argue with at Cheyney. Everyone loved us and had done every single thing they could for us—truthfully, at a level they really couldn't sustain. How can you ask somebody you love so much to give you something that they don't have? I was nothing but grateful, humbled by their support and their faith in us. But it was time for me to go.

It seemed like the University of Iowa was in the cards from the beginning. First of all, Ann's father had gone to podiatry school there, at a time when very few black men were granted medical degrees. My basketball coach at Slippery Rock, Dr. Ann Griffith, had gotten her doctorate from the University of Iowa, as had my field hockey coach, Dr. Zimmerman—two of the most important people in the world to me. In fact, Dr. Griffith was old friends with Dr. Christine Grant, the athletic director who had contacted me from Iowa. I was hoping Janice would tell me to drop it, but she knew all about Iowa because of their famed writers' workshop, and she encouraged me to look into it also. Even Coach Eddie Robinson had a connection to the University of Iowa. The stars were lined up, and I think that when things are meant to happen, they do.

Oh, I came up with every excuse in the book; I'm embarrassed now to repeat the things I said when I started talking to them. "Ohio, Idaho—who ever heard of Iowa? I don't even know where it is." I asked Dr. Grant if Iowa was where potatoes came from. More seriously, I knew that there were very few minorities there, and I was worried for myself and for my sons. But I knew in my mind that all this bluster was really fear of moving out of my comfort zone, and the one thing I won't let myself do is bow out of a challenge because of fear.

So we went out there for a visit. At the other schools I visited, the administrators would take me to the stadium so I could see the state-of-the-art courts and training facilities. There were fancy dinners, swanky hotel suites, high-flying alumni to shake hands with.

At Iowa, I got off the plane and was met immediately by a team of doctors—a neurologist, an orthopedist, even a dentist—who specialized in treating children with special needs. Dr. Healy, the director of developmental disabilities at the University of Iowa Hospitals and Clinics (UIHC), told me that he would personally coordinate this team to ensure that Nina got the best medical care possible and that he would come to my house at any time, day or night, if I needed him.

I felt that the people in Iowa really understood what I needed, not just as a coach, but as a mother and a woman. This, it was clear, was a place that would embrace us as a family. I didn't need to see or hear anything else to make my decision.

The last game I ever coached for Cheyney State College was an Elite Eight game at Penn State. It made no sense that we had to play at Penn State, because we were the higher seed, but we were used to it by then.

In the final minute of the game, we were set to win. We were down by one, but the ball was taken out of bounds, in our possession, under our basket, and we knew exactly what we had to do. They had no choice but to foul us, and we'd win the game.

But that wasn't what happened. They knocked her down while she was trying to take the shot to win the game, but the foul call never came. I can still see Debra Walker going up and falling down, with no call, and then going up again, and getting knocked down again—and the referee running off the floor.

The whole crowd went completely silent. You could feel the collective shame of everyone who sat there. I've never seen anything like it. If you'd said something in a regular conversational tone, you would have been heard at the very top of the stands.

The girls laid down on the floor and cried. They refused to leave the floor with that injustice standing. I ran after the officials, who had fled to their locker room. I banged on their door, begging them to come out and explain to me and the girls how they could possibly have done such a thing, in a game of such magnitude. "Please, please don't do this to my girls," I said. It's not my usual policy to argue with officials. I don't believe in providing my teams with excuses. As I always tell my girls, if the calls are excessive and unfair, it's our job to overcome. But I couldn't find a way to overcome what they'd done.

Finally, I stopped knocking. Ann picked the girls up and got them into the locker room. It was over.

For many years afterward, I wondered if they had been prepared. I thought they had been—I knew they had been. But I was nagged by doubts. In the summer of 2007, the Cheyney players and I went on a cruise to the Bahamas together—a long-planned reunion. It was a meaningful trip. We're all extremely close; we understood a long time ago that it is all for one, and one for all. We laughed and cried and remembered and reflected—just us.

On that trip, I asked them if they felt they had been prepared for what happened. They told me that I had given them that exact situation and time and score: 7.5 seconds left, the ball in our possession and under our basket. "When you called the time-out and we looked at the clock, we knew it was time to execute; we had gone through that exact scenario thousands of times. We just didn't know that they wouldn't call the foul." Thank God, I had gone over it.

But that day, when I got back to our locker room, which was a cramped, ugly, overheated facility, I saw that a little window in the corner, a filthy thing covered with iron bars next to the sink, was broken.

"Who broke that window?" I asked. The team sat there on that long bench, but nobody met my eyes and there was no answer. No one spoke.

"That is not how we react when things aren't right," I said, looking at each one of them in turn. I asked them one more time: "Who broke that window?"

No one said a thing, and I just couldn't make myself pursue it. They were so hurt already—as I was. And I knew that there was another heartbreak waiting right around the corner for them: the news that I was leaving them, and Cheyney, for Iowa.

Years later, on that cruise, when all the kids were in bed and all the husbands were occupying themselves somewhere else, Ann Hill asked the question yet again: "Who broke that window?"

Debra Walker said, "I did."

"I sort of thought you did," said Ann.

I arranged to take a sabbatical from Cheyney, which gave me a chance to explore this new place without losing the safe haven that was Cheyney forever. My brother Tim negotiated the one-year contract with Iowa. (He would later negotiate a historic deal for me there, in which I received pay parity with the basketball coach on the men's side. I know that he fought hard for that first because he loved me, but his advocacy turned out to be a very good thing for all female coaches.)

I don't remember telling the Cheyney players that I was leaving. I have always had the ability to block out things that are very painful, which has probably served me well. What's strange is that Ann Hill doesn't remember it, either.

I do remember the aftermath, though. One girl on that team told me that she'd been in and out of love a lot of times, but nobody had ever broken her heart the way I did when I told her I was leaving. I felt the same way. They were a great team, and I am grateful to this day that they loved me enough to let me go. You see, leaving was the best thing for us, and the best thing for Nina. We were still hoping that Nina would defy the odds, and we felt that if she had a chance at recovery, it would be in Iowa. So we packed our bags and moved to the Hawkeye State.

9

You Can't Go Home Again, but You Can Get Close

To this day, I think Iowa is the warmest place in the world. Everyone knows that the whole state is basketball mad, but the warmth we felt wasn't just for us as basketball people. You could see the genuine care and love that Midwesterners had for one another, and they valued things I could relate to, like an honest day's work for an honest day's pay.

I confess that sometimes Iowans were even nicer than I thought possible; I had to learn to relax a little bit. One day, I had to get some clothes cleaned in order to go on a recruiting trip. I stopped at a dry cleaner's that advertised same-day service. What they were actually promising was same-day *shirt* service, but I didn't see that on the poster. When I asked if I could get my suit cleaned the same day, the guy said, "Sure, Coach, anything for you." But when I got to Michigan and put the suit on, there was a stain that hadn't come out.

When I got back, I went in there guns blazing, expecting all kinds of arguments and excuses. But the guy just hung his head and said, "Coach, I'm sorry. I wanted to do anything I could to help, but I couldn't make it work, and I feel bad about that." He proceeded to give me a refund and a month's worth of free cleaning coupons, and he offered to reclean the suit and deliver it to my house. I was so embarrassed that by the time I left his store, I was apologizing to him! It was a good lesson for me. I thought, *Viv, you can't be bringing that East Coast competitive mentality to these people. They really do care!*

Another time, after a big storm, the skylight in our house started to leak, and there was water everywhere. You know what the guy wanted in order to fix our roof? A signed basketball. That was it. I'll tell you, the whole state was more like a giant family than anything else. If you got invited to speak, they didn't just drop you back at your hotel after. Instead, you'd find yourself sitting out in the middle of someone's property under the trees with a heaping plate of roasted corn and chops so tender you could bite through them with false teeth, as though you were a cousin who'd been away for a while.

Just as important, the University of Iowa was a beautiful place with a fantastic commitment to women's sports. This was a school that took Title IX one better: they didn't just give 50 percent of the sports budget to women's programs; they pledged that their financial commitment would match the profile of the student body. In other words, if two-thirds of the students were women, then women's sports would get two-thirds of the budget. And my boss, Dr. Christine Grant, had been president of the AIAW (the Association for Intercollegiate Athletics for Women), the organization that preceded the NCAA.

The icing on the cake was that Bill was hired as an exercise physiologist with the university, and his office was right across the hallway from mine. While he worked with a lot of teams, the key for me was that he worked with *mine*; he was the one responsible for getting my kids conditioned before the season started.

The situation was pretty close to ideal. As we had been promised, the medical care for Nina was without parallel. Dr. Healy and Dr. Nowak, Nina's brilliant special-needs dentists, were so important to us. You see, a special-needs-child's health is never completely stable, and doctors who know and care can make an enormous difference.

Let me give you an example. I took Nina to the hospital recently. Because she's over twenty-one, she's treated on the adult ward, but because she's never walked, her veins are minuscule, like those of an infant. Nina can't talk, so a blood test is the first thing they do when they're trying to figure out why she's in pain. But they don't have tiny, child-size butterfly needles on the adult ward. Unless I have a relationship with a doctor or a nurse on the ward, they're going to stick her over and over again, trying to find a vein, until I've convinced someone to go and get what they need from the pediatric ward. That's just one example, but it shows how important those relationships with her doctors are.

What's more, both Dr. Nowak and Dr. Healy were dedicated to treating the whole patient. It's hard for a parent to know what effect one procedure or medication will have on another, and it's nearly impossible to get a number of doctors on the same page at the same time. Dr. Healy coordinated all that for us. Let's say that Nina needed three separate surgeries—not an unusual occurrence in those years. Dr. Healy would look at what was scheduled; maybe the surgery Nina needed so that her teeth could continue to grow could be done while she was anesthetized for another procedure. Medicine has become so specialized that it's unusual to find a doctor who's looking at the big picture; I knew immediately how lucky we were to have these people on our team.

I really felt Iowa, and the Iowans. When the government wasn't giving the farmers the support they'd promised them, I felt the hurt personally. And to this day, when people make fun of the Midwest for being unsophisticated or square, I feel like someone has slapped me in the face. When you came right down to it, Iowa didn't feel all that different from Edenborn. Iowa City is a much bigger and more sophisticated place, but the values are very similar.

All the same, the move was not without strain for us. I was coming from a school right near Philadelphia, and I'd gotten used to being able to go see great jazz anytime I wanted to, or going out for a nice meal after a day of shopping. I've always loved bright lights and excitement, from the time I was a child. When I was about fourteen, my father tried to cure me of my dream of becoming a jazz musician by taking me to play my sax in one of the clubs. He put dark glasses on me so no one would guess my age. He wanted me to see how poor a musician's life was, with all the late nights and the cigarette smoke and the drinking. Unfortunately, his plan backfired—I loved every single minute of it.

So there was quite a bit of culture shock when I got to Iowa. The year was 1984, but the radio stations were playing music from the fifties and sixties, bands like the Beach Boys or the Platters. And the shops of Iowa City seemed to carry mostly Earth shoes and folk-singer clothing. I'd worn that when I was in college, but I wasn't going back to it! So I made a rule that whenever our team traveled for an away game, we had to stay at the hotel closest to a mall or a big department store, so that I could pick up some clothes.

These things—music and clothes—might sound trivial, but they're not. I'm talking about the kind of thing that makes you feel good about yourself, and I felt strained. Everywhere around me, it seemed like time had stood still, and I'll tell you, that part of it was hard.

Another, more significant concern was that at the time minorities accounted for just 2 percent of Iowa's population. Let me tell you what that meant in practical terms: wherever we were, we were almost always the only black people there.

In our first days there, I cornered one of the deans of the university, one of the few black men I had seen on campus, at a cocktail party. I had something urgent on my mind: "How do I find someone who can style my hair?" I ended up making an appointment with a woman who swore that she was used to working on black hair; she'd been the beautician for some musicians who had passed through Iowa City for a cultural series. I had a curl in my hair at the time, and I wanted to go straight. "No problem," she said, "I know how to do that," and I was absolutely overjoyed when I got out of her chair. She'd done exactly what I'd asked for, and my hair looked really pretty.

I was thrilled—for about two days. That was when large chunks of my hair started to fall out. It was bone dry, like straw scorched by the sun, and you could read a newspaper through what was left on my head. I practically went out of my mind. That stylist apologized up and down, but there wasn't anything to be done. She sent strand samples to the Redken product people in California and got the best minds at the dermatology department at the university working on the problem. But I was stuck in wigs and head scarves until it started to grow back. I still can't see it as funny, twenty-odd years later. How I look has always had a big impact on how I feel, and to lose my hair was terrible for me.

But by far the hardest thing for me about the move to Iowa City was not being able to find a church where I felt comfortable. I was accustomed to a more soulful rendering of the scriptures than what I found in the Midwest. I wanted to be touched; I wanted the words and music to speak to my very soul. That was something that never quite fell into place for us in Iowa.

I was also surprised to find that people would come up to me, before and after the service, to talk about basketball. It wasn't anyone's fault; Iowans just loved the sport so much. They loved the team, and they loved us. But I was still so raw, and in so much pain. I wanted to talk to God about how much I hurt, how much *we* hurt. I had so many questions about why Nina had been devastated the way she had been. I longed for a sanctuary—a place where I could be as expressive as I needed to be without feeling like people were looking at me, not another place to talk about what I thought Purdue was going to do on Saturday. I didn't want to be "Coach" at church.

When we were still at Cheyney, we had heard about something called "patterning," which was taught by the Institutes for the Achievement of Human Potential (IAHP) in Pennsylvania. Patterning is the idea that it is possible, in some cases, to reprogram even a very badly damaged human brain by taking the person through the normal stages of neurodevelopment. To give an example, proponents believe that a person has to learn to crawl before they can walk. The treatment involves intense and prolonged repetition, and it was the exact opposite of what we had tried with Nina until then. When you're with a coma patient in the hospital, the lights are dim and you're told to be quiet. In this system, there's a ball that flashes brightly colored lights to stimulate the visual part of the brain, and a bullhornlike siren to help startle the brain out of its comalike state.

For about a year, we believed that it was our only hope for Nina, but it was impossible to get into the training course. Wouldn't you know it, a month or so before we were due to leave for Iowa, we got one of the coveted spots in an intense course, which required hours and hours of attendance over the space of a week. We did some research and discovered that IAHP had a sister school in St. Louis, closer to where we'd be, but before we left we took the course.

It was held in a huge, ice-cold auditorium. Every one of the people in the audience was there as a last resort, and the stories broke your heart. One of the men we met was from Brazil; his six-year-old son had fallen into their swimming pool and been pronounced brain dead.

The stories we heard from the stage were nothing short of miraculous. Long after everyone else had given up, someone had believed, and that was what had made the difference. We heard about a mother who had continued to take her baby out in the carriage while she hung clothes on the line, talking and singing to him, and who had continued to play the piano to him, even though the child was thought to be blind and deaf. One night, that mother, lying in bed, heard a sonata coming from the piano in the living room.

They told us about a man whose doctors said he would never walk or talk again—and then we saw that same man walk out to the podium. When he walked onstage, his gait was stiff—as if it were something he'd memorized how to do, something that had never really become natural—but he was walking. It was incredible, and everyone in the audience applauded and cried for him, because we were imagining our own loved ones in his shoes.

Nina's limbs were stiff as the result of the brain injury. Four people—two on each side—had to move her limbs as if she were crawling, coordinating their movements to the beat of a metronome, and taking great care not to dislocate her hips or shoulders. It was physically exhausting after a period of time, not to mention that the bright lights and loud noises were enough to drive a sane person mad. Bill designed and built the special furniture we needed, including a patterning table and a sliding board that was tilted at a precise angle, so that if she moved her arms and legs, she could move toward us.

It took at least ten hours a day to do this work with Nina, so when we got to Iowa, we needed help, and a lot of it. My mother, thank God, had come with us, and she coordinated Nina's care. I have such gratitude to her, and to the people of Iowa who came out to help us. Each day brought another set of volunteers: neighbors, friends, college students, farmers, retirees. My mom and Bill coordinated this constant flow in and out of our house from our first days there; every hour or so, for eight to twelve hours a day, the bell would ring, and Bill or my mom would escort the new person to the room we had set up for Nina's therapy. The schedule that we kept during those years wouldn't have been possible if the whole family hadn't been working as one.

We would have kept going forever, I think, but Nina's hip got displaced. The head of her femur kept popping out of her hip socket and she had started to wince when she was sitting up in her wheelchair. The tendons had to be straightened and strengthened; there was no getting around the surgery, and we couldn't do the patterning work during her convalescence. We decided not to resume when she had healed.

It's so easy, when your child doesn't make a recovery, to feel that you somehow came up short, that you didn't do enough, or do the right things the right way. To this day, I wonder, could we have done more? I'll never know.

There was one more shock to come in those early days in Iowa. I had been coping with an upset stomach since we got there. I could not stop burping! I thought it was stress, or some change in the food. I even joked with Bill, "Gee, I'm really having some reaction to this place; it must be all the looks we're getting."

But it wasn't any of that. I was pregnant.

I could not believe it. If I'd had any idea this was going to happen, we never would have gone to Iowa. There was enough on my plate as it was. I had a new job, and all eyes were on me. We were traveling to St. Louis once a month for Nina, and coordinating eight hours a day of therapy. And everything was new and unfamiliar, even the house we were living in.

I admit I was also concerned about how the sports world would react to my pregnancy. Those were still early days in women's athletics; we weren't all that used to the idea of coaches who were also moms. But, once again, I had underestimated the state of Iowa. In fact, it was the reaction to my pregnancy that brought home to us how special this state was. When we went public with the news, we were flooded with gifts and cards from well-wishers. They sent so many little romper suits, our baby could never have worn them all. I still have the hand-knitted yellow-and-black afghan blankets that people sent, so that even the youngest Stringer would be wrapped in the school colors. There was a statewide contest to "Name Coach Stringer's Baby!" And the year after our son was born, the name Justin became one of the most popular names in the state. There was even a racehorse named after him.

Bill was a rock during those days. Whatever I dropped, he picked up. That was true at school as well as at home. I had my work cut out with that team—they'd had just seven wins the previous year, and we ranked 299 out of 302, if you can imagine. But I was free to do what I needed to do because Bill kept our life running smoothly. More than anything, he made the whole team, the girls and my staff, feel like his door was always open to them. If we were playing away, we'd get back at two, three in the morning, and Bill would be right there waiting for us.

When I wasn't coaching, we were together, though I regret that we missed a lot of opportunities, juggling Nina's care with the needs of the boys. I blame myself. Bill used to say, "Vivian, we need to have a nanny, someone who will allow us to move around a little more easily."

But I wouldn't agree. I thought that having someone there all the time would threaten our privacy and our family life. It was the way I was brought up; the Stoners were tight knit, and we didn't involve other people too much. And let's be realistic: where I came from, people didn't hire help.

I've since realized that if you find the right person, it doesn't have to mean losing your personal space. Hyacinth, the woman who has taken care of Nina for the past ten years, means everything to me. I wish that I'd listened to Bill. All parents must carve out time to be husband and wife. It's hard to do this, especially when you have a child like Nina, but it's essential, just as it's essential for parents of special-needs children to spend time with the other children in the family. Having the right person there would have allowed us more quality time with each other, and with David and Justin, too.

I was at a conference for the Nike coaches this year, and I met a young couple with a special-needs child. We talked about going to restaurants and places that say they're accessible but aren't, and a lot of other issues that the parents of special-needs children deal with every day. I could tell that they were relieved to talk to someone who understood, because most people simply don't know.

For example, I'm sure that over the years some of my colleagues have thought that I was standoffish or maybe even arrogant. I'm sure they wondered, "What's wrong with Vivian that she never hangs out with us, never stops by the bar for a drink?" But those kinds of relationships weren't possible for me. There weren't—and still aren't—many coaches who are moms; it's a harder job than most to balance with a young family. And while I know that most working mothers question the time they take away from loving and nurturing their growing children, that's something that never, ever changes for the parent of a special-needs child. Justin and David have their own lives now, but Nina needs me, twenty-four hours a day, seven days a week—and she will for the rest of her life.

I was grateful to have the opportunity to tell this young couple at the Nike conference that I regretted not hiring someone to help me and Bill when we were in Iowa. It was always important to us that David and Justin got to do the things they wanted to do, and we made sure that they did. But they usually did it with only one of us. Having someone to lend a hand would have allowed us to do more things together.

I let them know what it had taken me many years to accept: getting help does not mean abandoning your child. I shared with them a situation that I've been in too many times to count: let's say I want to go to church on Sunday morning, but I'm getting back from a recruiting trip or an away game on a flight that touches down at three in the morning. In order to get Nina ready for church myself, I'd have to get up at eight-thirty, which would mean spending the rest of the day exhausted. But if I can ask Hyacinth to have Nina ready at ten, then I can sleep a couple of hours, get up, get the van, and we can all go to church together.

I felt really good talking to that couple. It meant a lot to be given the opportunity to pass along insights that I wish someone had shared with me and Bill.

At Cheyney, if Bill and I got to feeling like we wanted time with his parents and our siblings, we'd just get in the car. But while my contract at Iowa allowed me to fly home a certain number of times a year, my coaching schedule didn't allow me to take the time away, and I started to feel seriously lonesome. My mom was in Iowa with us, but when you grow up close like we did, you start to hurt if you don't have a lot of contact with your brothers and sisters. At one point, I missed them so badly I even told Christine Grant I wasn't sure I could stay.

One day, I was on the phone with my sister Madeline, and we started to talk about how great Iowa was—what a great educational system it had and how many job opportunities. "Why don't you consider moving here?" I asked her. She talked to her husband, Rufus, and to our sister Ricky. Madeline and Ricky were like two peas in a pod. They had never been separated: When Ricky went to school, she went where Madeline was, and when they got married, they made sure they lived right next door to each other. So they all agreed to come and check it out.

All of us had valued growing up in a large family because it meant that we were always able to look after one another, and we wanted the same thing for our children. Ricky and Madeline each had two daughters, and I had two sons and a daughter. It would take the three of us putting our families together to give our kids the family we'd had.

So they moved to Iowa, and then it felt like I had everything I'd ever wanted. We saw each other every day, and every Sunday we'd eat dinner at a different sibling's home. We all had our special dishes. Bill was the chef of the family. He made French crêpes, authentic Chinese dishes, Louisiana gumbo—you name it, he cooked it, and it was all delicious. Ricky made giant cinnamon rolls. She had married Teapot, also known as George—the same Teapot I'd played ball with when I was young. He was a wonderful baker—his rolls would make the oven door pop open. Madeline made Hawaiian wedding cake. I was good with steaks and potato salad, and my mom fried oysters. Even the kids had little desserts they knew how to fix.

It was always the same: we'd sit down to a meal and then the real entertainment would begin. You see, the rule at these gatherings was that everyone had to perform. Everyone, from the littlest kid on up, had to prepare a piece of music, or a dance, or a song, or a comic monologue. And you couldn't bring any guests over to the house unless they were willing to perform, too. It was crazy, but that was the way it was.

The house that I had in Iowa was ideally suited for this. There was a balcony overlooking a great room and a piano upstairs in the loft; we even had a microphone. We would turn out the lights and put a spotlight on the performer, and the show would begin.

I loved seeing my nieces Erica and Leslie do a jump-rope routine to "Jump, Jump," and hearing David sing "Don't Leave Me" by Boys II Men. Bill—well, Bill wasn't a good singer, but he was loud. One of the songs he liked to sing was "Wind Beneath My Wings," which I learned to play on the piano to accompany him.

One time, after we'd practiced it together, I turned to Bill and told him, "You know, Bill, you really are the wind beneath my wings." It was difficult for me to express myself that way, and he wasn't good at accepting compliments, but I made sure he heard me. "You really are my hero. You've always been there for me, and I really appreciate everything you do. I've always known that if we went broke tomorrow, you'd build us a log cabin somewhere in the mountains. I just know you'd make sure that we were okay." It was true: I always had the feeling that he would take care of me and the kids, no matter what. He smiled and said, "That makes me feel good, Vivian, because you know I would."

The house in Iowa had the most festive atmosphere you can imagine. We had a basketball court outside; of course, the girls all thought they wanted to play. They played Ping-Pong and pool or danced in the basement. Some nights we'd play Monopoly or Scrabble or some other board game. On any given day, if you walked into my house, you might see Ricky cooking while Rufus fed Nina, Madeline and my mom sitting and talking at the kitchen table, while a big pile of cousins watched movies together in the den. It just felt so happy and busy, with the kids running in and out and everybody cooking and talking and teasing one another.

Bill was happy as could be. I loved to see him smoking a pipe and shooting the breeze with one of my sister's husbands. Maybe because he'd grown up on a farm, he was always happiest when he was doing something with his hands. He loved to work on cars and to build things. He had an enormous, immaculate, soundproof woodworking studio in the basement of our house, and he'd create masterpieces down there. For instance, he made a ten-foot-long table out of reclaimed mahogany salvaged from a bowling alley that was simply breathtaking; it's in my house to this day.

He also made a lot of things for Nina. Long before anything

similar was on the market, he made a three-wheeled rolling cart that attached to his bicycle so that the whole family could go for rides together, and he rigged up a special sunshade for her wheelchair so she'd never be uncomfortable, even if we couldn't find a spot out of the sun. If there was something she needed that we couldn't get, Bill usually figured out a way to make it for her.

In his quiet way, Bill was a real activist. He wrote a beautiful letter to our congressman to protest the inaccessibility of bathrooms, particularly for the fathers of handicapped children. It was just after an incident when the family had traveled to meet me, and he'd been unable to find any place to change Nina except on the floor in some remote part of the airport. There were changing stations in the women's bathrooms, of course, but no place for a father to change his daughter. His recommendation was a "family room." Well, who at that time had ever heard of a parents' room? But, of course, he was correct—as always—about human dignity and the rights of people to have the same basic conveniences as others.

We were one giant happy family and we did achieve what we'd set out to: our kids are superclose to this day. No matter how long it's been since Nina's seen her cousin Teonta, when she comes home, Nina gets the biggest smile on her face. Teonta won't sleep in the guest bedroom; when she's at my house, she just wants to watch movies and sleep with Nina. And Keonte, who looked a lot like Nina growing up, actually came to New Jersey with me to help while I was hiring someone to take care of Nina full-time. Ke's like a sister to her—the hospital we take Nina to knows to get in touch with her if they can't reach me. Those are the bonds we made in Iowa, and they're still tight.

10

No Crumbs from the Table

Not surprisingly, there wasn't a lot of support from the Iowa fans at the very beginning. The state is basketball crazy, and they loved the black and gold, but the team just wasn't there.

The Hawkeyes had been consistent losers the year before, with just seven wins. (The full name of the Iowa women's team was the Lady Hawkeyes, but I didn't use the *Lady* in Iowa—as far as I'm concerned, basketball is basketball.) The Iowans were kind about it—"Those girls sure did try their best out there, Coach!"—but with their record, there just wasn't that much interest in attending the games.

It was a change for me. By the time I'd left Cheyney, our games were standing room only; we often had to turn away people for safety reasons. Even in the early days, before we were so successful, I could always count on help rustling up an audience. I'd say, "Dean Miller, we're having Delta State [a powerhouse team at the time] down to play tonight," and the game would be announced in the dormitories. They'd go knocking door to door, and students would pour out to support the team.

Carver-Hawkeye was a much larger arena, but that only made it look emptier: I'd gotten a chuckle at an early press conference when I pledged to fill it, and there were times when I wondered if I hadn't bitten off more than I could chew. I got really excited one night because there were about three hundred people there. Then I realized that it was forty below outside—they weren't there to see us, they were just getting in out of the cold! In fact, when I looked closely, I saw that some of them were reading the newspaper. I didn't let it distract me. I was there to coach, and I knew they'd start coming once we got into gear. I hired Marianna Freeman to be my assistant. She had been my first All-American player at Cheyney, and she had the most terrific way with people. I needed all the help I could get.

The girls had nowhere near the skill levels that I'd gotten used to at Cheyney, but they did have one thing: drive. They *wanted* it. I'll never forget my first meeting with them. I'm not sure what I expected, but they looked as though they'd been thrown a lifeline, and that lifeline was me. "We're tired of losing, Coach. We don't want to lose anymore. We'll do whatever you tell us to do," they told me, and I could see that they meant it.

When I came in, there were four seniors on the team. One of them was Angie Lee, who would eventually become my assistant at Iowa, and whom I would recommend for the head coaching job there when I left for Rutgers. Right from the beginning, I could feel her commitment. "We just want to know what it feels like to win, Coach," she told me. "Just tell us what you need."

Angie had so much heart. The Iowa team's lack of finesse was highly frustrating for me, and during one practice when they were being particularly careless with the ball, I made a rule: every turnover meant ten pushups. They were so bad, I should have made the multiple lower—by the time I realized what was happening, they'd gotten themselves up to a hundred and sixty.

I had backed myself into a corner. I had to make them do the darn pushups because I'd said I would, but I didn't want to punish them—they had tried out there, pathetic though it might have been—and I had no idea how they'd do a hundred and sixty pushups without dying on me. So I thought, *At the end of practice, I'll just get busy with something and pretend to have forgotten.* And everyone was getting ready to go, when all of a sudden, Angie piped up, "Hold on, Coach—we've got some pushups to do!"

I was dumbfounded—I'd never seen anyone volunteer for hard labor. Marianna and I did everything we could to help them out. We counted really fast and dropped whole sets—I was frankly worried that they wouldn't be able to lift their arms at practice the next day—but wouldn't you know that Angie was keeping the right count? She was one of the purest, most honest, most hardworking people I've ever met.

That team might have been badly lacking, but they had the desire to make something of themselves, and that was all I needed. What I'm always looking for is effort, people who are driven to excellence and who will be tireless in their quest to achieve. It is not a sin not to know, as long as I can see that you're willing to learn; I will give you all the guidance you need as long as you'll do what it takes to be prepared. We didn't have strong offensive skills or a lot of talent, but building a strong defense just requires a tremendous amount of hard work, and that was something I could count on from this team.

Everyone gave their all. We'd play a game, put the team to bed, and then I'd go back to my office and go over tapes for the next game. Sometimes I didn't start until eleven or twelve, and I'd work straight through the night, drinking gallons of coffee to keep myself awake. They called me Video Viv. I went frame-by-frame for a lot of those games—diagramming every play on the floor, every movement, every pass.

For me, the *X*s and *O*s are essential. You wouldn't believe how many people I've interviewed for assistant jobs who don't know how to draw a play! But in a tight situation, you must be technically sound. You have to know what your opponent is likely to do, and you have to be able to draw it so that you can communicate your response immediately to the girls on the floor.

My other assistant, Linda Myers, loved the technical aspect of the game too. "Can I sit on the floor while you watch tapes?" she used to ask me. "I just want to see what you're looking at. You don't have to say anything to me; I'll pick it up." Sometimes I'd stop a pattern three or four times, looking for a little nuance, and she'd try to guess what I was looking for. If you'd stumbled into my office in the middle of the night, you'd have thought we were zombies, staring at the screen like that.

I broke the team's heart that year. Although no one would have called it a banner season, we had gotten just a little bit better, and as a result, we'd been invited to play in the WNIT, a postseason tournament that's not as prestigious as the NCAA. The girls were so excited, especially the seniors—they'd never been invited to do anything in the postseason at all. I remember Angie running up to me in excitement, telling me she'd seen the invitation in the paper.

I had to break it to her that we weren't going. "Angie, the crown jewel of athletic competition in women's basketball is the NCAA, and I don't want you or anyone else on this team to get used to accepting seconds. I know that this is your senior year and it means everything in the world to you to do something in the postseason, but never again will the Hawkeyes sit back and accept anything less than the best; we don't accept crumbs. We're going to have to say thank you, but no thanks."

She looked so sad. But it was her attitude that made her so special, both as a player, and later, as a coach. Sure enough, a minute later, she said, "Yep, you're right, Coach. I should have known you were going to say that. I don't want seconds, either. We're better than that."

Attendance grew steadily that year. Even before our results were really there, Iowans showed that they appreciated the effort we were giving to it.

We had the full support of the university. Too often, the women's program is viewed as competing with the men's program. But Coach George Raveling and the administration of the university understood that the two programs fed each other, and their marketing people were great at getting people excited about the teams. They arranged events where young people had the chance to meet the players, and they got journalists interested in doing feature articles about me and the players. Our schedule was on the grocery bags at the supermarket, under a big picture of my face! I've never seen anything like that, to this day.

We did our part too. The girls never complained about staying after practices and games to answer questions or to sign autographs. My own mother went door-to-door selling tickets for the games; she actually won a trip to Hawaii doing it! And I traveled across the state to speak at fundraising events, which were called I-Club functions. All the athletic programs participated, but the events traditionally hadn't been attended by women; they were seen as a time for the guys to get together and have a nice dinner and a couple of drinks with their buddies. So the representatives for the women's teams never went either.

I was excited about the program and wanted to tell people about it, so I asked to speak at a couple of I-Club functions. Some of those early ones felt very strange. This was Iowa, remember. You'd have 350 people in a room—350 men, basically—and one black person, me. But I was thrilled to have the opportunity to spread the word, and what I said was well received, so they started asking me to come on a regular basis.

That helped these events to catch on with women. "Who's speaking at the I-Club?" the wives of these big donors would ask, and when they heard that it was me, along with the men's basketball coach or the wrestling coach, they'd come along. In that way, we raised awareness about the program—and some money. When their husbands would stand up to pledge, you'd hear the women saying, "Wait, we're going to give all that money to the football team? Maybe we should give some of that to women's athletics."

It had been a really good year, and Bill and I felt that we'd found somewhere we could stay for a while. When I told Cheyney's president, Dr. Wilson, that I was thinking about staying in Iowa, he flew out to speak to the president, Dr. Freedman. He told him, "This woman means everything in the world to me and to Cheyney State College. She's not just a basketball coach—you've got to understand that. She represents the best, the brightest. I'm telling you now: don't bring her here if you're going to treat her like any other coach, because we want her back at Cheyney. Coach Stringer is special to us."

Iowa was smart. They announced that the president of Cheyney State College was in the audience at the game that night and asked everyone to show him how much the University of Iowa appreciated me. The crowd stood up and cheered and went crazy, and he understood. At the end of the game, he came to my office and said, "Little lady, I think they're going to take care of you. You're on top of the world, and that's where you're supposed to be. But if you ever want to come back to Cheyney, you pick up the phone and call me."

We recruited like crazy, and the teams got better and better as a result. Bill was the one to convince me to open up the house to the recruits. That was much more the way he'd been raised. We Stoners never had outsiders over to our house, growing up, and I was never comfortable entertaining; I'm still not. But I finally realized that I didn't have to cook; I could bring food in, and the kids could laugh and dance and play Ping-Pong and watch movies.

It was good for us. My mom thrived on it because she loves parties, Nina loved being in the center of all that action and liveliness, and the kids on the team treated the boys like their little brothers. It gave the players the chance to see me in a different light too.

Whatever we were doing worked; we got some great players to come to Iowa. One of them was Jolette Law. She was special from the very first, but I wasn't sure I'd get her. She came from South Carolina, and when she visited Iowa, it was about twenty degrees below zero. She was trying so hard, but even with her hands in her lap and her jaw clenched tight, her teeth kept chattering. I gave her my gloves and thought, *Well, she's a goner.*

She wasn't—but I had bigger problems than the weather. She wanted to come, but her father, to whom she was extremely close, didn't want her to go so far away. So I flew down to South Carolina to try to convince him to let her play for me. I told Joe Law that his daughter wouldn't be so far away, after all—he'd be able to hear her games on the radio. Our games were broadcast on WHO, and they'd always said that the games could be heard across the country. But I'd never put it to the test, until Jolette's dad reached under the sink, came out with this old radio, and threw it on the table in front of me.

"Fine," he said. "Find the station."

I started fumbling through the stations, moving the antenna—nothing. I asked him for a coat hanger, and I'll never forget him telling me, "Oh, I'll get you anything you want. But unless you get that station on the radio, I'm not letting Jolette go out there."

I laugh now to think of what I rigged up. It had just rained, and maybe that cleared the dust and helped me out, but sure enough,

I got the dial just right, and suddenly we heard, "This is Larry Cutler, the voice of WHO radio out of Des Moines, Iowa, home of the Hawkeyes." I was so happy, I smacked that thing. And Mr. Law gave me his blessing to take Jolette.

"You know you got a good one, don't you, Coach?" he said to me as he shook my hand good-bye, and I told him I knew that I did.

It wasn't the last time we bumped up against each other. In Jolette's freshman year, we were playing a game at North Carolina State, and her father brought a whole busload of relatives and friends to see her play. But I didn't put Jolette in, because the game was so tight, and I knew she wasn't yet prepared for that level of competition. I didn't want her or anyone else to have to cope with the burden of knowing that we'd lost the game because I'd put her in; you can really mess a girl up that way.

It got really quiet in the Law family section, and by the time halftime came, I could hear people muttering and mumbling, but I ignored them. My assistant coaches got a little nervous, but I told them, "When she's ready, I'll put her on the floor." By the end of the game, Mr. Law was getting pretty vocal with his dissatisfaction. I stopped and said, "Sir, can I speak to you for a second?" And I called Jolette over so she could hear me too. "She's going to be fine. Her grades are good, and she's doing wonderfully in practice. She's not ready now, but she will be, and when she is, I'll play her. Her future is bright, and that's all I have to say unless you're serious about her going somewhere else, in which case we need to have a conversation."

Jolette spoke up for herself. "I'm learning a lot every day, but I'm not ready yet. I love Coach and this is where I want to be." Her father loved her and he backed off. The next year, her sophomore year, Jolette won the starting spot over a senior, and we became the number one team in the nation. Her father was so happy and so proud.

Jolette was a very intense player and a dynamic one; she played with a real flair. Thousands of people would come to see her play at Iowa, and she went on to be one of the very few women to play for the Harlem Globetrotters before coming to be my assistant at Rutgers. She was a tremendous leader, on and off the court.

Michelle Edwards was a great guard, and recruiting her allowed me to attract talents like Franthea Price, Nadine Domond, Jolynn Schneider, Robin Christian, and many more. I'll tell you a funny story about recruiting Michelle Edwards that starts ten years before she came to Iowa.

When I first started coaching, I got a visit from a woman called Alfreda Harris, who founded the John Shelburne Community Center in Boston. Ms. Harris knows everybody in Boston, and everyone in Boston knows she loves the kids she coaches with all her heart. There's no graffiti on Ms. Harris's gym; that recreation center has been in the middle of the ghetto for years, but it looks brand new. When they're there, people respect one another, and you'd better believe they respect the woman running the show. When Patrick Ewing walks into Ms. Harris's gym, he takes his hat off.

One day at Cheyney, I was having practice, and she came and asked if I'd be interested in recruiting two of her AAU players. "I told them you're trying to start something down here at Cheyney and that you don't go for any nonsense." I didn't know the girls, but I knew that Ms. Harris had had some outstanding players over the years, so I said yes.

Well, she dropped them off, and right from the start I could tell that these two girls didn't have a clue about a Division I basketball practice. We'd be running, and one of them would start falling behind, and suddenly her shoelace would be untied, or she'd claim to have something important to tell me—a whole lot of garbage, and no running. So I'd give her a warning, and she'd step to it for a little while—and then the *other* one would start dragging and telling me why she couldn't get it done. Every time things got rough, these kids would give me excuses instead of what I needed. So finally, I just lost it and threw them both off the team.

I knew I'd done the right thing, but I was worried about the consequences. There's a lot of talent in Boston, and every bit of it goes through Ms. Harris. She'd entrusted me with these players, and I'd just kicked them both off the team. What was I supposed to say to her? "Ms. Harris, I'd love it if you'd think of me with players in the future and oh, by the way, I kicked the ones you just sent me out of my gym."

Finally I found my nerve and called her. "Ms. Harris, you know I'm trying to build a championship team, and those two young ladies just didn't want to work as hard as everybody else. I gave them a number of chances, but in the end, they weren't able to rise to the challenges in front of them. I don't know if you'll ever forgive me, but I had to do this: I threw them off the team."

There was a little pause at the other end of the line. And then, "Stringer," she said, "you know what? I'm not surprised. I told them before they went down there that you were not playing around. Don't worry. You are who I thought you were, and there will be other times." I was so relieved.

Flash forward to the University of Iowa, ten years later, where I was interviewing a young woman called Jennifer Bednarek for an assistant coaching position. She told me she'd just seen a player in the mode of the great guards that I had at Cheyney. "Coach, she is your kind of guard."

What does that mean? She's smooth, quick as a cat, and has an extremely explosive first step. She shoots the ball well, has excellent ball-handling skills, and her jumper is like yeast; once she starts into shot mode, she just keeps rising and rising. She's not an entertainer; she takes care of everybody else first, and herself last. She can see the game two or three moves ahead, and she's always talking, always teaching. If you're a halfway decent player, she's going to make you look good. *That's* my style of guard.

But it was the middle of the summer, and I had absolutely no way of getting in touch with this player; all I could do was call her high school every day, in the hope of finding someone who could help me get to her. Finally, I got hold of a janitor, if you can believe it. I was so desperate, I started talking to him about this player I'd heard about named Michelle Edwards. He interrupted me, "Who, Ice? Are you kidding me? That girl is the *truth*!" And then he tells me that her AAU coach is Ms. Alfreda Harris.

So I called Ms. Harris. "Coach," I say, "I know you're not going to remember me after all this time, but my name is Vivian Stringer, and we met while I was coaching at a little school called Cheyney." There's a pause at the other end of the line, and then in this wonderful rich, deep voice, she says, "It's about time, Stringer. She's only the best damn player in America."

With that, she gave me the go-ahead to pursue Michelle. That day, I was so happy that I'd cut those two players from the team at Cheyney. You can't ever know how something is going to work out; you have to do what you know in your heart.

When I first met with Michelle, she asked me to show her where Iowa was—literally, on a map. And when she came to visit, I thought we'd lost her, because when she was watching our practice, she dropped off to sleep. *That's what Iowa City will do to a Boston girl,* I thought. *This must be really different for her.*

But I guess she was just worn out from the trip, because when I was driving her to the airport, the best shooting guard in the country turned to me and told me she wanted to be a Hawkeye. "I feel like I can be the person I want to be on this team," she said. "This is perfect for me." She liked to ski and to read books, and she felt like Iowa was far enough away that she could be who *she* wanted to be, not who everyone else thought she should be.

I told her no.

"I wouldn't feel good about it if you accepted right now," I told her. "I want you to go visit USC and Texas and Tennessee," and a couple of other schools she'd been talking to. "When you've visited, you can make the comparison, and if Iowa is still first in your heart, then I'll be happy to sign you."

She hadn't even gotten home before Ms. Harris was on the

phone to me. "Have you lost your mind? This is the best guard in the whole country! She's telling you that she wants to make a commitment, and you're sending her to other schools?"

I felt very calm about it, although truth be told, you're never really calm when you're talking about a player like Michelle. But I don't believe in railroading these girls into doing something they're not ready to do. "She needs to check out all those other schools," I told Ms. Harris, "and then she can make an informed decision."

I soon found out why they called her Ice. She was the most mild-mannered, soft-spoken, unassuming, and humble player, but if you got into a tough situation, she would just knock those shots down. She went on to be the National Player of the Year for me—and the only female Hawkeye to have her jersey retired. She works with me to this day as director of basketball operations at Rutgers.

I loved those kids. But that doesn't mean they didn't give me a hard time. You have to earn trust from your players, and you get that by being consistent, not by letting the kids play you. You've got to be for real, and I will say that that has always been a strength of mine.

It starts even before they come to play for me. One fall, I went to see Necole Tunsil, one of the biggest recruits in her year, at her high school, but Necole wasn't there. Can you imagine? We'd come from Iowa to Florida, but the girl we'd come to recruit hadn't bothered to come to school that day. That night, we went to her house, as arranged. Her parents were there, but no Necole. Half an hour late, she saunters in. As soon as she was through the door, I said, "You're probably going to ask me to leave your house after I say this, but I'm going to say it anyway. Unless you address your academics, you're not welcome at the University of Iowa."

I can still see the look of shock on her face. I turned to her mom and said, "Mom, did you think that Necole was in school today?" Her dad spoke up: "Of course she went to school. She left the house this morning like always." "No, sir," I said. "She left your house, but she didn't go to school. Did you, Necole?"

She just looked at me. "I know that you're angry right now, and I'm sure we're not going to be one of your schools for consideration," I said, "but you have way too much talent to play the games you've been playing with your education." I found out later that she'd pulled a no-show on the last four or five coaches who'd flown out to see her, and not one of them had said anything to her parents.

Her parents knew that if I'd tell them what she wasn't doing, even when she wasn't mine, I darn sure would when she was. Necole graduated from Iowa as one of the most decorated players in the history of the school and played for a few years in the WNBA. And, I'm proud to say, she is now a schoolteacher in Florida.

You're not guaranteed a starting position on my team. Starting is an honor and a privilege; you represent all of us out there and set the tone for the game. But anything less than your greatest effort will not be tolerated, and I don't care how talented you are.

I remember playing one game against Indiana when I was at Iowa. We always had trouble there, and this was no exception: it was the worst mess I'd ever seen. I had a couple of All-Americans on the floor—Jolette, Fran Price, Michelle—but they weren't putting any effort into what they were doing. I got so angry, I took the whole group out of the game. We needed them in, even with the way they were playing, but at that moment, I didn't care if we won or lost.

Our score started to suffer fast. We were down by five, then ten, then fifteen, and the girls on the bench were just losing it. Suddenly, Indiana is leading us by twenty points, and the starters are begging me to put them back in. Finally, at twenty-five points down, I told Fran Price and Jolette they could go back in. Jolette took her warm-up pants off so fast, she almost took her shorts with them, and they ran in like lightning. They would remember that lesson for the rest of their lives, and you can be sure that the team never approached the floor in that manner again.

That's the way I've always coached. You will not play for me unless you are playing to the best of your ability, with all the intensity you can bring. Going halfway is disrespectful to me, to your teammates, to your opponents, and it is disrespectful to the game.

I do believe that if you play it a certain way, the winning and losing will take care of itself. But winning and losing will never mean as much to me as making sure that you honor the game and the people who have worked alongside you. If we lose but I know that we played the game right—that we were prepared, that we were intense, that we executed what we said we were going to execute—then I can sleep. If you don't, then I can't, and you won't either.

Bill, of course, always believed. Teapot would say, for example, "I hear Ohio State is coming in here with a lot of talent." Bill would shoot right back, "You don't need to worry about that—she's got them covered. They are not going to be a problem. My wife is smart; nobody can handle what she's got planned."

I would get so upset with him. "Bill, why are you talking about it like it's nothing?" After all, I spent hours looking at tapes in the soundproof office in our house in order to prepare for games like that one.

He'd say, "Because it *is* nothing. You know you've got this." When we'd win the game, often by a pretty decent margin, everyone would start teasing me: "Man, you always cry wolf. You wouldn't play games with us because you were studying, and then you go and beat them by twenty-five points?"

Bill was always our biggest fan. Every game, he'd be in his usual seat with Nina and the boys beside him. David and Justin would come to the locker room to give me a hug, but I always wanted them back in their seats by the start of the game. It was important for me to walk out and see them there.

The TV stations loved to show my family sitting in the stands, and that was significant. You didn't see a lot of people with special needs on television at that time—in fact, you still don't. We got hundreds of letters from other parents thanking us for allowing the media to cover Nina the way they did.

One year, we were playing a tournament in Florida. First we played Auburn, the number seven team in the country, and we beat them. The next day, we played Virginia, the number three team in the country, and we beat *them.* The next day—three games in a row, mind you—we were set to play Texas, the number one team in the country. They were a powerhouse team, with the National Player of the Year and another girl who was about six foot nine. It was literally like David going up against Goliath.

Well, I spent the whole night before the game thinking about what I could say to make the team believe they could beat the number one team in the country. Ann Hill used to call me "Preacher Stringer" because of the lectures I'd give before the games at Cheyney, but I knew I had to give this Iowa team a motivational speech they'd never forget. I had a book of tremendous feats, a collection of stories about accomplishments that had been earned against all odds and through the immeasurable strength of the human will, and I turned to it for the basis for my talk.

The subject was faith against the odds. I told them about the mother who was given superhuman strength to lift a car to save her baby. I told them about the woman who swam the English Channel even though she had no arms. I told them about the man who had broken the mile record, even though he'd been so badly burned as a child that nobody thought he would live, let alone walk—or run. But his mother never gave up on him, just like I'd never give up on this team, just like they could never give up on themselves.

"Nobody believes in you. That's why *you* have to believe in yourselves. Belief is faith in things not yet seen. You can't see the air, but you know it'll be there when you go to take a breath. You don't understand how the sun comes up in the morning, but you know it'll be there tomorrow when you wake up. You have faith that these things will happen, and they do! And I have faith that you can go out there and beat this team.

"We're here for one another—all for one, one for all. The sun shines through a small thing like a bottle, and that focus is enough to start a fire that can light up the world! A finger can't do anything, but we've got the power of the fist, five fingers working as one! As one, we're the most powerful team in the world!"

I went on like that, working them up into a frenzy. "You see this bumblebee on my lapel? He shouldn't be able to fly—*he's too fat to fly*. His wings are too small; his body, too big. But nobody told that to the bumblebee, and neither will anybody tell us what we can't do. We will fly."

Finally, I turned to the blackboard, which was unmistakably black, and cried out, "You know that blackboard is green, don't you? Why? Because I said it's green! What color is it? It's green!" I swear, the whole team was sitting there, looking at this blackboard, with their heads cocked to the side like the RCA dog, and they were agreeing with me. They could hardly contain themselves: "It's green, Coach, I can see that it's green!"

At the end of our silent prayer, we always said, "Team Unity!" But that day, I'd gotten them so worked up that they leapt up into the air when they yelled it. And as they were tucking in their shirts to get ready to go out there, I heard Jolette say, with wonder in her voice, "It's green, isn't it? It's really green!"

At the tip, our center rose up like she had wings. And you better believe that we won that game against Texas, to go from being unranked to the number one team in the country.

11

Dig Deep

By 1992, women's college basketball was finally on the radar for the notoriously rabid Iowa fans, and Hawkeye mania was at a fever pitch. The black-and-gold women played to packed arenas, and we led the nation in attendance. One game day, I looked out my office window and saw a long line of cars stretching as far as I could see down the road to the highway. "Oh my God, I think there's been an accident out there," I said to one of my assistant coaches. She just smiled. "There's no accident, Coach. They're coming to see us play!"

At the same time, I was personally getting a lot of recognition, and it wasn't entirely comfortable for me. It's one thing to have fans calling your name in the arena as you walk across the floor to join your team at the bench, and something else entirely to be recognized wherever you go. It was incredibly flattering, but I've never been a person who's comfortable with a lot of attention, and I was pretty overwhelmed.

The trouble was, it changed the way I felt I could act in public. I love to sing and play music loud and laugh and clown around. When we first met, Bill would get so upset with me: we'd be walking in a park and I'd start singing or dancing without caring what I looked like or who was looking. I'd just laugh; he was a strait-laced kind of guy, and I was a free spirit. But when we were in Iowa, I started to feel like I was on display, no matter where we went, and that I had to look a certain way and act a certain way, even if I was just running errands or fooling around in the mall with my kids. I couldn't leave the house without my hair and clothes being just so, and I didn't feel that I could dance around a parking lot, because inevitably I'd hear, "Hello, Coach Stringer! Great game on Saturday."

This took some getting used to. I couldn't get angry with the Iowa fans; they were nothing but loving and supportive, and I was thrilled that they cared about the team. But as minorities in a state with very few black people, we already stood out. George Raveling, the coach on the men's side, said that for a six-foot-seven black man, living in Iowa felt like living in a fishbowl. He used to go shopping at two or three in the morning so that no one would say anything to him. I, too, sometimes found that swimming in that fishbowl could be a little intimidating; I often wanted to be home when I wasn't coaching, because at home, I knew I could just be me.

It was the blending of the personal and the private that I minded, especially where my family was involved. One time, I took David to a department store to have his picture taken with Santa Claus. As he climbed up onto Santa's lap, the guy said, "I bet I know what you want for Christmas—you want your mom to win that game on Sunday!" I just smiled at the guy, but inside I was furious. *No, that's not what he wants,* I thought to myself. *He wants what every little boy wants for Christmas: trucks and a new train and more Legos.* I felt so angry that David couldn't have this quintessential, classic childhood moment—a Christmas photo taken in Santa's workshop!—without basketball intruding.

When I started out as a coach, I never thought for a second that there would ever be so much written or so much said about my work. I had always been driven, but by a love of the game and a sense of responsibility to the teams I coached, not by ambition. I was going to be a gym teacher, and Bill was going to be a gym teacher, too. We were going to have a white picket fence and two children and a dog, and live happily ever after. That's a pretty decent level for us, I thought—more than what our parents had had, for sure, and enough to make them proud.

The rest of this—well, who would have guessed?

When David was in third or fourth grade, there was an incident that hurt me deeply. It showed me very clearly what I was sacrificing by bringing up my boys in a state where they really were in the minority.

We'd driven all the way from Iowa to Philadelphia to take David to John Chaney's basketball camp for the first time. It happened to be my niece Tesha's birthday, so we thought we'd stop off at my brother Tim's house to sing and have cake with her before dropping David off at camp. Just inside Philadelphia, we pulled up beside a card store. I told David to go ahead into the store to pick out a card for his cousin while Bill and I stretched Nina out in the backseat and changed her. David didn't budge. I started to get Nina out of her chair, but he was still just sitting there, looking out the side windows of the van.

"Boy, what's wrong with you?" I asked him finally, exasperated with how long he was taking. "Get out of the car, and go get your cousin a card!"

He shook his head, and in a quiet voice he said, "I'm afraid they're going to hurt me."

I looked out the window. On the sidewalk near the van, there were three street vendors. They were black men wearing dreadlocks, talking with one another in front of mix tapes and jewelry laid out on trays—a common-enough sight in an urban setting. They weren't doing anything threatening or out of the ordinary, but David was afraid. My son—*my son*—was worried that the men on that street were going to hurt him.

"I'll take him," Bill said, looking at me, and they got out.

I was so hurt, it brought tears to my eyes. I wasn't angry with David; he was just a scared little kid. But he had been born not forty miles from where we were standing! The fact that he was frightened of people of his own color, his own race—that he didn't recognize himself in them—broke my heart.

When they came back, we all had a talk. "Why did you think that those men were going to hurt you?" I asked David. But I knew the answer. Like the rest of America, his perceptions had been shaped by what he'd seen on television. He'd had no experience of urban street life. He'd never seen someone with dreadlocks, or someone selling something on the street—all things that are part of the culture of the American city. He didn't have a lot of experience, to be honest, with black people, and the few he did know were university people.

That incident told me a lot. I thought I spoke freely about acceptance in our home, and David had certainly seen black as well as white players on my teams growing up. But television is a powerful medium, especially when people aren't actually exposed to different ethnicities and cultures. This was a young black man, growing up in a black family, but he didn't identify with the black men he saw on that street—instead, he identified them as people likely to hurt him. So it doesn't surprise me at all that white youngsters who aren't exposed to different types of people would think the same thing.

As a parent, I had always made clear to my kids that they ought to feel good about who they were. But that incident made me wonder if I had put enough emphasis on helping them to *know* who they were, and not just feel good about it. Right then and there, Bill and I promised each other that we'd spend the summers exposing both the boys to a much wider range of cultures and races than we could find in Iowa.

Although the encounter in Philadelphia had left me painfully aware of what might have been missing, the boys were blissfully happy in Iowa. Both of them are good athletes, something that has always made me happy. I was never looking for either of them to be the next Michael Jordan, but it was important to me that they participate. A person who knows how to join a pickup game in the park or how to bowl is a person who holds the key to a whole realm of social interactions. I am so glad that Bill and I exposed the kids to skiing, to golf, and through their schools, to team sports. We need to strengthen the spirit of our young people, and sports can be a great way to do that. But we never pushed them, and that was deliberate.

I feel very concerned when I see how competitive it is for young athletes. There are millions of dollars in professional athletics (on the men's side, anyway); I can see how a parent could be tempted to do everything possible to make his or her child the next Magic Johnson. But something has gone wrong when a seven-year-old is worrying about his trainer and strengthening his left hand instead of having a proper childhood. To me, it's far better not to keep score and to make sure that everybody has an opportunity than to tell little Johnny that he can't play today because you need a win.

Sports have given me countless hours of pleasure in my life, and I'm glad I was able to pass along that pleasure to my sons.

David dropped by my house the other day to pick up his brother's golf clubs for his cousin; they were going to spend the day out on the course. I smiled to think about them out in the trees, getting some exercise, talking and getting their heads clear. That is a nice way to spend the day.

The team I put together for the 1992 season was thought to be one of the strongest out there. We had some great players: Tia Jackson, Necole Tunsil, Laurie Aaron, Toni Foster. And they were in amazing condition—faster, stronger, and capable of jumping higher than any team I'd ever had.

I tried something with that team I've used ever since: I inverted the starting lineup, so that the so-called starters—traditionally the strongest players on the team—began the game on the bench. I called the five players on the floor in the beginning of the game the tone-setters. They'd work really hard and show great enthusiasm, wearing out the other team's starters, and after ten minutes I'd put in our starters.

It was a very effective strategy. First of all, it made everyone on the team understand that they had an important role to play. The tone-setters worked hard and played to the best of their ability to show that they deserved the honor they'd been given, and the starters came in fresh, appreciative for what their teammates had done. Of course, it was psychologically devastating to the other team, especially if our tone-setters had managed to score some points. Imagine how you'd feel if you were already down by eight, only to see three All-Americans come off the bench!

Simone Edwards was a player on that team. Simone had grown up in Jamaica, where they didn't have basketball; she was in her junior year of high school before she'd even heard of the game. But she was tall—six foot four—and athletic, and a track recruiter brought her to a junior college in Oklahoma, where I found her.

She might not have had experience, but she made All-American her first year. (When she got the plaque, she thought they'd made a mistake: "I'm all-Jamaican!") After two years of junior college, she was one of the most widely recruited girls of the year. I was so touched by her—all alone out there in Oklahoma, so far from home and everything she knew. When you meet someone really special, you know it right away, as I did with Simone. She was probably the least talented player on that team, but she started for me because no one worked harder or gave more of herself. She didn't know any of the names of the plays, but I could never get mad at her for mixing them up—she was like a sponge, trying to learn. And even if she didn't know red from blue, she would get out there with those long arms, and she'd be all over the court trying to stop the ball.

Simone had virtually no money, and she didn't like the food in the cafeteria, so she started losing weight like crazy. It broke my heart. The NCAA rules (with good reason) prohibit coaches from giving kids money or gifts of any kind. I couldn't even buy her a sandwich! All I could do was let her know that I would never be too busy to stop and listen to her concerns. It might not have been food, but it was nourishment of another kind.

This wasn't the first time the NCAA rules had given me trouble. I fully understand why they're in place, but people make millions of dollars off these kids, and a lot of them have to go without. Once in Iowa we had a girl whose only winter coat was a summer baseball jacket. Temperatures could easily get to twenty degrees below zero, with the wind chill factor making it feel like forty below, but this kid had no money to get anything more substantial.

I told my athletic director to find her a coat: "I can promise you that that girl is not going to walk out of here in a baseball jacket. Find a way to get her something better, or I am going to get into trouble for breaking that rule." Someone in the office had the nerve to ask, "Why doesn't she ask for a coat from home?" Amazing. Home for this girl meant standing in the kitchen and looking through the gaping hole in the floor to the apartment below. I've never been so mad in my life, but all I said was, "Find a way, or I'm going to break that rule." They petitioned the NCAA and it got done.

In Simone's case, I was at least able to "find a way" when the recruits visited. During those visits, the girls were allowed to come and eat at my house, and I always made sure that there would be something Simone liked and that she had a heaping plate.

In her freshman year, we played the University of Southern California, against the magnificent Lisa Leslie. There was less than a minute on the clock, and we were down. As we stood in the huddle for our last time-out and for USC's last possession, I felt someone tugging at my hand. It was Simone. She was a rookie, and there she was, asking me to put her in! "I'll get you that rebound, Coach, I'll get it for you, I will."

There was something in her face that made me believe her: she wanted it as much as I've ever seen anybody want it. I'm sure everyone around me thought I had lost my mind, putting this rookie player in at such a crucial point in the game, but I knew what I'd seen. And wouldn't you know she got the rebound, passed it out to her teammate, and we won that game by a single point.

Later, I went to New York to be there with Simone when she was trying out for the WNBA. She was up against three hundred of the most talented women in the country, and she didn't have as much of a name as some of them because she'd spent a lot of her college career injured. The powers-that-be must have seen that nobody had Simone's heart, because two girls were chosen, and she was one of them. She went on to a distinguished career in the Seattle Storm, and to found a children's charity called Simone4Children. She's now co-captain of the Jamaican National Basketball Team and a coach at Radford University.

Felicia Hall was another player who might not have been the most talented, but who had the heart of a winner. She came from the projects in Louisiana, and I didn't know for sure if she could play, but I could see that she was a quality person. Sure enough, she worked harder than anyone I ever saw. She wouldn't wait for her turn during a drill; she'd be working on her footwork in the line. Fedi reminded me of myself. She was living proof that it's not where you come from, it's where you're going that counts, and I could see that in her from day one.

She wanted to be a lawyer. The dean of the law school at Iowa followed our games, and one evening, he asked me for a recommendation. I told him that I knew she would be a stellar student, one who would distinguish herself in her class. I guaranteed not only that she would graduate with a law degree but that he'd have cause to mention her within the first ten minutes of that graduation ceremony.

Sure enough, when I flew up to see her get her law degree, the dean was at the podium talking about Felicia in the first five minutes. She has her own motivational-speaking company now. One night she called me: "This girl from the projects in Louisiana just introduced Secretary of State Madeleine Albright, Coach." The smile on my face was so big, I thought my face would split. I always get her to come back and speak to our teams, because she always tells them what I believe to be true: "It's not about the basketball; it's about giving everything you can."

It's a shining moment for any coach when a girl finally understands what you're trying to do. At Iowa, I had a great player from Connecticut by the name of Nadine Domond. She was young, and at the beginning she didn't know what she needed to do to function at the level we were playing at. But over the course of the year I saw her begin to understand the level of commitment and discipline required, the sacrifices you need to make.

She was in there every day that next summer, working in the gym or studying tapes. She would ask me, "When did we lose momentum here? How could I have sensed that and turned it around?" I really enjoyed talking to her and teaching her; she was a great student of the game.

One day we were in my office. She wanted me to know that she finally understood what it meant to play at this level, to be a point guard, to lead her team, and she was explaining that to me. Suddenly, she stopped and looked at me, and she said, "Never mind, Coach. I'm not going to say anything more. I'm not going to talk about it; I'm going to do it. You'll see."

I just smiled.

12

The Best of Times, the Worst of Times

In 1992, Bill and I and the three kids piled into the van and embarked on a twenty-five-day trip to points west. We'd never done anything like it, but at the end of my season, Bill told me he'd planned a big trip for us.

He was always the one who made things like that happen, and I counted on him to do it, although I always gave him grief about it. "Bill," I'd complain, when he'd organized a couple of days away in the summer, "you know I need to be getting ready for next year." He'd just say, "Well, I've got the car, I've got a cooler full of sodas, and I've got Nina's medication. Everything's set—all we need is you. Boys, grab your mom's hand, and let's go."

That trip was the greatest gift

he could have given me. Twenty-five whole days, completely removed from my daily responsibilities—it was heaven. Nobody had cell phones then, of course, so you weren't expected to be available when you were away; I called into the office a couple of times, and that was it. I remember drying clothes at a Laundromat on the road and telling Bill how nice it was, just to waste time together. Of course, I know now that we weren't wasting time at all.

We saw such amazing things on that trip: Muir Woods, Yellowstone Park, Mount Rushmore, the Grand Canyon, the Continental Divide, and the Badlands of South Dakota. I'd never seen a landscape like that. We fed deer and buffalo by hand.

Bill was absolutely meticulous in his planning. He always knew where we'd be staying and what we could expect when we got there. And we needed to know, because we were traveling with Nina. Not only did we need wheelchair access, but the hotel needed to have a section in the restaurant where we could sit away from people who might distract her from eating. At that point, we were still trying to feed her by mouth, and all of her food had to be pureed, so we either had to bring the puree, or the restaurant had to puree it for us. Feeding Nina took an hour and a half or two hours, so one of us would feed her while the other one was outside playing with the boys.

David was twelve; Justin was eight. They were so young! We used to make them run in the hotel parking lots, to get rid of some of their excess energy. I'd often look in wonderment at my sisters' girls, bouncing their dolls on their laps, while my boys bounced their balls—and sometimes their bodies—off the walls. David and Justin liked to compete with each other—they still do—and that became one way that we could get them to do what we wanted quickly. We'd set little goals for them: "Okay, run to that tree, climb it, and then run all the way back!" We laughed with such pride and love as they huffed and puffed back to us.

When we were satisfied we'd worn them out, we'd bring them

into the room, and by the time they'd had a bath and something to eat and written in their travel journals, they were out like a light.

On that trip, we went to the Carlsbad Caverns in New Mexico; Bill stayed in the van with Nina while I took the boys. Now, I have always been claustrophobic. Any house I live in has to have an open feeling to it, and I don't like a lot of clutter; I want things in their place and against the walls. Still, claustrophobia or no, I wanted to see what those caverns looked like, and they were spacious enough that I thought I'd be all right.

The boys and I were the first ones in. I'd seen photographs of those amazing rock formations, stalagmites and stalactites, but they paled in comparison with the real thing. It was another world.

As people came in behind us, I started feeling very uncomfortable. Thoughts rushed through my mind: *I'm closed in; I can't get out of here. How am I going to get out of here?* David and Justin were wrapped up in the tour and oblivious to my growing panic. Suddenly, I felt really hot, and when the guide said it was time to move on to the next chamber, I realized that there was no way I could make it through the tour. I put my hand on David's shoulder and tried to get him to come with me, but he was confused—we'd just gotten there, why would we leave?—and I was unable to talk. I finally choked out, "Wait here, guys. Wait here," and then I tore out of there as fast as my legs could take me. I swear, it felt like I was losing my mind.

When I got back to the van, Bill was feeding Nina. He took one look at me and got up to go for the boys; neither one of us wanted to deny them the experience. As he was walking away, he said, "You know, Vivian, I wondered how you were going to get through that." I told him how much I'd wanted to see those amazing caves. He said, "I know. But you know what? You would have been okay if you'd stayed in the back." He was right. I would have been fine without all those people between me and the exit. Bill always did know me better than I knew myself.

Some of my best memories of that trip are of the van. With most people, you don't even notice the way they drive—or if you do, it's because you feel unsafe. But driving with Bill was like dancing; he was brilliant at it and he loved it. When he was in medical school, he always teased me that he was going to drop out and go to the Skip Barber Racing School. One time for his birthday, I got him tickets to the Indianapolis 500, and he was like a little kid. Another time, I bought him an old Triumph Spitfire and got it restored. I put a big bow on that car and made him the happiest person in the world.

Bill did all the driving at home, too. It meant that I never had to worry about being late. My general nature is to wait until the last second to try to get something done, but Bill hated lateness of any kind. He'd find out when I had to be somewhere and he'd set the departure time. More often than not, I'd give him half an hour to make a forty-five-minute drive. He'd complain—"Woman, do not put me through this stress again"—but somehow he always got us there on time.

Some nights on that trip out west, if we were pushing through to get somewhere for the morning, we'd fold up the seats in the back, take Nina out of her chair, and the boys and Nina and I would cuddle on blankets in the back and watch movies while Bill drove. I remember watching *The NeverEnding Story* countless times—that unicorn was so beautiful and so unreal, and it felt so perfect at the time.

The only request Bill made of me on that trip was that I not work in front of the kids, so I didn't. But as soon as they went to sleep, I'd take out my tapes—instructional videos, or clinics, or old games—and watch them until two or three in the morning, while Bill drove and the kids slept. In that van, I felt like I had the best of both worlds: my family and my work. Many, many times, I thought, *This is the best time of my life.* And it was.

Bill was the picture of health, but when I thought back on it later, some things stood out. I'd noticed over the summer that he seemed to be sweating an awful lot over the smallest of physical tasks. He also started carrying Tums with him, which was odd because he never took any medication at all, not even aspirin. But when I asked him about it, he just said his stomach was a little upset.

After our trip, we settled back into our fall routines and the hectic blur that the beginning of a season always is. The next thing I knew, it was the day before Thanksgiving.

I was fixing spaghetti for dinner, just something quick so we could start to focus on getting ready for the holiday. Off our kitchen, there was a beautiful room with a big picture window, decorated entirely in white. We called it the white room. Bill was in there, and he called to me, "Vivian, could you come in here for a second?"

"Bill, I'm busy," I called back. "Why?"

"It's the first snowfall of the year, and I want you to see it. You move so fast; you're always doing something. I just want my wife to sit down and relax and spend some time with me, okay?"

So I sat down next to him, and he made me admit that the snow out the picture window was pretty, and the two of us gazed out at the scene and hugged.

Of course, when the boys saw Bill hugging me, David wedged his way in between us, and Justin grabbed my leg. Bill said, "Let's all just sit here and be quiet." So the whole family sat there for ten minutes, hugging one another and looking out at the snow.

Then I said, "You know that the Stop and Shop is going to close, and if you don't get those things, there's no Thanksgiving dinner," and he said, "All right, all right—I know. I'm going to go."

I went to finish my cooking, and Bill took the car and went shopping. When he came back, he sat down in his favorite leather chair and took a nap. The boys were downstairs playing, and I was plaiting Nina's hair. All of a sudden, Bill jumped up from his chair, as if he'd been startled in his sleep, and walked over to the kitchen counter. I saw him lift the top off the turkey pan, look at it, and then replace the lid. I had just spoken to my brother Tim, and without looking up, still working on Nina's hair, I began telling Bill some piece of news that Tim had shared, but he didn't respond. Still with my head down, I said, *"Bill"* to get his attention.

Then I heard a crash as he hit the floor.

I ran to him. He wasn't conscious, so I started to give him CPR. I remember thinking that I didn't want the kids to see their father down on the ground, and yet I knew that I needed to keep working on him. How was I going to call EMS? My mother was downstairs in her room. I think I screamed at the top of the steps, and then I got on the phone, frantically trying to tell the ambulance where we were. My mom came up, and then I called my sister, or maybe my mom called her, I don't know. Someone had to stay with Nina and the boys.

I don't remember the order of things after that. I didn't know what to do; I kept trying to give him mouth-to-mouth, then I pounded on his chest. I didn't realize that David had come up the stairs from his room until he started yelling, "Why are you hitting Dad?" My mom took both boys upstairs and my sisters had come to the house, but the ambulance still hadn't arrived. I remembered that the man who lived two doors down from us was a paramedic and I ran out into the snow to see if he could help.

By the time I got outside, the fire trucks and ambulance were pulling up to the house. Teapot got into the ambulance with Bill. We went to Mercy Hospital, the closest one to us. As soon as we got there, I called the radio announcer for our games, whose father-in-law was the chair of the cardiac unit at the hospital at the University of Iowa, and begged him to ask his father-in-law to come over to help my husband. Bill's regular doctor was on his way, too; I knew he'd be okay as long as he got some help.

But then the emergency room doctor came out, looked at me, and said, "I'm so sorry." I didn't even know who he was, and he was telling me that my husband was dead.

At forty-seven, my best friend, strongest supporter, the father of my children, and the love of my life had succumbed to a massive heart attack. In a moment, my whole world had fallen apart.

I don't have any memory at all of where I was or what I was doing during those first days. There was a memorial service at the university. I came in through a side door and sat in the front row. I never looked at the audience, but people said it was packed, and that my colleagues and former players and Bill's friends had come from all over the country to pay their respects.

I knew that I wanted to take Bill back to Pennsylvania, to be close to his family and where we were from. My sister arranged for his body to be flown there, and all of us flew back together—my sisters and all of their kids. Bill's mom chose the church for the service there. His brother Mark, a music major, asked me what music I wanted him to play. I chose Simon and Garfunkel's "Bridge Over Troubled Water," because it was the song that our friends had sung at our wedding, and the Bette Midler song "Wind Beneath My Wings," because that was what Bill had been to me.

After Bill died, I felt terrified, insecure, and helpless. I had depended on him for everything. He was always trying to teach me something—how to change a flat, where the fuse boxes were—but I was never interested. I thought he'd always be there to take care of things for me.

When I used to lose about twenty pounds during the season—you can see my skirt rolled around my waist in pictures of postseason games—Bill would scold me about my habits by teasing me: "You don't eat well, and you don't sleep enough. It's unfair for you to leave this earth before me and expect me to raise these kids all by myself. I need you to take care of yourself. I'm telling you now so you know, if something happens to you, I'm going to find a new wife to do Nina's hair. Nothing I say makes you act different, so maybe that thought will get through to you and make you do better." But it had always been a joke—one of us wasn't supposed to be left behind.

My mom lived with us for twelve years, and if you asked her today, she'd tell you that she never heard Bill and me raise our voices to each other. I might have walked into a stadium to a standing ovation and been carried out on the crowd's shoulders, but twenty minutes after the game, I'd be bathing our daughter or pressing our sons' clothes. There was never any competition between us, only full cooperation. We were a team. No matter how hard it got—and we were tested by what happened with Nina—I always knew that we would be able to make it together.

Now that certainty had been taken from me, and suddenly I didn't know anything at all.

Again, I thought back to what that priest had told me after Nina had gotten sick, about being a source of strength and comfort for others who are suffering. But I didn't want it; I didn't want to be strong. This was too steep a price to pay.

I couldn't have gotten through the next six months without my family and so many others—some of whose names I don't even know, but to whom I'll always be grateful. Ricky and Madeline and my mom cooked the meals and cleaned the clothes and dressed the kids. My brother Tim came up to sort out the finances and pay the bills and to figure out where everything was; Bill's recordkeeping, like everything else, had been meticulous.

I asked Madeline and her family to move in with me for a while. The house was big enough that the kids could have their own rooms. I knew it would take away from the privacy she had with her own family, but I felt desperate to have her there; she and her husband and their daughter made the house feel full. I remember Madeline telling me that she wouldn't let me fall, and she didn't.

I know that women from the Cheyney team reached out and told me they'd do anything I asked. They were willing to coordinate their vacations so they could take turns coming up to care for the kids, so that I would always know that they were safe and with people I trusted.

And I know that Iowans grieved as well. Bill had always been able to talk to anyone about anything, from knitting to retooling vintage cars. After he died, it seemed like every single person whose life he had touched came forward with a card, or flowers, or a donation in his name. My sisters and the basketball staff answered all the condolence letters and thanked people for the cards and the flowers. They protected me from so much. I couldn't have looked at any of it; I still can't. I know where all of those letters are, but I have yet to open the box. One day I will, but I'm not ready yet.

It was a good thing I had kids, because without them I think I might not have survived. The other thing that sustained me was thinking about and talking to my mom. Bill had died twenty years—almost to the day—after my father had passed. My mom had lost her husband when she was right around the same age—I was forty-four—but she had none of the resources I did. I could support my family; she'd struggled to feed and clothe the kids still at home. Whenever I thought I couldn't go on, I'd think of her example; sometimes, it was the only thing that kept me going.

I was so insecure and fragile, I could barely function. About a month after Bill died, I realized that I had forgotten to cancel a speaking engagement to a group of hotel workers in Cedar Rapids; suddenly, there it was on the calendar. I hadn't made arrangements and I couldn't find anyone to take care of Nina.

Finally, Ricky said she could watch her, but I didn't want her to come pick up Nina because she had taken some cold medicine that had really knocked her out, so I was worried about her driving. I got Nina ready and drove across town. At this point, I was barely keeping myself together, heart and mind. Just getting myself dressed and into the car was a challenge.

There was no ramp at my sister's house, so I had to carry Nina up the steps, even though we'd been told not to lift her by ourselves. I was wearing a white suit, and halfway up, I could feel a muscle pull in my stomach. As I laid Nina down beside Ricky, I thought, *God, I can't take this. It's too much.*

I had about twenty-five minutes to get to Cedar Rapids, and it was snowing pretty hard. Now, even at my best, I have a notoriously terrible sense of direction, and sure enough, after about fifteen minutes, I looked up at a sign and realized that I'd been driving in the wrong direction the whole time. I pulled over to the side of the road, put my head down on the steering wheel, and cried.

Driving in the wrong direction was a perfect symbol of the way that I felt at that moment in my life—how disoriented and lost I was, at a time when I couldn't afford to be lost. I literally did not know where I was or what I was doing. *What am I going to tell these people?* I asked myself. *They want me to come and talk to them about the importance of being accountable, of doing what you say you're going to do, about preparation and the importance of teamwork, and I'm driving to Des Moines.* There were no cell phones, so I couldn't call without finding a pay phone, and even if I turned around, I still didn't know the way there. "I can't make it; I just can't. Just leave me alone," I felt like saying.

I had lost my confidence. I didn't know who I was without this person who had supported me, guided me, and made my life so much better at every turn. It wasn't as if he'd done my thinking for me. In a way, he'd done something even more important: he had amplified the quiet voice within me, so that I could always hear my dreams. Losing him overwhelmed me most because, suddenly, it felt like I couldn't hear myself anymore.

But that didn't mean I wasn't in there somewhere. I'd made a commitment to show up, and people had taken their lunch hour to come and hear me. So I told myself: "You know what you do? You go there and tell people the truth. Tell them that you couldn't find someone to take care of Nina. Tell them that you got lost. Maybe they've gone through something like this in their own lives." I dried my face, asked for directions from a gas-station attendant, and got to where I was going. I was more than half an hour late, but the audience had waited for me.

At first, I cried. I apologized, explained about my poor sense of direction, and told them that I wasn't much good at anything but basketball. I spoke from my heart and told them the truth, and I felt as though the people in that audience and I made a connection for a lifetime. They understood what I was trying to say, which is that we're all human. Whether you're a cook, a chambermaid, or a basketball coach, all of us are simply trying to live our lives, often in the face of challenges that feel like more than we can bear.

Life might be unfair; you might be blindsided by bad luck or misfortune. Nobody knows better than a basketball coach that you might not reap the rewards of your hard work, and that you don't always get what you deserve. But with the support of other people, you get through it. We need one another, and if we stick together, we can get through anything.

13

Lost

In time, the kids went back to school. But the longer I went without coaching basketball, the easier it seemed it would be to walk away from it forever.

I couldn't imagine when I would be able to face basketball again. To play sports is a celebration of life at its highest level; death is at the other end of the spectrum. How could I celebrate life on the court when in my heart and in my soul, I was hurting more than I ever had? How could I reconcile those two emotions, mirroring and mocking each other?

I took about a month off, and I got very quiet. I was trying to hear the voice inside me, so I would know what I was feeling. But it was so faint! You can't read about the place I went to after Bill's death; you can't hear about it and understand. You can't go there unless you've been taken on that journey, and it's a place nobody chooses to go.

The team did go on, of course. Marianna Freeman, my brilliant and compassionate assistant, took over in my absence. I never worried; I knew that I could always count on her. Angie Lee was there with her, too, along with Linda Myers. They were loyal, trustworthy, and hardworking, and we loved one another. We were a team, and it didn't matter who got the credit so long as we won—that had always been our motto, and it was never more true than in the months after Bill's death.

I listened to the games on the radio, and afterward, when the girls were being interviewed, they'd say, "Coach Stringer, we love you, we miss you, please come back!" That would break my heart because at that point, I just couldn't do it; I couldn't answer their call. I was so weak; I couldn't lift my chin and put on a strong face like I had always done. I wasn't ready, and I wasn't sure I would ever be.

One day, I took David over to the recreation center for his own basketball practice. There was a bad snowstorm, and his coach couldn't make it; he'd gotten stuck on the other side of town. All the kids were standing around, and one of the dads came up to me and said, "Coach, could we ask you to help these boys out?" Everything in me resisted, but David said, "Mom, please—just say something and give us some drills to do." So I led them in a little practice; I don't even remember what I did. Looking back, I wonder if that whole episode wasn't staged to lure me a little closer back to the game.

Then, over the Christmas holidays, Marianna got a serious case of food poisoning and couldn't make it back from Delaware. The team asked me, again, to come back.

I knew that my mother felt strongly that I should return to work. But the thing that most helped me to make up my mind was when my sons came to talk to me. When Marianna got sick,

Justin and David came into my room and sat on the edge of the bed. Justin said, "Mom, you need to go back and coach. That's what Dad would have wanted. Besides that, what do you love the most? You know that you should be coaching—that's you, Mom. What else are you gonna do? I mean, what else *can* you do?" I almost laughed. Even at eight, Justin looked exactly like Bill; he still does. Sometimes now he reminds me so much of him that it's scary; his mannerisms and way of speaking and moving are so similar, even though he was so young when Bill died. Then David reminded me of how Bill had always been in the stands at my games with a smile on his face.

There was never any question in my mind that Bill would have wanted me to keep coaching; I just didn't know if I could do it. But the conversation with the boys made me decide that I would try.

The day I went back to practice, I asked my niece Keonte to go with me. I couldn't be alone very much.

Those early practices were very difficult; it reminded me of the way the kids at Cheyney had been when I came back after Nina's injury. You've never seen people try so hard. They tried so hard to make every shot, every cut, every pass perfect, to please me. They'd forget a play and look like they were going to burst into tears.

I realized that Bill's death had been a loss for them, too. Every one of them, both the staff and the girls, had known him and loved him; many of them had treated him like the father they'd never had. And he had been as proud of that team as he'd been of his own children. He had always been there for them, to offer a kind word or some support after a tough practice or a defeat. And now he wouldn't be.

Truthfully, even when I was back, I couldn't feel any enthusiasm for what they were doing on the court. I was physically present, but I know that I had a sort of blank look on my face, and I spoke in a very slow, very soft, deliberate tone of voice—not what you might think of as a "coaching" voice. But basketball has always been able to get to me. One day in practice, one of the kids failed to execute something that we'd just gone over, and I said in a loud, clear tone of voice, "Wait, *wait,* just wait a minute."

It was like I had dropped an atomic bomb. Everyone in there, players and assistant coaches, stopped in their tracks and looked at me. I realized that it was the first time I had spoken in my real voice, with power and emotion. They didn't even care that I was annoyed at them; they were just happy that I was back.

The court became, once again, a place of refuge and recovery for me. The only time my mind was clear and at rest was when I was on the floor coaching. As my mother kept reminding me in those days, life has to go on. It doesn't mean you're any less grief-stricken, but you can't stop living. Members of my staff like Dianne Murphy, who is now athletic director at Columbia and still a dear personal friend, took care of me in a lot of small ways and shielded me from condolences, which were still too painful to hear. I didn't know this at the time, but John Chaney asked my assistant to fax him my schedule every day to make sure that I was scheduling enough rest and time to eat. After practice, I would close the door to my office and cry.

The run-up to the tournament is a blur for me, but I do know that the fire and resolve that our team exhibited were completely unmatched. The only thing you can do when times are tough is pull together and let it make you stronger, and that is what we did. Our hearts ached and we let it all out on the court. They gave me near-perfect play, winning seventeen consecutive games in a row.

Tennessee was one of the NCAA games we played en route to the Final Four that season, and their coach, Pat Summitt, told me later that she'd never seen a more determined or stubborn team in her life. She said, "It seemed that every time we thought we had an answer, your girls said no." She told me that at one point, she started to get up to call a time-out, and her assistant told her to sit down. "It's out of our hands. There's nothing for us to do. There's no way that this team will be stopped."

I couldn't believe what I was seeing myself. The effort they were putting up made you cry as you sat on the bench. It truly demonstrated the power of the human spirit, and there was no question in my mind: they were doing it for me and for Bill.

But basketball is a game of runs, and if you can't sustain the runs, that's what determines who wins or loses. All of a sudden, Tennessee went up ten points in short order, and we couldn't stop them. I have to say, the atmosphere in that auditorium was eerie. The fans would never have dishonored Tennessee; the team was, as all of Pat's teams are, extraordinary. But it was more than a game to the people in the stands that night, and our team's fans—the citizens of the state of Iowa—would not be denied. It was as if we were supposed to have that one special moment together.

I looked across the floor to where Bill always sat with Nina and the boys and my brothers and sisters and some other special-needs children whose parents he was friends with. I saw everyone there in their usual spots, and I can't explain it, but I felt like Bill was there, too. I felt that he had somehow helped us to this place, and a tremendous calmness came over me. I wasn't the only one; everyone there felt his presence.

They set up a line press for the last play. One of the kids broke, and we scored for the win.

The place erupted; there wasn't a dry eye in the house. It was over. Just five months after Bill's death, we were headed to the Final Four, the first time a Division I coach had taken two teams from two different schools.

Our rivalry with Ohio State was legendary. There had been more than twenty-two thousand fans in the stands to see us play them the year before, the biggest crowd ever assembled for a women's basketball game, and our first game against them during the regular season had been the very first advance sellout in women's college basketball history. State troopers had to stop people from coming into Iowa City; restaurants and bars were filled with people watching the game on TV. After his own big win, Coach Raveling had promoted our game on television; instead of basking in his own success, he had used the platform to raise awareness about the women's game. "The shoulders of the state are broad enough to support men's and women's basketball," he told the cameras. "I want you all to come out to support. Let's make this a historic event."

It was odd—that game against Ohio State didn't feel like a Final Four game to me. We'd beaten them handily a couple of times during the season and we'd beaten Auburn and Tennessee, teams I had been far more worried about.

Unfortunately, we lost. The irony was that the game-winner was hit in overtime by a young lady who had wanted to come to Iowa but whose skills I felt would be duplicated on our team. She went on to play for Detroit in the WNBA. She had never played well against us until that game—and then she hit the basket that won it.

Our teams were staying in the same hotel, and I ran into her in the lobby shops in the middle of the night; I guess neither of us could sleep. She gave me a big hug. "I'm so happy for us—but I'm so sorry!"

As I walked into the arena to watch the final game of the tournament between Texas Tech and Ohio State, everyone in the sold-out auditorium rose to their feet and applauded me. My grief, combined with the tremendous outpouring of love and respect from the wonderful people in those stands, was almost more than I could bear.

After Bill's death I grew more reluctant to be away from the kids when I didn't absolutely need to be. Coaching took me away too much as it was; now the I-Club functions I had once asked to be a part of made me feel that I was stealing time from my family.

I tried to explain that I was all the kids had now. I had to rely on my sisters and mom to take care of Nina, and what about the boys? Children don't grow like plants. Someone has to *be* there. In the past, that person had been Bill, more often than not. Now there was only me.

Everyone said they understood, but their actions said otherwise. They'd commiserate about how many demands there were on my time, and then they'd just add to the pile. Everybody takes your time to tell you to take time, and nothing is more stressful than that. How can you tell me to relax when you've just gotten finished telling me where and how I'm going to spend my weekend? It became clear to me that I had to put some limits on what I was prepared to do. I no longer wanted to travel halfway across the state to meet with a few people to raise a little bit of money for the program.

I still regret that I wasn't there sometimes when I should have been. For instance, when David started playing football, he was really excited. But after a little while, I noticed that he was very quiet when he got home from practice. A mom can always tell when a kid is disappointed, and when I pressed him, he told me that the starting quarterback wasn't throwing him the ball.

I didn't want to approach the coach, so I suggested that David speak to him in order to get some answers. He did, but I could tell that he wasn't satisfied. So I went to practice one day and saw what was going on with my own eyes. Either the quarterback couldn't throw or he wasn't seeing open receivers. Or was he just not seeing David? And why was the coach still playing him with this blind spot? David was one of the most talented kids on the team.

I just couldn't understand it—until David finally told me that there was a group of dads who would stick around after practice to hang out with the coach, and their sons were the boys who played. I never let David see, but I cried a little bit about that. If Bill had been alive, he would have been there, and that coach would never have been able to fall short the way he did. Even if he had, David would have been able to look out into the stands and see that someone was there for *him*.

David did go on to distinguish himself as one of the outstanding high school football players in the state, but things like that haunted me throughout the boys' childhoods, as I imagine they haunt all single mothers. On another occasion, the school called to notify me that Justin would be reading during the school assembly. He was eight or nine, and it was a great honor to be chosen. But on that day, we had a game at Michigan, and I had to leave the night before, so Madeline went instead. I felt so upset about that: you could have bet your last dime that Bill would have been there. But I comforted myself as best I could: at least someone who loved Justin was there.

The only thing that mattered to me in those days was that the kids felt safe and okay. Many times, I'd walk in the door to find Justin lying on the couch with his head on Madeline's lap while she stroked his hair. It always made me feel good to know that even though our family had gone through this major tragedy, the boys still felt that everything was under control.

Bill had been everything to Nina. We could never really be sure how much she heard and understood, but there was never any question of how she felt about her dad. He picked her up from school almost every day, because I was usually practicing in the afternoons. There were sometimes as many as fifty people in that classroom at pickup, but the teachers always told me, "Mrs. Stringer, it doesn't matter how many people are in this room; when Nina hears her daddy's voice from across the room, the smile comes all the way across her face." She had lost her best friend.

After he died, when I had to be on the road, I'd call and ask Madeline to put the phone up to Nina's ear so I could say hello to her. I'd always pretend to sneeze, to get her to laugh. If anyone ever overheard me, they probably thought I was crazy or stupid, but I didn't care; the one thing that has always made Nina laugh is the sound of me sneezing. That was the last interaction we had in the hospital before she went into the seizure that led to the coma. I sneezed, and she laughed; I blew my nose, and she laughed harder, and then she got this really funny look on her face and she was never the same again.

Because Nina can't talk, Madeline would always hold the mouthpiece very close to her mouth so I could hear her breathing. When she's excited, her breath gets louder and quicker. That's when I'd sneeze, trying to make her laugh, because I'd always just want to hear a little bit more. "I hear you," I'd tell her. "I hear you. Mom loves you." Madeline would get back on the phone and say, "You should see the big smile on her face right now."

Sometimes, when I couldn't hear her breathe, I'd ask Madeline whether she was smiling, and Madeline would always tell me that she was. I wonder sometimes if she wasn't just telling me what I needed to hear so I wouldn't hurt more than I already did.

Bill had also been the point person for Nina's medical care; I had relied on him to talk to the doctors about what she needed and how it would work. That year, Nina had a number of medical problems that had to be dealt with right away, and dealing with those things alone tested me beyond what I thought I could bear.

Nina had scoliosis, a curvature of the spine, which was becoming severe enough that it would soon compromise her breathing. Her chest was literally caving in. She needed a set of rods—they're called Luque rods—put in her back to keep her spine straight, allowing her lungs room to breathe. It was major surgery.

If he'd been alive, Bill would have researched it and told me what we should do. Without him, I felt overwhelmed and unable to cope. I could never bear the thought of surgeons cutting Nina.

But I had no choice: the spring after Bill died, I got a letter from Nina's doctors saying that she had to have the surgery by April or they wouldn't be responsible for the consequences.

Once again, I leaned on my family to support and protect me. All eighteen of us—the whole clan—would descend on the doctor's office when Nina had an appointment. And when she was in the hospital, she was never alone; we needed all the chairs we could gather to accommodate everyone in her room.

Support came from unexpected places that year as well, and I was always grateful for it. After her surgery, Nina needed a new wheelchair. Getting fitted for a new chair is a complicated process I hadn't been through before. If he'd been alive, Bill would have taken Nina for all the appointments and asked all the questions. But Bill wasn't there, so I found myself turning to all quarters—even twelve-year-old David—for advice. The evaluating orthopedic physical therapist assigned to Nina was a woman named Margaret Alston. She would step in, and indeed, turn out to be one of my close friends—but not right away.

It takes as many as five or six fittings to get a wheelchair right. Nina needed a custom-molded insert and a whole lot of things I didn't know anything about then. But we were in the middle of the season and things kept coming up, so I had to cancel the fitting appointments a number of times. Finally Margaret showed up in my office to tell me, face-to-face, just how irritated she was by the clear evidence that I didn't value her time. But in the little while it took for me to be able to see her, she saw what it was like in my office, and by the time my secretary waved her in, she was apologizing to me! She promised that she'd do whatever she could to help me out.

Luckily for us, she's incredibly detail oriented, knowledgeable, and caring. She did what was necessary to get that wheelchair right—she paid attention even to the color of the cushions!—and in so doing, took a tremendous weight off my mind. She was an angel of mercy for us then, and later, too.

There was another incident that summer that reminded me that I wasn't alone, no matter how I might have felt. The woman who was supposed to watch Nina had a family crisis of her own, and I had a nearly impossible time finding someone I trusted to replace her on short notice. The upshot was that I showed up a day late to a major recruiting event. When I finally got to the gym where the girls were playing, I was exhausted, and I climbed to the top of the bleachers to be alone. It had been such a struggle to get there. I was sitting there, watching the event through tears and wondering how I could make it through another day, when a woman climbed up and introduced herself.

She didn't need to; I recognized her right away as track great Willye White, the five-time Olympian. So I put on my "everything's okay" façade, shook her hand, and told her what an honor it was to meet her. But she saw right away that I wasn't all right, and she asked if she could help. I found myself telling her how inadequate I felt at that moment. "I'm moving as fast as I can and I still feel like I'm drowning, like I'm failing as a mom and as a coach," I told her.

Out of the clear blue, this woman sat down and spent a little time with me. "You're not going to be the best coach all the time, and you're not going to be the best mom all the time," she said. "You are going to come up short, and that's okay. You're doing a great job of juggling all these things. All you can do is your best, and then forgive yourself for the rest."

It was simple advice, but it really took some of the weight off my shoulders—that day and in the years afterward. Many years later, Ms. White and I attended a Women's Sports Foundation luncheon together; I knew she was there, but I was unable to find her in the crowd. It is one of the great regrets of my life that I wasn't able to tell her before she passed how profoundly her words affected me that day on the bleachers.

Before Bill died, I couldn't have been happier in Iowa. The basketball-crazy state had embraced me and my family, and I had done what I came to do professionally, turning the Hawkeyes into one of the best teams in the Big Ten. During my time there, they collected six Big Ten titles and made nine NCAA tournament appearances.

But now all the happy memories we'd made were like daggers. I had to pass Bill's office at the athletic center daily to get to my own. For months, I avoided the kitchen, and I never could go near the place where he had fallen. All those bake-offs with my family, every happy dinner we'd shared, every game he'd come to with the kids—those memories made my day-to-day existence impossible.

And we were so visible in Iowa! Everybody knew who I was. It was helpful to know that people cared, but I felt that the boys and I would never be able to heal because someone was always telling us they were sorry. Sometimes I'd be out shopping and having a comparatively good day, and someone would offer their condolences, and I'd find myself in a dressing room, crying again. Eventually, even the most enjoyable activities felt like pouring salt into an open wound.

It made me miserable that my kids saw me so sad. I had always rejoiced that Bill and I were young parents, with so much energy and enthusiasm for life, and I had been so lighthearted. Before they were born, I had imagined playing football with them on the lawn, going for bike rides, barbecuing, and being together. But then Nina got sick, and some of that lightheartedness went away and never came back. Because of her situation, we didn't always have the freedom to do the things we wanted to do, and I immersed myself in my work. Now Bill was gone, and I could barely keep my head up.

Suddenly, I felt really angry at the sport, as if basketball had robbed me. I had spent so many hours on the road and away from my family for this game. I had to ask myself, had it all been worth it? My husband, the most precious person in the world to me besides my children, was gone, and basketball had taken up a lot of time that we could have spent with each other. Instead of going on vacations with my family, I had traveled around the globe in the service of this game.

The truth is, coaching basketball can be all-consuming. Sometimes it feels like the most important thing in the world, especially if you believe, as I do, that it's more than a game. But sometimes you look up and realize that it really *is* just a game. Just this past summer I took a trip with my mom, and right in the middle of a lovely conversation in beautiful surroundings, I got a call from a girl I'd been trying to recruit. Sure enough, my mom's lunch got cold while I asked this teenager about her back-to-school wardrobe and what kind of music she liked to listen to.

We got through that first summer after Bill's death, and the season started again. I threw myself into it, not with love but with anger. Part of me was thinking, *You better give it to me, because I'm hurting here. You owe me, and now you'd better pay me back.*

That year, we had what people said was the finest class that had ever been recruited in women's basketball—they called them the "Sensational Seven." I'd never had so many great athletes at one time. All the elements were in place: they were well developed, their conditioning and skill level were where they needed to be, and their grades were good.

Marianna had accepted a head coaching position at Syracuse University—I could not have been more appreciative of her loyalty or her commitment to me and the program. Angie and Linda were joined by a young man called Tim Eatman. He had impressed me with his work ethic, his drive for excellence, and his expertise, both in recruiting and on the courts.

But I had to ask: what did it mean that the Lord would give

me a team of that sort following the death of my husband? I had spent my whole career waiting for this team—I had done so much with so little, by comparison.

Now they had come. And what I found was that it didn't matter.

Don't get me wrong: I loved that team. They were great athletes, and I loved them as people; we went to church together. But basketball, as important as I had thought it was, wasn't that important. I still went home, and my sister Madeline would hold my head while I cried. It didn't matter how many points we held the other team to, how many games we won; I was still alone with that hole in my heart.

And so I started to think about what life would be like somewhere else. I needed to know that I could be independent, that I wouldn't spend the rest of my life imposing on others. Nina's situation would never change; I'd never be able to run out to the market for a pack of gum without having to rely on someone to stay with her, so I had to figure out how our family could achieve a reasonable quality of life, taking that situation into account.

I also felt a new responsibility to help my sons find their identities as young black men, which was going to be hard for them in Iowa. I needed to prepare them for life—*real* life—and that meant giving them a more realistic understanding of the way the world views young black men. They didn't know that most people who passed a cluster of boys like them hanging out on a street corner would think they were getting ready to start some trouble. I worried that the safety and the security of Iowa would disarm them. If they spent their whole lives there, would they be ready for Boston or Chicago or New York or Los Angeles, or wherever their professions took them?

I knew, too, that they felt a strong responsibility to take care of me. If they saw me as a widow, would they always feel obligated to stay? It would have been different if Bill had been alive; he wouldn't have wanted them to grow up in a city. A few years before, I'd gotten a serious offer from Temple, and he'd said very clearly, "I'm not going to worry about you leaving this stadium at night and getting knocked on the head; you don't pay attention. And I don't want my children to be raised in a city. I am not feeling this, Vivian Stringer." That was fine with me—I was a country girl myself. But now Bill was gone, and in order for my sons to grow, I had to leave—or I was afraid they never would.

I knew I was leaving the most stable situation imaginable for my children; my sisters and their husbands, who had seen us through so much, would stay in Iowa with all their kids. I was leaving the best team I'd ever had and a state that had loved us and held us in its heart. By the time we left, I felt as deep a sense of pride and allegiance to it as if I'd been born there, and I know my sons still consider it their home.

But I felt that we needed to get our lives started again, so I did what I often tell my teams they must do: accept the hand that has been dealt and take a step into the unknown.

14

Play Your Way Out

The decision to leave Iowa was professionally controversial. The general consensus was that if I stayed, the championship would simply be a matter of time. We had recruited the best class in the country; if I stayed with the program, I could bring it to maturity and reap the harvest I had worked so hard to sow. I knew that many of my colleagues had found tremendous success by staying in one place, building and refining their programs over a period of years. But as much as I loved the state and the school, I couldn't stay.

Rutgers, I believed, was a sleeping giant: a large research university with a great academic reputation, situated in the East, where the majority of schools are small. I had gotten many wonderful players from the East over the years, and I knew that it would definitely be easier to convince a talented girl from the East Coast to come to New Jersey to be a Scarlet Knight than it had been to get her to come to Iowa.

What's more, Rutgers basketball had enjoyed a great deal of fan support over the years, and I did not think it would be difficult to revive it. People told me that the East was a place for professional sports, but that there wasn't a lot of interest in college ball, but I never believed that. After all, they'd told me that no one would ever be interested in anything but football and men's basketball in Iowa, and that had turned out to be nonsense. I believed that the people of the great states of New York and New Jersey were simply waiting for a winning team, and that they would reward us with tremendous devotion and support if we could oblige.

It felt right to come back east in order to begin again; after all, this is where I was from. My brother Tim and his family were in Philadelphia, and I was excited to be a quick train ride away from the jazz clubs and shopping in New York, Philadelphia, and Washington. With a home base in New Jersey, I could be at the ocean, in the mountains, or in the first row at a Broadway show within an hour.

But that didn't mean that it was easy. In fact, even after I had accepted the position, I was so afraid that I'd done the wrong thing that I thought seriously about changing my mind. The day we made the announcement on the Rutgers University campus, I put in a call to my old friend Bobby Cremins, the Georgia Tech men's basketball coach who had announced his decision to go to the University of South Carolina and then rescinded it. I felt that he might be the only person who could understand what I was going through.

We talked for a while, and he told me what I already knew: that the most important thing was to follow my heart. "In time, people will forgive you," he told me. "Don't worry about what everybody else thinks. You have to make the decision that *you* can live with."

He also asked me why I was having doubts, and I spent the

rest of that long night thinking about the answer to that question. I had weighed the decision carefully and I had felt strongly that leaving Iowa was the right thing to do. I still did, but I was also deeply afraid. By the time the sun rose, it was clear in my mind that my fear was the reason I was having second thoughts.

Fred Grunninger, the athletic director at Rutgers at the time, picked me up at my hotel the next morning, and I couldn't stop crying. Why would I move my family when they were so safe and comfortable in Iowa? Why would I make a change at a time when Nina had major, life-saving surgery scheduled? I needed my family and the team of doctors we had come to trust to help me handle that.

Fred saw the state I was in and told me I could do whatever made me comfortable. I could come to Rutgers after Nina's surgery, as late as I wanted—October or November even. Instantly, I felt better. I've never liked the feeling of being cornered, and he must have sensed that. I respect and love that man to this day because he wasn't angry with me and because he didn't want me to do the right thing for Rutgers if it meant doing the wrong thing for my family. I was always loyal to him because I knew that he personally cared about me, not just about what I could do for him or for the school.

In return for Rutgers' faith in me, I pledged to make the school a national power, calling it "the Jewel of the East" in my first press conference. I meant no disrespect to the other teams in the conference or in the East—to the team at the University of Connecticut and their brilliant coach, Geno Auriemma, or to past Rutgers programs, especially the one coached by Theresa Grentz, whom I had known for years and considered to be a friend. I simply meant that I saw the tremendous potential this school had and hoped to help it live up to that potential.

My niece Keonte agreed to move to New Jersey with me. Ke had always been a major part of our family. If Bill was flying to meet me somewhere, Ke would travel with him to help him handle Nina. She's like a niece, daughter, and close friend rolled into one. Honestly, it was only when she agreed to come to New Jersey that I knew I would be able to handle it. She was like a mom to the boys, and she helped me find a nanny for Nina. Finding the right person was hard; we went through a number of people before we found Hyacinth, who takes care of Nina now. In the meantime, Nina began to lose weight. It took hours to get enough calories and nutrients into her, but I didn't want to stop feeding her by mouth; I didn't want her to lose the pleasure of taste. While we were looking, I never worried, because I knew Ke was there. I truly thank God for her.

But even with Ke there, the landing was rough, personally and professionally. There was, as there had been in Iowa, a great deal of attention; Rutgers is in the largest media market in the country, which meant that games were routinely covered by ESPN and the *New York Times,* with as many as ten papers at a time represented in the press box.

My brother Tim had once again negotiated a historic contract, and the press got wind of the fact that I would not only be making more than the men's basketball coach but also more than the *football* coach. I was surprised to see that it wasn't only the sports media that were interested; there were articles in the *Economist* and the *Wall Street Journal*—neither of them known for their sports coverage. The article in the *Economist* was titled "Looking Down on Tall White Men." I hadn't been looking to make history, and the fact that my salary was now public knowledge was a source of embarrassment to me. I hadn't even known I would be making more than the football coach. When I asked my athletic director if it was true, he said, "Yes—and why not?"

By coincidence, I'd had a chicken-or-the-egg conversation with a journalist right before I left Iowa: should fans come out to see a team before they're successful, or is it necessary for a team to be successful in order for the fans to come out? We never did determine the answer. In Iowa, the fans came out to support a great effort, even before we'd started winning for real. In New Jersey, it seemed, the fans were taking a wait-and-see approach. I welcomed the challenge. Once the team started performing the way I knew they could, we'd fill those seats.

I still ached for Bill, and the logistics of being a single mother without my extended family overwhelmed me. One afternoon during a meeting, I was interrupted by a phone call from David. He was out of school, and where was I? In Iowa, the kids had always walked or ridden their bikes home from school, and there was always someone—Bill, one of my sisters, or my mom—waiting for them. If they needed transportation, Bill organized it. I don't think I even excused myself from that meeting; I just ran out of there, feeling like the worst mother on earth.

There's no question that the move was hard on the boys. Mostly, it was the little things. In Iowa, we'd lived on a block with lots of kids all around us, and of course they'd had their cousins. In New Jersey, we lived in a cul-de-sac where there weren't any other kids their age to play with. Once, soon after we'd arrived, I was driving with the boys to do some errands and I was a little slow pulling out of a stop sign. The driver behind me went crazy, honking and carrying on. I looked in my rearview mirror and could see the driver giving me the finger—all this over a one- or two-second delay! I shook my head and got out of there—but then Justin piped up from the backseat: "Mommy, Mommy, slow down! They're waving to you!"

You see, he didn't know what the gesture meant. It never occurred to Justin that someone might be coming at us with aggression or impatience or hate. We were used to the way things had been in Iowa—"Coach, you don't need to wait in line; why don't you come up to the front here?"; and "Coach, you know your money's no good here"; or "Why don't you bring your boys in the house and we'll get them something cool to drink?" We were used to people telling us to have a nice day *like they meant it.* But we weren't in Iowa anymore.

I didn't take any of the class I'd recruited for Iowa to Rutgers—although some of them begged to come. I didn't take any of my players or my assistant coaches from Cheyney when I left, either; I don't raid the henhouse. When I'm on salary at a university, I'm the representative of that university, so when I recruit someone to play for me, I expect them to attend that school whether I'm there or not. Maybe that's not good thinking on my part, but I have always wanted to leave my teams in good order. And I could never have robbed a program I loved the way I loved Iowa. But it did mean that I had a whole new set of players to win over.

The Scarlet Knights lineup I was working with wasn't as strong as it could have been, but I'd been there before. We didn't have much offensive talent, so while we were recruiting more offensive-minded players, we hung our hats on shutting down the opposition. The one thing I have always believed is that you can address defense very quickly. For me, defense is Team personified. No one person gets the credit; it's not one player scoring twenty points over the course of a game, but the whole team working together to prevent a player on the other team from doing so. The team gets the credit, because they have to work together to earn it. And I've always believed that defense wins championships, so that's where I focused our energy.

We had a losing season that first year, and the next, but there were immediate signs of improvement, and I knew that I'd eventually have the chance to make good on the promise I'd made. In the meantime, I put together my team.

I hired my great player from the University of Iowa, Jolette Law, to be one of my assistants, a position she filled for twelve years. (She went on in 2007 to a head coaching position at the University of Illinois.) At one of the very first Rutgers practices we coached together, I told the players that they had to run five sets of a sprinting drill called a double suicide. Each set had to be run in fifty-five seconds, but they found themselves needing five more seconds on the last set, and I held the clock so they could make it. I've never believed in punishment for the sake of punishment. If you're giving your best effort, why on earth would I make you do it over again, when I know you won't be able to recover? The only thing to be gained from that is a broken spirit, and that's not the business I'm in.

Jolette was outraged! She couldn't believe I was cutting them a break. I laughed so hard. I finally had to tell her, "Jolette, whether you want to accept this or not, you guys did *not* run those suicides the way you think you did." She was furious. "Yes we did, Coach! Yes we did!"

The recruiting situation that first year was unique. Recruiting is traditionally quite a long process, one that takes place over months and even years. For example, I first saw Cappie Pondexter play when she was in high school, at least four full years before she came to play for me at Rutgers.

Usually, you attend camps in July where you can evaluate talent. You're not allowed to speak to the athlete or her family during those trips, so you have to make very sure that your potential recruit sees you watching her from the stands. During the periods when you are allowed to speak to the recruits and their families, you get to know them a little on the phone, and by e-mail. During their senior years, you can visit their high schools and their homes, and they can come to campus as well. By August, you're usually working to hold on to the relationships you've developed over the past few years, and hoping they'll use one of their five visits to see your school.

That first year at Rutgers, I was at a major disadvantage; I hadn't signed my contract until August, and because of Nina's surgery, I had been at very few recruiting events. My brilliant staff—Jolette, Betsy Yonkman, and Larry Lawler—and I had a vision of making Rutgers one of the national powers. So we decided to bring six kids up to campus all at once, and to share the dream we had for building this team.

I gave a lunch on campus so that the president of the university and some of the deans and vice presidents could meet the prospects. But instead of the administration interviewing the girls, I found that several of them had such outgoing personalities, it was working the other way around! I always laugh when I think about Usha Gilmore that weekend. She was vibrant, engaging, and funny, the life of the party, and *she* was asking the questions. I looked at Jolette and laughed.

When we were alone with the kids, we made our pitch. "Look around," I told them. "You're looking at the future of Rutgers women's basketball. I have a great vision for this team, but I need you to help me make it happen. *It starts with you.*" I told them that Rutgers was a great university and explained the successes I had enjoyed in the past. They believed in one another and in us—and five out of the six of them came.

Tasha Pointer was one of those recruits. Tasha was an extraordinary player: she had four triple doubles in her career, a Big East record that she holds to this day. But she also possesses a real leadership quality and a tremendous amount of energy, which made her an enormous asset for our team. Tasha is someone who leads and calls for others to follow. She could have gone to any number of schools, but I felt that she belonged at Rutgers with me. I told her that she could go and follow in the footsteps of those who had been at the other great programs or she could come to me and make a path of her own, and I'm so happy that she did.

Jolette was great with the kids, and she always knew precisely what the dynamics were on the team. We always try to switch it up so that everybody has a different roommate when we travel. If we're going into a game where we know the centers are going to be carrying the brunt of the work, we might put the guard who's going to be responsible for delivering the pass they need in the room with them, so that the center can ask questions about specific patterns. Or if we think an older player could help a younger one who's struggling, we'll put them together. (We never ever put freshmen together.) Jolette always knew how the personalities were meshing at any given time, and what combinations would be best for the team. I miss her greatly; it was like losing a piece of myself when she left for Illinois, but I loved her too much to hold her back. I had always known that day would come, and I believe in my heart that she will be one of the great coaches of the future. But in those early days at Rutgers, we were all new and we were all fired up, with big dreams and plenty of energy to put into chasing them. We were starting a little behind, but I felt sure that persistence and hard work on the court would get us where we needed to go.

If there was one thing that fell right into place in New Jersey, it was church. When we moved back east, I got letters from a number of pastors, but after Iowa I wasn't going to settle for anything less than a church I could feel, and I didn't want anyone selling me anything. So we began visiting a number of churches without telling anyone we were coming.

It was very important to me to expose David and Justin to a religious tradition. Like music, I think that religion is one of the greatest gifts you can give your children. God is a friend that you can always count on, even when it seems like you have no others. I hadn't yet been able to provide that for my kids, and I felt a sense of urgency about it, especially since they wouldn't have Bill's guidance as they grew.

Well, the First Baptist Church of Lincoln Gardens was an immediate fit. From the first time we attended, Pastor Buster Soaries was addressing the things that really mattered to me. In fact, in that first sermon, I heard him say something I have always believed, which is that what you do Monday through Saturday is as important as the praying and tithing you do on Sunday. I was impressed by his emphasis on church scholarships and on having young people come up and speak. The choir touched me, and I could feel myself getting emotional during the prayer. It was the uplifting experience I'd been searching for.

On the way home, I asked my boys what they'd gotten from the sermon, and we spent the rest of the ride back to the house deep in conversation. Pastor Soaries had discussed the issues of the day in a way that truly engaged them, heart and soul.

Old habits die hard; we still came late and left early, so that we wouldn't attract any special attention or have to talk basketball. In fact, we attended the church for about a year before I even met Pastor Soaries. But in the years since, he and his wife and family have become great friends to my family and to my teams.

Finally, I had brought David and Justin to a place where they could learn to find comfort in God. In that respect, at least, we were home.

I was moving so fast and so hard in those first years at Rutgers that I put off having an annual physical. Finally, I went in for a workup, but after about a week, they called me and asked me to come back in because there had been some kind of technical glitch with my mammogram. I was irritated, thinking I didn't have time to do this thing over. My friend Margaret had moved to Maryland and was helping me with my plans to build a new house. When I told her about the mammogram, a bell must have gone off in her head, because she said, "Schedule it for Friday, and I'll come with you. I've been wanting to come up for the weekend anyway."

During that second round of tests, they saw again what they'd seen the first time, and I was diagnosed with breast cancer.

My immediate reaction was anger. I was very scared, but I was angry, too. I'd come to Jersey to try to start my life over, but I'd gotten so wrapped up in giving this job my all and making sure that the boys and Nina were taken care of that I hadn't taken care of myself. I'd never neglected myself that way before—but of course

I'd had more time before, because Bill had been on top of everything else that needed to be done.

I flew to Iowa because I felt so comfortable with the doctors and the medical center there. I didn't tell anyone I was coming in, but my sister Madeline happened to call my office that morning, and my secretary told her I'd gone to Iowa. Now Madeline knew that I had no reason to be in Iowa unless I was there to see her and Ricky, and I hadn't said a word. So she waited at the airport for me to come in and followed me, without me knowing it. And when she saw me going onto the oncology ward, she started screaming.

I wasn't trying to be secretive, I really wasn't. It was just that the thought of worrying the people who loved me made what I was carrying even harder to bear.

The doctor in Iowa recommended a mastectomy. I scheduled the surgery, but Margaret begged me to meet with a doctor from Johns Hopkins she'd heard on the radio. His home phone number happened to be in the book, and when she called him on a Sunday, he picked up! She told him that I was scheduled for a mastectomy, and he said, "Please don't let your girlfriend do that. See if she can delay the surgery by a week, and I'll see her tomorrow." So she came up and drove me to Baltimore.

Dr. Dooley, the doctor at Hopkins, didn't think I needed to have a mastectomy, even though my doctor in Iowa felt that I was taking too great a chance. But I wanted to believe Dr. Dooley's advice, so I had a lumpectomy and started a course of radiation.

I came out of the hospital and recovered for a day or two at Margaret's house so that none of the kids would see the bandages. I didn't tell anyone at work that I was sick except my athletic director, Bob Mulcahey, and my assistants, so they'd know why I was so tired and where I was all the time.

Practice was over at eleven-thirty, and I had to be at the center in Philadelphia for treatment at twelve-fifteen. I'm late for every doggone thing in this world, but knowing that people were coming from all over the area to get treatments, I wasn't going to be the one making them wait. I used to look at the women in the waiting room, the anxiety and fear written on their faces. It was like every one of us was sentenced. I'd always wonder about the stories in their heads and hearts, and try to use that time to hold on to just a little bit of gratitude for what I had.

Radiation takes a lot out of you. Margaret or Ricky or Madeline would come right after practice and drive me to the cancer center. I'd lie on that metal bed, watching the bright lights of the scanner move over me, stopping at the target the doctors had marked with a tiny, permanent dot. I'd always think about the other women in the waiting room, lying in the dark just like me, frightened and tired, just hoping the machine was doing what it needed to do. After a while, your skin changes color. There's a dark discoloration like a bruise, or a burn from the inside, which I guess is what it is.

I slept in the car going there and back, but I never caught up. I was completely exhausted all the time. One of my doctors told me it would be years before I felt like myself again.

Because I had told only a few people in my inner circle about it, no one knew why I was so tense and tired, or why I'd be out the door the minute that practice ended. The press was upset; they didn't understand why I wouldn't stay and give them a quote or an interview, and it showed in the way they wrote about me and the team. Many of the articles from that time painted me as cold, unfeeling, and arrogant.

I remember one in particular, headlined THE MANY FACES OF STRINGER. In the photograph that ran alongside it, I looked like a criminal. They published the article the weekend that we hosted the Big East Tournament at Rutgers, one of only two times we've done that since I've been at Rutgers. Everyone in the sport was there, all eyes were on us—and that was what ran in the paper. It was a real embarrassment, and the other coaches were appalled. It stung terribly, but I couldn't explain to the press why I couldn't give them more time without telling them my situation, and I didn't want to do that.

Why didn't I talk openly about it? I considered it to be a private issue, and I still do. But I'm a public figure, whether I like it or not, and if I had started talking about it, there was no way it would have stayed private.

My biggest concern was for the people closest to me. I didn't tell my sons for years; they had gone through too much already. All my medical records went to Margaret's house; the cancer center never even had my address. I told my mother only while I was working on this book; there's nothing I wouldn't have done to spare her the anguish of worrying about me. As for the rest of the world, I guess I wasn't looking for anyone to tell me whether this was something or nothing. I didn't want to have to look into people's faces to see whether or not they understood. I didn't want sympathy, or empathy, or anything at all.

At a Nike recruiting event in Indianapolis, I pulled my friend, Kay Yow, the legendary North Carolina State coach, into the stairwell to talk. I told her how much I admired her decision to speak out about her own struggle with the disease. "You've given hope to so many," I told her. "Talking about this would hurt my family too much right now, but I promise you that someday I will." I didn't want to burden her, but our talk helped me enormously, and when she hugged me, I could feel that she was powerful and strong, just as she had always been.

The experience took a tremendous toll, both physical and mental. I had to find a different way to think about things. My doctors had told me to expect to put on about ten to fifteen pounds, but gaining the weight still made me angry; I'd always maintained a certain weight, and during my season, I'd always lost some. But I was picking it up, and at a rather rapid rate, and I didn't like it. I thought to myself, *Instead of being so angry about gaining all this weight, why don't you think about what it will mean when you lose it, when you're past all this?* And I remembered that being overweight had actually saved Nina's life; the doctors told me that if she hadn't been such a chubby baby, she wouldn't have survived. You have to be careful what you wish for, since you never really know.

There was a song by Yolanda Adams that I played again and again, called "The Battle Is the Lord's." The lyrics went, "There is no pain Jesus can't feel, no hurt He cannot heal. No matter what you're going through, remember that God is only using you, for the battle is not yours, it's the Lord's." I listened to that song over and over, letting the words inspire and console me.

Throughout this time, the only person who was able to bring some measure of peace to me was a woman I had never even met who had had breast cancer. I'll call her Susan. We were connected through a friend, and although we never did meet in person, we shared some very important hours on the phone. It was such a relief to me to talk to someone who had been there. She was conversant with terminology I was just learning and she explained what it all meant.

Susan gave me a tremendous amount of encouragement, too. "You need to get your rest, you need to eat properly, you need to get your checkups," she'd say. It was common sense, but it was still good to hear someone else say the words, maybe because they were the kinds of things Bill would have told me. Perhaps most important, she understood how scared, how angry, and how betrayed I felt. She'd had all the same feelings, but she was on the other side of it. Sometimes she didn't say anything, she just listened.

We didn't talk more than three or four times, but I cried with her and was comforted by her. It was through our conversations that I came to fully understand what that priest had told me when Nina was in the hospital—that sometimes we are tested so that we can go on to help others. Susan was just wonderful—a real angel, who carried me at a very critical time.

It's with Susan in mind that I am finally talking about this now. I've been healthy for almost ten years, thank God, and it's time for me to reach out and offer comfort to those who are suffering as I did.

Life slowly got back to normal. Nike hosts annual retreats for the coaches they sponsor, and Bill and I had always gone; they were a nice way to relax a little during the summer while getting to spend some time with my colleagues. When Bill died, I stopped going, but after a few years, I started going again with David and Justin.

On one of those trips, about five years after Bill had passed, my friend Bobby Cremins approached me while I was spending some time by the pool. Bobby had given me a lot of good advice over the years, and I respected him both as a coach and as a man. He always seemed to have a real love affair with his wife. He was one of those men, like Lute Olsen and Steve Fisher, who wouldn't think twice about leaning over to give their wives a kiss or to ask them to dance, even in the most macho environment. Bill had been like that.

"I don't want to pry, but I wondered if you'd given any thought to dating again," Bobby said to me. I must have looked taken aback. "Nobody's suggesting that you could ever replace Bill, Vivian; he was a heck of a guy, and nobody's denying that. But I hope you'll leave yourself open to the possibility of meeting someone. You're a vibrant woman, and you deserve to have someone to spend time with. I know that Bill would not have wanted you to live the rest of your life alone."

I didn't say much. I certainly didn't have to tell Bobby about the difficulties of a coach's schedule. But the tremendous demands of my job made up only a fraction of the responsibility I was carrying. With Bill gone, I felt strongly that I had to be both mom *and* dad to the boys, and I knew that Nina would need me every day for the rest of her life.

Still, I appreciated Bobby talking to me about it. I'm sure that many people wondered, but nobody said anything. And I often thought about my mom, who never did date after my dad died.

Her kids were everything to her, and she remained completely devoted to us, even after we were all grown and had families of our own. She was so beautiful, and had always looked so young, and yet the romantic side of her life was something she never pursued again. Like me, she's someone who enjoys going out to do things; I love to hear music, travel, see movies and plays. Part of me wondered if I would always have to do those things alone, as she does.

I wondered also how my boys would react to the idea of me having someone in my life again. So one night, when David was about seventeen and Justin twelve, and we were all on vacation together in Mexico, I asked them the question at dinner.

"How would you boys feel if I started thinking about dating again?"

They were both shocked—and then angry. "Why would you say something like that? How can you even think about it?" David asked me. They were not even willing to have the conversation. "We are not going to discuss this," David said, and Justin said, "No, we are not going to talk about this anymore."

I took this in quietly, but I left them with this thought. "I don't have anyone in mind, guys. But the love that you give—and get—from your children is different than the love you give and get from another person. Grandma loves her children to death, but we all have our own lives and children, and she gets lonesome; it would be different if she had a gentleman friend. You're going to grow up and have your own families eventually. What will I do then?"

They just sat there, silent, looking upset. I excused them from the table—it had been a late dinner anyway—and we didn't say another thing about it that night, or the next day, or the day after. We raced speed cars, swam in the pool and the ocean, and saw the sights, and I thought the subject was finished.

But a few days later, the three of us were sitting down to another quiet dinner, and David spoke up. "I apologize, Mom," he said. "We were just shocked. But we've been thinking about it and talking about it, and you're right: we don't want you to spend the rest of your life alone. If you found someone great, we would welcome that." I was so relieved that they had forgiven me, and that I had their blessing. I knew that they'd want what was best for me.

There are a lot of things I'd like to do in my life, and I don't necessarily want to do them alone. But even though I have the boys' blessing, I haven't dated anybody since Bill.

For one thing, a coach's schedule makes it really hard to have a personal life. I see it all the time with the people who work for me. During the summer, we travel all over the country to do recruiting, and during the season, we don't do anything at all aside from basketball. When I'm recruiting, I often don't know what city I'm going to be waking up in the next day. Who's going to have the patience to deal with that?

I'll need to know that someone is with me for *me*, not because of any ulterior motive. I went to one of David's football games after signing a new contract. My salary had just been published in the newspaper, and as I walked onto the field, some joker in the stands yelled, "Vivian, I'll marry you!" Okay, fine—it was a joke. It wasn't like I heard it and thought, *I'll never date*. But it's an issue that successful women struggle with.

Aside from that, I know that any man I'd be with would have to be very strong, very confident, and very secure in himself. I'd hope that he's passionately interested in his own work, as I am. And he'd have to be aggressive, because I've never been any good at flirting. I often think that I don't know what would have happened if Bill hadn't been as committed and persistent as he was.

Of course, there's another factor, too. Nina and I are going to be together for life. It's going to take a special kind of person to accompany us on that journey—someone compassionate and knowledgeable about her condition, or willing to learn. Bill and I never had to question our commitment to each other or to her; it was just "This is our child." Any new person would have to be someone who would embrace Nina as I do; I would never allow anyone to put her in second place.

I'm open to dating; it just hasn't happened yet. Maybe I just haven't met anyone as special as the man I married.

After high school, David was recruited to play football for North Carolina State.

It was interesting for me to be on the other side of the fence—the parent of a recruited kid, as opposed to the one doing the recruiting. I sat in on each and every one of his interviews, because I wanted to see with my own eyes that the coach he went to play for saw him as a human being first. Was this a person who was going to help my son grow and develop, or was this someone who was going to treat him like a piece of meat? I'll tell you: it's tough to be the parent of a college athlete, and being on the other side of it gave me cause to think about the relationships I've had with some of the parents of the kids I've coached.

Every parent wants the same thing, to see their child happy. When a kid wants to play, it means the world to them, and it's hard to know there isn't a thing you can do to help: you can have all the money in the world, but you can't get your kid on a team. You can give them the best genes, make sure they have the best gear and the best trainers, and ensure that they go to the best camps, but you can't get them playing time. Ultimately, that decision isn't up to the parent.

I'm sympathetic to the parents of the girls on my teams; there were certainly times when I questioned the decisions of David's coaches. What I try to remember is that the instincts of a coach and the instincts of a parent are diametrically opposed. A parent wants what's right for their child, while a coach wants what's best for the team and the overall success of the program. That may not be the best thing for a particular individual—in fact, it often isn't. But how do you help any one person or parent to see that?

My own policy is that while I will gladly discuss anything personal or academic with a parent, I will not talk about playing time, and I will not talk to them about how their daughter measures up against other members of her team. I ask them, as I am asking their daughters, to trust that I am making the best decisions for everybody, working to make the program something that their daughters will benefit from being a part of.

It's not always easy for them. One gentleman was a high-level executive with a Fortune 500 company. His daughter was talented—not the most talented, but a good person and an extremely hard worker. That wasn't enough for Dad. He would scream terrible things at her teammates and give instructions from the sidelines, hollering at the other girls to pass the ball to his daughter, as if I hadn't just prepared them for exactly who was going to pass what to whom, and when.

It got bad enough that I asked to meet with him. I explained what a terrible position he was putting his daughter in. She had to apologize to her teammates, on his behalf—that wasn't the way it should be. But the comments from the sidelines continued, and so I gave instructions to the ticket office: no matter what tickets he requested, he shouldn't be seated close enough to be heard on the court. Still, he found a way.

Most of the girls on the team had been insulted, and I knew his daughter was going to start to worry that her teammates were blaming her for her dad's bad behavior. So after a particularly bad incident, I addressed the issue: "We're a team first. None of us asked to have the parents that we have, and sometimes they don't make us proud. They do love their daughters, but sometimes they say things that create a heck of a strain. None of us holds any individual responsible for what she can't control."

Saying it might have eased things between her and the team, but it did nothing to contain Dad. During one Big East Tournament, his tirade about the other players was so abusive that one of the other moms actually got up and left. So her daughter not only had to endure this man's abuse, but she had to see her mom, who had taken a day off work to see her play, put on her coat and leave. But that didn't stop him: "They should fire that coach!" he kept yelling, and my niece Keonte, who was sitting nearby, got into it with him. He retaliated with some very hurtful personal insults, forcing her fiancé at the time to stand up. Some of the Cheyney players were also there, and Debra Walker gave him what for: "Those girls are out there, working hard and sacrificing. Not only is the team struggling, but you're up here making a scene in front of all the other team's fans?"

What happened afterward was the saddest thing of all. When we got to the hotel, that father was waiting for us, and when he saw his daughter, he opened his arms to give her a big hug. With a look I'd never seen on her face, she put her hands out to stop him. "Don't say anything to me," she told him, and she walked right by him. He'd hurt her team, and she wasn't going to stand for it.

I had a very talented freshman on another team. She was a starter, but she wasn't used to memorizing plays, so I'd sometimes take her out for someone with a little more experience.

At one game, her mother wasn't happy to see her daughter come off the floor, and she loudly called me a couple of names that I won't repeat, telling anyone and everyone, "I didn't bring my daughter down here to have her sitting on some bench. Who says that coach knows what she's talking about anyway?" For good measure, she added a couple of ugly things about the girl I'd sent in to replace her daughter. Afterward, I went over to her and said, "I just wanted to let you know that your daughter is working hard and doing very well. She's a credit to you, Mom. We do things a little differently in college than her coaches did in high school, but she's learning fast, and I feel sure that she's ready to take that next step if she can just get your cheer." I added that I hoped she wouldn't make things rocky for her daughter with her new teammates by continuing to speak badly of them. If her mother had something to say after that, I didn't hear about it.

I thought about those parents many times when I was watching David out there. As a parent, it's very hard to be objective. All you can do is promise yourself that you'll be quiet for a second and let things happen, and mostly, that's enough.

One time I was coaching a very talented kid; we were pretty sure that she was going to be drafted after her senior year. But I also knew that she wouldn't have the credits she needed to graduate on time. The draft comes out in April or May, and once you've hired an agent, you're no longer an amateur, and the NCAA won't pay for any more school. She didn't come from money; if her school wasn't paid for, she wasn't going. The long and the short of it was that if she didn't go to summer school between her junior and senior years, she wasn't going to graduate. It was just that simple.

I didn't anticipate a problem. Getting a degree was the point of all the work she'd already put in. And surely she would see that even the best professional career doesn't last forever; a degree would stand her in good stead, no matter what she wanted to do afterward. But when I told her that she needed to start signing up for summer-school courses, she refused. Instead of catching up on the credits she'd need, she wanted to rest.

It might have sounded funny coming from a basketball coach, but I couldn't stop myself from asking her: "Why are you going to let athletics use you up like that? You played, you represented your school, and now you're going to walk out of here without a degree?" But I made no headway. So I took the next step and got in touch with the grandmother who had raised her, expecting that at least she would support me. I expected she'd tell her granddaughter: "Sure, take a little vacation, but use your scholarship; graduating on time is the most important thing."

But the grandmother wouldn't hear a word of it, either! "She needs to come home to me this summer," she told me.

Well, I pitched a fit. It didn't make any sense! "Are you really telling me that you're not going to allow me to pay for her school?" I asked. I could believe that the kid wanted to take a rest, but I couldn't believe that her grandmother—an adult, someone who was supposed to know better—was going to let her walk away from her education just because she didn't want to take a few classes over the summer. But no matter what I said, I couldn't change their minds.

Everyone around me urged me to let it go. But even if I couldn't stop this girl from throwing away her education, I could at least make sure that she and her grandmother knew exactly what they were doing. So I drafted a document, very similar to the release you have to sign if you check out of the hospital before your doctor thinks it's wise for you to go.

"I understand that if I don't go to summer school this summer, I will not graduate on time, and run the risk of not graduating at all," it read. And then I made the two of them sign it.

I don't take any pleasure in telling you that it worked out the way I feared it might. The girl did get drafted, and she never did finish her credits. Unfortunately, her professional career didn't work out the way she hoped it would, and she had no degree to fall back on; I don't even know what she's up to now. I will say that I do not understand when someone who ought to know better refuses to step up and make a young person do what they should.

Sometimes parents won't let their kids grow up. I had one kid at Rutgers who was badly homesick; every time her mother would come to visit her, she would pass out in the lobby crying: "I can't live without my mom!" And the mother, for whatever reason, encouraged it. I thought she'd toughen up after her first year, but then the girl told me she'd made a decision to go home.

I told her straight out: "You're making the biggest mistake of your life." But she couldn't hear me. So I sat her mother down at my kitchen table and asked her some hard questions. "Mom, if you tell her she can come home just because she's lonesome, then how is she going to grow up to be a strong individual, to stand on her own two feet as you know she will have to in this life? If you let her come home, how is she ever going to understand that she has to commit herself to fulfilling the responsibilities she's taken on? She needs to grow up. You need to cut those apron strings. I know it's hard to let go, but nothing bad is going to happen to your little girl. I gave you my word that we would look after her, and we will."

But her mother had another plan: "She's going to get a job to pay for school back home," she told me.

I couldn't believe my ears. The girl already had a job! Her job was playing basketball. Her job, which earned her a free education and provided a roof over her head, was playing a sport that she loved. Basketball was a job that made her mind and her body healthy, and one that put her on a team full of girls who loved her and cared about what happened to her. This was a job with a future—because even if she didn't make it in basketball, she was learning what it meant to be part of a team, to work hard and give something her greatest effort. When it was all over, she'd be walking away with a degree, if not a professional career. And all she had to do was come to practice and go to class.

"Look, you're not kidding me," I said to Mom. "That kid is done. At least promise me this: if she decides to withdraw, make sure she does it properly, so that she'll keep her grades and be eligible to transfer to another school. I have the feeling she's going to come up against the reality of this situation and want to change her mind; at least make sure that she can use her talents to get her school done when she grows up a little bit."

But she didn't withdraw properly, and wouldn't you know it, a year later, I get a call. She doesn't want to wake up at the crack of dawn and go out into the freezing cold to do her job at Jiffy Lube anymore; she can't make enough to support herself and to pay for her school credits, and she misses coming back to a dormitory filled with people.

I told her I'd be happy to have her back, but only under certain conditions: "If you pay for your credits over the summer, and if you earn only As and Bs, I will reconsider you for a scholarship," I told her. She could borrow money from the school or from the bank to do it, but I wasn't going to take her back until I knew she was willing to make a significant personal sacrifice. I couldn't afford to let the team go through all that drama again, and I didn't want to saddle them with someone who had shown me that she wasn't ready, when they had shown me they were.

My conditions scared her off; I guess she still wasn't ready. That girl is working at Payless now. Instead of pulling on a pair of top-of-the-line Nikes that would be given to her just for playing, she's putting shoes on someone else's stinky feet, two pair for twenty-five dollars, with nothing in her future but more of the same. It's a sad story, isn't it?

When I was diagnosed with breast cancer, I'd been in the process of designing a house to live in, with our house in Iowa as a model. You see, Nina's bedroom was just off our bedroom in our house there. It was very easy to go in to give her a kiss good night, even if I got home late. In the house I ended up choosing in New Jersey, Nina's room is downstairs, and sometimes I'll get so caught up that it'll be a couple of hours before I've said hello to her.

A lot of times, when I'm really happy after landing an important recruit or a big win, I'll go into Nina's room and do a silly dance for her. She thinks it's the funniest thing in the world when I grab her hands and move them around and twirl around her chair. She loves to see me laugh. Sometimes she laughs so hard, her face gets red and I have to stop so she can catch her breath.

Other times, I'll just lie down next to her and play with her hair, or we'll watch a movie together. And sometimes, when I'm really hurt, and I don't think anyone will understand how I feel, I'll go down and tell her what's on my mind. And then I'll tell her that everything's all right. I don't know that she understands, but I feel better telling her.

I love shopping for Nina. She looks so pretty in her clothes and jewelry. I always come home with giant boxes full of things for her. She does love to get dressed up. No matter where I am in the world, I make sure to be home for the prom at Nina's school.

She looks beautiful with her hair down and curled, and we always make sure we're a little early so she gets a good long look at herself in the mirror before we head out.

One of those early Christmases in New Jersey, I brought home the same gown in two colors, thinking she'd choose one for her prom. "Tell me which one you like, Nina," I said, holding up both of them. "Move your eyes to the right if you like this one," and she moved her eyes to the right. "Are you sure? What about this one?" I put down that dress and held up the other one—and she moved her eyes to the right again.

The boys and Hyacinth practically fell over laughing. "Just like her mom—she wants both!"

Unfortunately, David's football career at NC State came to an abrupt end. In 1998, David attended a party at his girlfriend Maggie's house (she is now his fiancée). Maggie is a gymnast, and there were a lot of athletes there from a number of different sports. Two wrestlers, leaving the party, heard a pop; one of them looked down to see that his shoulder had been nicked and was bleeding. He thought he might have been shot by a BB gun, so a group of his friends went over to the house across the street to see what was going on.

Time passed, and they didn't come back, so David and two other football players went over to the other house to investigate. The door was open, and although they called up, they didn't hear anything in response. As they discovered when they got up the stairs, they hadn't heard anything because their friends were being held hostage by a young man crouching just inside the door with a gun—a real one—which he was swinging back and forth.

David hit the gunman in an attempt to knock the gun out of his hands. One of the wrestlers grabbed the armed kid and got him on the bed, and while they were struggling, the gun went off. The shot killed the boy who had been holding the gun. David's roommate picked up the gun and took it with him back to their apartment. David told Maggie what had happened and asked her to call the police and tell them where he and his roommate lived, and that they had possession of the gun. When the police arrived at David's house, he and his roommate gave them the gun, and then went with them to the station to give their statement.

I was getting ready to play the University of Texas when I got the call from my sister that David had been involved in a shooting death. It was one of the most horrible moments of my life. By the time I got to North Carolina, David had already been released—and so had the pictures of him sitting in a police car. The first newspaper reports were printed a few hours later. It was bitterly unfair to David: none of the other athletes' names were mentioned, not even the boy who had been wrestling with the shooter when the gun had gone off. But every single press report mentioned David's name and said that he was my son.

People make assumptions about all athletes, but especially about football players. According to the media, this was a story about testosterone and aggression, when it was anything but. The irony for us was the knowledge that David has always been incredibly shy and soft-spoken. I could count on the fingers of one hand the number of times that he went out in high school—it just wasn't him.

That lack of killer instinct had actually been holding him back in football. In fact, one of his coaches, Dick Porte, had called my house less than two weeks before to compliment me on the way David conducted himself. "Your son is a very talented athlete, and a real gentleman," he said. Ironically, he had assured me that David's future with the team was bright—as long as he could become more aggressive.

David was charged with breaking and entering and assault and battery. The door had been open, and any assault had certainly been justified, but those were the charges. The football coach decided to suspend all the boys who had been associated with the incident until there was a resolution, so David's scholarship was suspended.

I hired a prominent attorney in North Carolina—Wade Smith, one of the lawyers who defended the Duke lacrosse players, in fact. Now, nobody knows better than me that the clock starts ticking on a college athlete's career when they start playing. Wade Smith explained that preparing for and holding a trial could take up to two years, which meant two years that David wouldn't be allowed to play. He recommended that David plead guilty to the misdemeanor charges; they were so minor that the hearing would be held in traffic court, he told us. That way, David could get on with his life and his dreams instead of squandering the opportunity he'd been given.

I knew that David wanted to play more than anything in the world, so after a lot of thought, I agreed. The hearing did take place in traffic court, and Wade Smith didn't even appear, further underscoring how minor the whole thing was.

Immediately after the incident, David moved back to New Jersey and kept up with his coursework at a nearby community college. Ultimately, he didn't want to return to North Carolina. He was accepted to Rutgers and earned a place on the Rutgers football team.

It was a terrible experience. In fact, it was precisely what I had been afraid of my whole life—what the mother of every young black man is afraid of. I worried that I had sheltered him all that time in Iowa. "Why would you go over there?" I kept asking him. David had never seen a gun or had to cope with violence. If he'd been a little more street-smart, would he have stayed in the house and called the police, instead of getting involved?

On the other hand, could I really blame him for coming to the rescue of his friends? What would have happened if he hadn't struck the gun out of that boy's hands? The police later discovered that half the bullets were missing from the gun—presumably fired into the darkness before someone was hit. How much worse might it have been?

Once more, it was the support of the people around me that got us through that incident. My Cheyney player Debra Walker flew in one afternoon just to give me a hug. I'm not kidding. She flew in around three, watched the first half of our game, and caught me coming out of the tunnel at halftime. She walked up to me and said, "I'm not here for basketball, I just wanted to give you a hug and tell you that I love you."

I was so shocked that I could hardly speak. All she said was, "You saved my life. You got me at the point when I could have gone left or gone right, and you made me go straight. You gave me my life and I could never repay you for that. I'll help in any way I can." I got my hug, and she turned around and got the next flight out so she could work that night.

The young man who was directly involved in the shooting did take his case to trial. He was, of course, completely exonerated; it took a year. But David, who pled guilty to the misdemeanor, never had the chance to clear his name.

It still angers me to write about this. Bill and I had the same kind of ambitions for our children that everybody has. We wanted to make sure that every last thing that surrounded them was *right*. David, to his credit, has always been a model son: I have never had even the smallest thing to say about his respect for our family, our house, or for me. So yes, I do resent that his life was hijacked. Like a lot of young athletes, he had dreams of playing at a higher level. We'll never know if that might have been a possibility for him, but I do know one thing: he will persevere and be successful in all that he does. I know that.

I wonder daily if we made the wrong decision, and most of the time I think we did. But even if we did, I think there's a life lesson to be learned: that life does get disrupted, no matter what you do or how careful you are. Yet even when you get pushed down, you have to pick yourself up and go on, believing that other good things are in store for you.

15

Do You Know Who We Are?

We made it to the Sweet Sixteen in 1998—the first time Rutgers had gotten that far in the NCAA. And every year after that, we moved one rung closer to the National Championship, until 2000, when we went to the Final Four. It was significant for the team, and it meant a lot to me: I was the first coach, in the men's or women's game, to take three different teams to that level.

I believe that the success of that team, beyond the hard work and the attention to detail, could be attributed to our *sway.* The girls on that Final Four team embodied my own attitude. Ever since the earliest days at Cheyney, I had never felt small in front of anybody else, no matter who they were. I didn't think there was any coach who had a better mind, or who was willing to work harder than I was. I don't mean to say that there aren't better coaches, simply that I never doubted my own dedication or determination.

The girls on that Final Four team were confident to the point of arrogance, and you could see it as soon as they walked out onto the floor. They were led in this by Tasha Pointer. She was a great player, but what made her magic was her attitude. She always believed in herself and her team.

Shawnetta Stewart wasn't just a tremendous talent; she had a tremendous heart, and she would never be perceived as a quitter in anything that she did. One day we were running, and she was carrying too much weight. She fell before she reached the finish line, but even then, she refused to stop. She *crawled* to the line, and I could hear her saying, over and over, "I am not a quitter." We had to take her to the hospital that day to get her rehydrated, but her mind didn't quit, even after her body had. Much of that team's ability to sustain had to do with mental toughness, and hers was something to see.

Tammy Sutton-Brown was also on that team. When you recruit, you bring your highlight tapes with you to show the kids and their families; you watch them again and again, until you know every second by heart. That year, one thing caught my eye: Tammy was always restrained in her emotional demonstrations, whether the occasion called for celebration or disappointment.

Emotions run high in sports; it's natural for a girl to have a reaction when she does something great. I would never tolerate an unsportsmanlike display, but there's usually a big smile or a high-five with her teammates to tell you she knows she's done something substantial. With Tammy, there was only restraint. She'd make a reverse layup on the baseline that would take us up by one, and she'd hide her smile. She'd go to pump her arm, but she'd get it up only halfway.

I was always sorry about that. She was a terrific player and she distinguished herself not only at Rutgers but also later in the

Above: When I started coaching at Cheyney, we didn't have much—there weren't even enough leather balls to go around in practice!—but we knew we were bringing hope to the have-nots, and that meant everything to us.

Left: John Chaney and I met at Cheyney and were the first to practice the men's and women's teams together. He went on to a Hall of Fame career and has been my great friend and mentor for more than thirty years.

Above: The Cheyney Final Four team *(left to right)*: Sharon Taylor, Faith Wilds, Val Walker, Ann Strong, Yolanda Laney, Deb Walker, Rosetta Gilford, Karen Draughn, Lena Dabney, Paulette Bigelow, Sandra Giddens, and me.

Left: Jolette Law played for me with great flair at Iowa; she later spent twelve years as my assistant coach at Rutgers. *(Jeff Myers)*

My coaching staff at Iowa *(left to right)*: Linda Myers; Angie Lee, who played for me at Iowa; me; and Marianna Freeman, who played for me at Cheyney. We took care of each other like a family.

This shot was taken after the Tennessee game that took the Hawkeyes to the Final Four. Everyone in that arena felt Bill there with us, and there wasn't a dry eye in the house.
(University of Iowa Athletics)

DUKE
NCAA
35

In 2007, we upset the number one seed, Duke; earlier in the season, they had beaten us by forty points, and on our own court. But, as I always say, it's not where you start, but where you end up, and that game took us to the Elite Eight. *(Rutgers/Grant Halverson)*

Matee Ajavon led this team—five freshmen, no seniors—to the Final Four victory against LSU in 2007. It had been twenty-five years since one of my teams had played for the championship.
(© Matt Sullivan/Reuters/Corbis)

Tennessee may have stopped this young team at the championships in 2007, but we still had much to be proud of. Little did we know, our greatest test was yet to come.
(Dan Bracaglia/Daily Targum photography editor)

The Scarlet Knights, in April 2007, at the press conference we held to address the Imus issue. *This* is who we are. *(AP, Mike Derer)*

We win and we lose, but we do those things together. As long as you've given your greatest effort, you can be at peace. *(Lamar Carter/Daily Targum Staff Photographer)*

I celebrate my 700th win in 2004 with Nina. She inspires me every day that I walk out onto the floor, and gives me strength beyond what anyone could ever imagine. *(Rutgers/Larry Levanti)*

Olympics and as a WNBA all-star. But I wish I could have given her the key that would have allowed her to let herself go.

Dana Boonen was from Belgium; she had an unstoppable work ethic, the most positive attitude you can imagine, and such a generous heart. When I went to Belgium to visit her when I was recruiting, her mother excused herself, and we could hear sobbing from the other room. Her little girl would be going away, and her heart was breaking. "She loves me enough to let me go," Dana explained. It is moments like that one that remind me to take my responsibilities seriously: I know that when a parent agrees to send their child to play for me, they are placing their very heart into my hands.

Dana used to walk around campus picking up litter. One day, I heard the team teasing her—she'd picked up some garbage and deposited it in the big blue "can" on the corner. That was the kind of person she was: she hadn't been in the country long enough to recognize a mailbox, but she was cleaning up the trash! I loved that girl.

These were extremely ambitious, high-spirited, and independent young ladies. They were also very bright—the grade point average that year was a 3.3. But when you have so many strong personalities on a team, it isn't surprising that we ended up holding an awful lot of team meetings that year. We had to come to know ourselves.

Linda Miles was a gorgeous athlete, but she could be insensitive to the shortcomings of others, and her bluntness hurt people's feelings. Tasha could be sharp with her teammates sometimes, too, though I never had to worry about her bringing her best game; Tasha always came to win. I always said that if you had eleven Tashas on a team, you'd be guaranteed the championship. But I did have to teach her some patience.

The real role of the point guard is to feel everybody out and to make sure that they have what they need when they're on the floor. Tasha needed to learn to see when one of her teammates needed a little extra time, a hug, or a conversation. "Why don't they come ready?" she asked me, when I pulled her aside to point out that someone needed a little extra attention. "Not everyone is like you," I told her. "And your team doesn't go unless you bring them with you."

Sometimes I needed to get everyone's attention and call them back to order. At one point, I was so frustrated by their willfulness that I came to a meeting wearing a sheet and some sandals and carrying a tablet, like Moses coming down from the mountaintop. "If you won't listen to your coach, maybe you'll listen to Moses," I said. They were shocked and then they laughed—and then they sat up and listened to what I had to say.

But all the same, you had to appreciate their spirit. I never had to worry about their desire or their willingness to work hard. I teach my players never to bend over and hold their knees while they're catching their breath. It's a sign of weakness, and it tells your opponent that you're tired. "We will never allow you to see us breathing hard, with our tongues hanging out like dogs. Even if she really feels like she's about to fall over in exhaustion, a Scarlet Knight always stands straight, with her eyes forward and her head held high, looking like she's ready to play the game all over again," I always tell them.

I never had to say anything of the sort to *that* team. It was something they just instinctively understood. Nobody on that team wanted to hear about waiting their turn: as freshmen, they believed that they should be competing at a championship level. Their attitude was "Our time is now," and that was the way they played.

I remember watching them play at Iowa State, with fifteen thousand people in the stands—everyone on the court was a freshman, except one. Tammy came from the corner and blocked what would have been the other team's game-winning shot; Miles caught it in midair. They ran off the floor hugging each other, and I thought, *Look at them! They're just kids! They don't even know what they've done.*

What they had done was hush fifteen thousand people with their talent and effort.

The 2000 Final Four was widely covered. Part of that had to do with the fact that it was being held in Philadelphia, and three out of the four coaches—Geno Auriemma of the University of Connecticut, who grew up in Philly; me, who had coached at Cheyney State, a few miles outside; and Rene Portland of Penn State—had a connection to the area.

Tennessee was there, too, and they were the team that stopped us. It surprises some people that Pat Summitt and I are true friends—why, I don't know. It's hard to make and maintain friendships on a coaching schedule, and as a result, it can be a very lonely profession. If anything, I'd like to see more reaching out among the coaches in the women's game. It means a lot to get a phone call from a colleague remembering a birthday or commemorating a milestone. I try to reach out that way, even if it's to say, "I know things look bad out there right now, but you've got a fan in me."

Pat is one of the warmest, most caring people I know. Being friends doesn't mean I'm not going to try to beat her, because I am—the very next time I see her. But I'm also going to hug her after the game.

It would be easy to get frustrated. "Where's my reward? I've been working at this for thirty-odd years, and I don't have a national championship." But if I really thought that way, then I would have quit this game twenty years ago. The way I see it, if your ultimate goal is winning that national championship, then you're going to give up anyway. What's going to keep you coming back once you've won?

You can't ever rest on your laurels; it's about what you do in the here and now. It's got to be about the process, not the destination. You realize that every year really is a new start. That's what makes basketball so exciting. Even if you're returning with the same people, the kids on the other teams will be different. The skills, the strategy, the breaks—all these things continue to challenge you.

And I believe that basketball is just a vehicle. None of it means anything unless you give back by way of example. That's why I'm always asking my girls, "I know how great a basketball player you are, but can you handle this next step?" I don't just want them to walk out of my program as better basketball players, with degrees in their hands. I don't want them to be selfish; I want them to give. Our young people are held up as examples—for female athletes and for all women. I want to be sure that we carry ourselves a certain way, in victory and defeat. When we speak, I want everyone to feel proud.

In 2000, after the Final Four, my family experienced another calamity.

It was the second day of September, the morning of David's first football game at Rutgers. I was cleaning up and making food for the tailgate; Justin, who was a junior in high school, and his cousin Brendan were helping. Eventually, the boys grew restless and asked if they could get David's girlfriend, Maggie, to drive them to the game a little early.

I agreed; I'd bring Nina and my friend Margaret later. We packed the food into the car, and as they got in, I said, "Maggie, please be careful. If anything happens, I will have a fit." Justin, sitting in the backseat, teased me. "Mom, you're always fretting."

I was so happy when I went back into the house. The day was gorgeous—clear and sunny, what I always think of as a real football day—and I was going to see my son play. Everything seemed perfect. I put on "Smooth" by Carlos Santana, and danced around the house while I finished tidying and packing the last bit of food.

It wasn't ten minutes later that the phone rang. It was Maggie, completely hysterical. "There's been an accident. Brennie's okay, but Justin, I don't know, I don't know." I tried to get her to tell me where she was, but she couldn't see any signs, and knew only that they were somewhere on Route 27. Margaret stayed with Nina while I got into my own car, heading to where I thought they might be. I've never driven so fast in my life.

I came over this little hill, and I could see the van, completely flipped over and resting on its top, our tailgate picnic scattered on the road.

The first person I saw was Brendan, who had blood all over his face. "It's not as bad as it looks," he told me, and I could see that it was true. I ran to the van. Justin was trapped in the backseat, moaning. I could see a huge cut on his head, and a tremendous amount of blood. The police kept trying to move me, but I stayed and held his hand while we waited for someone to cut him out of there.

When the ambulance came, we were rushed to the hospital. The trip felt like it took forever; we were trapped on these narrow country roads. And David never even knew we weren't in the stands.

The car had been heading north toward New Brunswick. It had been broadsided, and rolled forty yards, eventually hitting a telephone pole, which prevented it from going over a hill. Brendan and Maggie were fine, but Justin had been seriously hurt.

By the time we reached the hospital, he was unconscious, in a coma. The doctors did a quick assessment and told me that he'd unquestionably suffered brain damage. "I think you should prepare for the possibility that your son will not be the same as he was before the accident," the doctor told me—virtually the same words they had used about Nina, twenty years before. That broke me completely.

The whole family flew in, from Florida, Atlanta, Iowa, wherever they were. Everyone was there within six hours. Ann Hill came, and John Chaney. I remember John saying to me, "He won't do this to himself, or to you. He's going to be okay." In the dark of night, I heard one doctor say, "They need to get a rehab center. He's not going to function again like he did," and I thought I was going to die.

The hospital made rooms available to us, which I was thankful for; the whole family stayed for days. Justin eventually began to come out of the coma, but he wasn't Justin. He had a blank look on his face all the time. He walked, zombielike, on his tiptoes. He could talk, but he didn't; the single-word answers he did give were in a monotone, and nothing he said made you feel there was much of a thought process going on.

Physically, he was like another person. His reactions were completely gone. I kept thinking about his lightning-quick fingers, beating everyone at the video games he loved, but when David or his cousins would bring those games and play them on his bed, he'd watch as if he'd never seen them before. He had always been a natural athlete, but he couldn't even kick a ball you rolled at him; by the time he'd gotten his leg out, the ball would be two or three feet past him.

He was also highly irritable. He didn't want to eat, and light bothered him. When the nurses would come in, he would pull the covers over his head and turn away from them; sometimes he would yell at them to go away. That was so hard to see. Justin is, by all accounts, a sweetheart. He'd always been very outgoing and charming, and it had always been easy for him to make friends. He was also incredibly affectionate; he'd always put his arms around me, no matter who was there. When David was in sixth or seventh grade, he let me know that the time when I could make a fuss and kiss and cuddle him like a little kid was over. Justin never stopped—to this day, he'll always give me a hug or hold my hand, and it doesn't matter who's watching. The boy in that bed didn't feel like my son.

The doctors told me to do anything I could to wake up his brain, to stimulate his interest in living in the world. So I called

Charles Barkley. Charles had always had a lot of respect for Bill. In fact, I laugh to think about it: we played a game of golf with him right before he got married, and he asked Bill if there was really anything wrong with going out with the boys after a game. Bill asked him if he really wanted to know what he thought, then told him: "It's fine for you to socialize, but those days of parties are over. When you turn into a family man, you have a responsibility to your wife." To this day, I'm not sure that was what Charles wanted to hear!

When Bill died, Charles made it clear that he'd do anything for the boys, and while I have never liked asking for favors, I thought a call from Charles might lift Justin's spirits, maybe even wake him up. It meant so much to me that Charles took the time to make the call, but even with his idol on the phone, it was just, "Uh huh, uh huh, uh huh," on Justin's end.

In the meantime, we were making preparations for the house to be retrofitted. Obviously, it was already set up for Nina's wheelchair, but Justin's bedroom was upstairs, and he was still walking very clumsily. Rearranging the house really tested me; I couldn't believe this was happening to us.

I took Nina to the hospital on her birthday, September 14. My sisters had gone to the cafeteria to get supplies; we were going to sing and have a cake. I told Nina, "Happy birthday. You're here with your brother Justin." And it was the most incredible thing I'd ever seen: Justin sat up in bed, focused his eyes, and said, in a near-normal tone of voice, "Happy birthday, Nina."

By the time my sisters got back to the room, they found Justin sitting up and talking, with me in the bed, laughing and crying and hugging him, and Nina laughing to beat the band.

The next day, the doctors had a meeting. What had happened was nothing short of a miracle, they told me, and they showed me the brain scans. "He is not supposed to be doing this," one of them kept saying, shaking his head in amazement. Nobody was more surprised by his transformation than the nurses. "My goodness! Your mother told us you were a pleasant person, but we didn't believe her," they teased him.

Talking to Justin about the time he spent in that twilight is chilling. He doesn't remember anything about the accident; his last memory is seeing a car cut in front of them. When he woke up, he told me he felt that he was "in the world, but not of it." He could hear things and wanted to respond, but he felt like he was invisible. He says now that he didn't connect things like not being able to kick a soccer ball to the brain injury. "I just thought I wasn't having a good day." The doors to the ward had the letters BTU on them; it was a month before he realized that BTU stood for "brain trauma unit." I think it's probably a good thing he didn't understand, because it meant he never gave up hope.

We weren't out of the woods yet; in fact, when he was talking a little more, the extent of the damage became clear. One time he asked me, "Mom, does a potato have seeds in it?" I pretended I was doing something so he wouldn't see the tears in my eyes. It was like he was a child, learning things all over again.

We had to make a decision about where he should do his rehab. There was a world-class facility in Newark, but it was a long drive. We'd all gotten into the habit of swinging through the hospital when we passed by, and that wasn't something we'd be able to do if he moved. I thought that being close to his family would motivate him as much or more than great doctors, so we kept him at the JFK Johnson Rehabilitation Institute near us.

After a few weeks at the rehab center, Justin began to do word puzzles and to react a little more swiftly to the soccer ball. Right from the beginning, he wanted to go home and get his life back to normal. One time, we were sitting on the grounds, and he grabbed my car keys and started to walk across the street. He was in no condition to walk, much less drive.

When he was released from rehab, he went to a special center instead of right back to school. We fought a lot about that. He's such a proud person, and he didn't want to acknowledge that he needed any extra help at all. He wanted to forget that the accident had happened, and I wanted to make sure he got all the help and support he needed. But he was back in school by January, and has since made a full recovery. It is something I give thanks for every single day of my life.

It turned out that the fellow who'd caused the accident had no license; there were eight people in the car at the time, and they didn't even realize what they'd done. There were lawyers who suggested that Justin could be set for the rest of his life, but he wasn't interested. "I'm fine—there's nothing wrong with me," he told them. It didn't surprise me at all; Bill would have been the same way.

Sometimes I think Justin is proud to a fault. He can take it too far. After the accident, his school suggested that he wait to take his SATs. He not only wouldn't wait, but he waived the extra time he was entitled to. And in the interview with Morehouse College, which he ended up attending, the interviewer expressed some concern about his attendance record. I sat there, incredulous, waiting for Justin to say something, but he didn't. Finally, unable to stop myself, I explained to the interviewer that he'd been involved in a serious car accident, which had put him in a coma and entailed six months of rehabilitation. If I hadn't been there, he wouldn't have been accepted.

The day that Justin graduated from high school was a proud day for all of us. At the ceremony, I turned to hug David and was surprised to see that he was crying. I hadn't seen him cry since he was a child. "I feel like a parent," he said to me, with some amazement in his voice.

It has always meant a lot to me that the boys are so close, and that they've been able to rely on each other over the years, even though they're very different. David is a little more conservative, and more of a loner, while Justin is more sociable. But I will tell you something that you can count on: if the two of them are talking, you will hear them laughing. No matter what, if those two are together, they have smiles on their faces.

That day I looked at David, and at Nina next to him, and Justin up on the stage, with "Pomp and Circumstance" playing, and I thought, *We did it.* The four of us, with Bill watching over us, had made it through.

In 2000, we were ranked number one going into the season. We had graduated some great players, including Shawnetta Stewart, but there were some terrific players remaining, including Tammy and Tasha.

That season was interesting for another reason. I had been contacted by Peter Schnall, a documentary filmmaker who wanted to capture the ups and downs of a season in women's basketball. I agreed to let the cameras into the gym and the locker rooms because I wanted to bring attention to the women's game, even if it meant losing some of our privacy. It was important to me to show the world how hard these young women worked.

The result was the Emmy-nominated documentary *This Is a Game, Ladies.* I still don't understand the title; as every one of my players can testify, what I'm known for saying is, "It's *more* than a game, ladies." For me, basketball is a way to address some of the bigger issues in life, a vehicle for me to take young girls and help them to become young women—women who will go on to become accomplished leaders. I think you see that very clearly in the documentary. If it were just a game, why would I call my team out for their apathy, lack of heart, and lackluster performance after a win with a margin in the double digits?

It was odd and uncomfortable for us to have the cameras there; although the girls adjusted pretty quickly, it took me a little more time. I remember how alarmed I felt, seeing the kids stretching, with cameras filming them from every angle. This team had always had fun when they were stretching; it was a time to talk and laugh. But I found myself wondering, *Is this the way a top-five team stretches?* I was looking for us to be America's team, and when I thought about it that way, I didn't want them messing around in the middle of the floor; I wanted them serious and in uniform, stretching in formation, counting how long they held those stretches.

Changing was a mistake. It sounds like a small thing, but those moments were important. Stretching was a time for the girls to be together, without the pressure they felt in practice. We laughed, but we talked about serious things, too. And we did get our stretching done.

I realize now that I came dangerously close to taking away our identity. We weren't a team that lined up and counted one, two, three, four on the right as we stretched; we were a team that made jokes and conversation. Making jokes didn't disqualify us from being America's team—America's team, I know now, is the team that does what they need to do in order to win.

If I have one complaint about the documentary, it's that they focused more on the troubled elements of the team than on all the ways in which we were a cohesive group. I understand that a girl who's flamboyant or one who's not succeeding makes for a better story than the one who gets straight As, does everything she's supposed to in practice, and goes to church on Sundays, but I still believe there was an imbalance, with the emphasis on the negative. To set the record straight, I don't have a problem with Mandy, the girl with the orange hair who was featured so prominently and who is shown quitting the team. I heard from her a few times this summer, most recently with an invitation to her going-away party.

The other player who figured largely in that documentary was Linda Miles. She was a fierce competitor, someone who had a very low tolerance for people less skilled than she was, and even less for people who didn't try. That type of girl is a challenge to coach:

you have to direct her enthusiasm without killing her spirit. That season, I put Linda off the team several times, and left her home a few times—even though it meant throwing twelve rebounds and ten or fifteen points out the window. When we went to Orlando to play in the inaugural game of the season before a nationally televised audience, I left Linda—and a win—home. But I have always thought that it's the lessons that we learn as people through basketball that are going to be what's most important, and I've got to be true to myself and what I know is right. It's more than a game.

Linda and I are still in touch, too. Last year, on Mother's Day, I picked up my phone to hear her on the other end. She told me she was on her way to church, calling all the women who'd made a difference in her life. "You had a soft voice and carried a big stick, Coach, and you touched my life in a profound way. I know every day of my life that I'm stronger for having known you."

I was moved. It doesn't matter if I've had an issue with a player—all coaches do, sooner or later. Ultimately, my players know that I love them like a mom, and they always come to understand what I was trying to do. I can't count the number of young ladies who have called me after graduating to say, "I never thought I'd thank someone for riding me as hard as you rode me, but I think about what you taught me every day."

Our season ended with a game against Southwest Missouri State that featured the NCAA's top scorer. Notre Dame won the championship that year; we were one of only two teams to have beaten them during the regular season. Tasha and Tammy and Usha were drafted by the WNBA; Tammy and Usha went on to play, but Tasha was cut. Her heart was broken, but she rallied, in typical Tasha style, getting her master's degree and going on to be an assistant coach at Xavier and Columbia. These days you can find her at my right side, having replaced Jolette as my assistant.

I first saw Cappie Pondexter when she was in the eighth or ninth grade. Even at that age, she was an amazing athlete, as you'd expect from someone who has gone on to be a two-time WNBA all-star. She was agile, quick, had excellent ball-handling skills, and was an elevated jumper who seemed to defy gravity. She made great passes—and better still, she had incredible decision-making skills. It's rare to see that much talent in one person.

There she was, playing in the state championships, the youngest player on the floor, surrounded by much bigger, much older girls. But even with all the contact and the height around her, she still had the confidence to take her shots and the heart to rebound. Her team was down, but Cappie was going to find a way to win. Every time she put her hand on the ball, she forced a drive and made the clock stop. Then she stepped up and hit her free throws, maybe eight in a row. As she shot her last set, I saw the tears streaming from her eyes. Clearly, it was more than a game to her, too. She ended up being High School National Player of the Year.

In the other positions, all you have to do is take care of what's in front of you, but when you're a point guard, you're like the mother of the whole team. Cappie is, to my mind, one of the great guards, in that she makes everyone else on the floor better.

When it was time to recruit her, I went and spoke to her mother, who had exactly the right attitude, in my opinion. "I don't need anyone telling me how great a basketball player she is, because everyone in the world knows that," she told me. "I don't need somebody who's going to build her up. I need someone who's going to give her strict discipline and guidance—and tough love, if that's what it takes."

She was speaking to what has always been one of my core beliefs: that it is my job to develop the whole person, not just the athlete. As I tell every girl who plays for me and every girl I try to recruit: by all means, appreciate the opportunity you have to be involved in sports, but *don't let it define you.* I'm not just a basketball coach; I'm a woman and a mom and a friend. I love books;

I love music. I care deeply about politics and social issues, both in my own country and in the world. There's far more to me than simply being a basketball coach, and my girls are far more than just basketball players.

I have always loved the Rudyard Kipling poem "If"—especially the line that reads, "If you can meet with Triumph and Disaster / And treat those two impostors just the same." There's only one way you can do that, and that's to know who you are *as a person,* not just as an athlete—or a lawyer, or a model, or a racecar driver, or whatever you might be. Those things might be what you do very well, but they are not who you are.

You help a young lady to understand this by always treating her like a real person. The kids who come to play for me know that I love them for them, not for what they can do for me on the court. I'm a monster when it comes to basketball, but if you come to my office, we're going to laugh and talk about other things.

It was always clear that Cappie would do anything for the team. She started one season late, but when it was time to start her, she said, "No, Coach—let the chemistry of the team stay." I could be within two inches of her, saying everything in the book with spit coming out of my mouth, and the only thing that girl would do was drop her head and ask, "What can I do, Coach? Tell me what to do and I'll do it."

My work with Cappie was always in getting her to understand how good she was. "You might be small, but nobody has a bigger heart," I always told her. I really believe that there is no guard in the country who can stop her—something the rest of the nation saw when she guided her WNBA team, the Phoenix Mercury, to win the national championship this year. (She was named Most Valuable Player in the winning game.) And she's still the most humble person I've ever met.

Cappie came at the same time as Chelsea Newton, a first team all-American. I don't think I'll ever get another Chelsea; I've never seen someone deliver effort so consistently. She suffered a broken nose, a broken finger, and several concussions playing for me, truly exemplifying what it means to play hard all the time. Chelsea is the only player I've ever coached who had an award named after her: they call it the Chelsea Newton Heart Award. The fans will give this award as long as Rutgers is an educational institution; Chelsea should be so proud. I'm sorry that we never won a national championship, but I'm proud that I had the chance to cheer with Chelsea when the Sacramento Monarchs won the WNBA championship in her rookie year. No one could have been more deserving.

Both Cappie and Chelsea were starters in their rookie years on what would turn out to be national-championship teams. Honestly, when I think about those kids, tears come to my eyes. They came to Rutgers because they were supremely confident. Instead of taking an easier path, they chose to make it happen here, and I thank God every day that I had the opportunity to know and to be inspired by them.

16

Team of Destiny

It was obvious, right from the beginning of the 2006–2007 season, that we were not even remotely prepared for the road ahead.

On one hand, I felt very fortunate: my coaching staff was the finest and most experienced in the country. Jolette had been with me for twelve years; Carlene Mitchell, for seven; together, the two of them had put together a great recruiting class, and knew my every thought, sometimes before I did. Marianne Stanley, an esteemed coach with experience at both the college and the professional levels, had just joined us. They were great strategists and tacticians, with a genuine love for the game and the young ladies who had been entrusted to us.

But the team was a disaster.

We started out behind the eight ball, considering three of the few upperclassmen we did have—there were no seniors on the team—were hurt. Junior Essence Carson came back from USA Basketball with a knee injury and wouldn't start playing until November. Kia Vaughn returned from USA Basketball with a partially torn rotator cuff. Matee Ajavon, another junior, was recovering from a recurring stress fracture in her leg and would be out until late December. Those injuries robbed us of three very important starters, leaving only junior Katie Adams and sophomore Heather Zurich on the floor—along with five freshmen.

My teams had always been made up of strong personalities. It could be a struggle, but at least you knew where you stood. This team seemed very passive, right from the beginning. At one of our early meetings, I gave them the following scenario: "There are two horses at the starting gate; one will need to be whipped to get started, while the other is chomping at the bit, waiting for the bell to ring." Then I asked each player in turn: "Are you a 'giddyap,' someone who needs to be pushed every inch of the way, or a 'whoa'?" By the time everyone was accounted for, there were about three whoas in the group; the other seven were self-proclaimed giddyaps.

"Yeah," I thought to myself, with my head in my hands. "That sounds about right."

Unfortunately, the freshmen were used to falling back on their natural athleticism and talent. Now, talent will get you through at a high school level. You can carry too much weight, or have slow feet, or a weak left side, and your natural gifts will sustain you. Frankly, just being tall in high school can be enough. But at the college level, *everyone* is really talented, and the contests are decided by effort, skill, conditioning, and intensity, not what the good Lord gave you. Mental weakness can make you a prisoner of your body; you can't even get into the physical condition you need to be in. If you don't commit to training, to building your skills, to working harder and better than everyone else out there, then you're going to see all those other really talented girls dancing circles around you.

Sophomore Kia Vaughn had lost more than forty pounds and was in the best shape I'd ever seen her in. One day, the year before, a reporter had called me for a reaction to a quote he'd gotten from Kia at a media session. She'd told him, "I'm just a freshman. I don't have to pull out all the stops right now—I've got the next four years to develop."

I practically fell out of my chair. "She said what?"

This reporter is a good guy, and he didn't want to embarrass an inexperienced eighteen-year-old in her first interview. "You want me to scrap the quote, Coach?" he asked me. I thought about it, and then I said, "No. Go ahead and run it. Let her see those words in print. Let her have to explain what she meant to her teammates. Let her have to explain it to me. And then let me explain to her that if she doesn't give me a hundred and ten percent, she won't be part of the team at all next year."

She'd gotten it; her first year with us had clearly had an impact. But the rest of the girls, especially the younger ones, weren't in proper condition, and I could very clearly see that they weren't doing what they needed to do to get there.

These girls made every excuse imaginable to explain why what I asked of them was impossible. Of course, I knew that they *could* do anything they set their mind to; what they were telling me was that they *wouldn't* stop eating whatever they wanted to eat, and that they *would* be getting up when they wanted to get up. So it wasn't entirely surprising that Jill Pizzotti, a Nike representative who came to watch an early practice, told me afterward that she'd never seen a team so out of condition in her entire life. I couldn't be upset with her for saying it: it was the simple truth. Their minds were weak, and their bodies were making them cowards. We were preparing to play one of the toughest schedules in the country against some of the biggest teams, but we weren't ready, and I knew it.

I've had a rule ever since I began coaching: no player can attend the first day of practice unless she can pass three tests proving her basic conditioning level. In 2006, that deadline arrived, and only four of the players on the team could pass.

I've never been so mad in my life. It was as if they had figured out that there was strength in numbers, telling themselves, "Well, she's got to have five players out there on the floor, so what's she going to do if none of us make the grade?" For the first time in my career, I modified the rule and started practice. At least if we were practicing, I could make them run.

Chelsea Newton, our graduate assistant (she is now playing in the WNBA), was so frustrated with the team that she called some of her former team members, who flooded me with calls wanting to know if I was getting soft: "You never would have let us step out on that floor without those tests, Coach." In fact, Cappie reminded me that I'd kept *her* out of practice for a week.

Some of those players reached out to the 2006 team. Mariota Theodoris called Epiphanny Prince, one of our freshmen, and asked her, "Has Coach got you practicing the fifty-five?" referring to the very difficult full-court press that is one of my trademarks.

"Nah, she said we can play the fifty," Epiphanny told her, as if it were no big thing. These girls were so young, they didn't even know what they didn't know—but Mariota knew exactly what it meant. "Don't you understand? Coach doesn't even think enough of you to put in the fifty-five. She doesn't think you can handle it."

You'd have thought they'd do everything in their power to make it up, but they continued to straggle, and when one of the upperclassmen expressed her exasperation with them, they acted offended—as though *she* were the problem. I was so disgusted, I told them that they had to pass two of the tests on the same day if they wanted to go to the Virgin Islands, our first scheduled trip. "Some of you are going to spend Thanksgiving in a coat and hat, and some of you are going to spend it in a bathing suit," I said.

I had one of the assistants put a photograph of a gorgeous

tropical beach in each of their lockers. "That picture is as close to that beach as you're going to get if you don't start running," I told them. They had about five days to prepare.

I'll tell you, I was really worried I wasn't going to have enough of them to make a team. But sun and surf are powerful motivation, and by the time we were ready to go to the Virgin Islands, everyone who didn't have a medical excuse had passed two tests.

It didn't matter. Our early results on the court were absolutely dismal. It hit the girls hard; they weren't used to losing. One freshman was in hysterics after our second loss; we were only two games in, and she'd already lost more games in her college career than she'd lost the whole time she was in high school. The kindest commentators called it "a building year" for us; I was less diplomatic and told them they were the worst team I'd ever coached.

Then, at the beginning of December, we lost our home opener to Duke. The score was 85–45. We lost by forty points on our own court.

I'm not exaggerating when I say that it was one of the most humiliating defeats I have ever suffered in my years as a coach. As the time on the clock ticked away, I called a time-out, but it wasn't to talk *X*s and *O*s. "Turn around," I told the huddle. "I want you to look at all those people putting on their coats and walking out of this game. Those are your fans, but you're not seeing their cheering faces; you're seeing their backs *as they walk away from you.* They are showing you no respect because you have not given yourselves respect. You don't deserve their support or their time."

After that game, I took action. If they didn't want to work to deserve the privileges they were awarded as part of the team, they could see what life was like without them. "You think you can show up with your natural skills and read yesterday's newspaper clippings?" I said. "Wrong: you don't automatically inherit the accolades of those who came before you. Privileges are conferred to the team. If you don't act like a team, they can and will be taken away."

In practical terms, that meant I didn't allow them in the locker room; they had to dress in a hallway or in a bathroom and return to the dorms to take a shower. I also took away their laundry privileges, so they had to wash their own clothes. Next I took away their practice uniforms, and if it hadn't been an NCAA rule that teams have to wear uniforms during games, I would have taken those away too. If you'd come to one of our practices in those weeks, you would have seen a bunch of ragamuffins wearing mismatched shorts and shirts, a Division I team looking like a bunch of bums off the street. To my mind, that was pretty darn near the truth. Why pretend to be a team? We weren't acting like it, or practicing like it, or playing like it. Teammates make sacrifices for one another, and these girls hadn't.

In order to succeed at this game—or, I believe, at anything—you have to see yourself as an essential part of the win. Years ago, when I coached at Iowa, I looked down the bench for someone to put into our Final Four game against Ohio State. I looked in particular at one kid—and she looked away. Later, I asked her, "The night before that game, did you see yourself helping us? Did you see yourself sinking the winning basket? Did you see the sweat on your clothes, and the confetti?" She said that she had been convinced that we would win—but that wasn't what I had asked her. She saw other people doing the work, she didn't see herself there, and, sure enough, when it came time for her to step in and make a difference, she couldn't do it.

I saw something very similar with this team. They had come to play for Rutgers because they wanted to be part of a program that was respected by everyone. But for each of them, there was a crucial piece missing: they didn't see themselves having to do the work to earn that respect. As they were learning, the Scarlet Knights can disappoint as much as any other team if the people on that team don't work hard to uphold the tradition.

Aside from the fact that the team was doing so poorly, it was a difficult period of time for me at home. Nina's condition had been relatively stable for a number of years; I always said that she'd gotten fewer colds than the boys when they were all growing up. But in 2006 and 2007, she developed a number of problems that led to three or four unscheduled hospital stays. There were a few games I didn't think I was going to get to at all.

Ordinarily, the basketball court would be a place of refuge for me, but what I had been seeing in practice and at our games wasn't making me feel better; it was making me angry—until they started to turn it around.

I believe that there were three different turning points during the season. The first happened, appropriately enough, on New Year's Eve.

The kind of leadership I'd been looking for often comes from the seniors on the teams, so the coaches and I told the upperclassmen that we were making them all honorary seniors; maybe, we thought, we'll get the equivalent of one whole senior out of it. But our real senior leadership came from a surprising quarter: some of my former players.

We'd had a practice in the morning on New Year's Eve, and met up again at three for dinner in the locker room. At four-thirty, I was lecturing before we went back out onto the court, when suddenly Tammy Sutton-Brown and Cappie Pondexter walked into the room. They'd just gotten off a plane from Turkey, where they'd been playing on the same team. Concerned about what they'd been hearing, they got right to work. Tammy shared with the team how weak in mind, body, and spirit *she'd* been when she came to play for me, and how much better and stronger she'd become. She talked about the kind of respect that the other players in the league had for a Rutgers University player and what it meant to be a meaningful part of a team.

I asked the two of them if they'd like to participate in practice. "That's what we came to do, Coach." When we got out to the floor, I saw that they weren't alone. There was Nikki Jett, who was working at the time as a basketball coach in New Jersey. There was Michelle Campbell, who had been playing in Israel. There was Maury Horton, back from playing in Europe. As soon as she saw them, Chelsea quickly changed from her office clothes into basketball shorts too. And before we started, each one of my former players took two of the younger ones to a corner or to a basket to talk.

The practice was an education. When the centers saw Tammy flick a chest pass almost three-quarters of the court with crisp precision, they finally saw why I'd been so impatient with the soft, slow, sloppy passes they'd been making. When they saw her cut across the lane and sit down in the post, so wide and so graceful and with such a powerful presence, they saw how different it was from the timid, small stance they'd been taking.

When Cappie ripped the ball out of Epiphanny's hands at half-court, she asked her, "Didn't Coach tell you not to move the ball into the coffin corner? And didn't she tell you to step the dribble off just before you make that pass?" Piph smiled in amazement: "You said it in the exact same way Coach did."

Brittany Ray, who never could seem to get herself free for a shot, heard Maury Horton explain how to put her top leg on top of the defense, sit, seal with the inside hand, and explode out at an angle to catch the pass. "And be sure you show that hand the whole time," she told her. Brittany dropped her head: "Yeah, that's just what Coach said."

After what seemed like a minute, I looked at the clock, and realized that it was actually ten-thirty and it was New Year's Eve! My former players had only three days at home, and yet, on the most festive night of the year, they were sweating in a gym, demonstrating, by word and by example, what it meant to have real sisterhood in the Scarlet Knight family. When I saw how much had been accomplished, I could only be grateful that these former players had given of themselves one more time. I felt the pride of a mother watching her older kids helping the younger ones. My team understood I wasn't asking them for anything I hadn't asked of these all-stars, and they saw what they could achieve if only they'd listen. They saw the love and respect I had for my former players, and I believe they wanted to know what that was like.

The next turning point took place during the game against Mississippi, when all of our starters fouled out. All of a sudden, it was the babies who had to play this game against a top-twenty program—and they stepped up. Three freshmen with three overtimes, and they managed to win that game. I was absolutely stunned. You hope your players are prepared, but you never know what's going to happen in a do-or-die situation.

After that game, the whole team dynamic changed. The upperclassmen looked at the freshmen and said, "Wow." When their backs were against the wall and they had nothing but themselves to rely on, the freshmen had come through. More important, the young players gained a great deal of confidence from seeing what I had been telling them all along: that they were capable of making a difference.

The third turning point was in a game against the University of Pittsburgh. The only way we could possibly win the game was to play the 55, our famed full-court press. I knew that they knew how to do it, but I also knew that they had never worked hard enough to master it. This particular press is very effective in forcing your opponent to make mistakes, but it is also extremely taxing for the players. If it's going to work, you can't be slow or lazy.

We stood in the huddle, and I said, "We can't allow them to set up at half-court. There's only one way to win: we have to go into the fifty-five." I asked them if they were ready. I knew they were; I could see it in their faces. They had lost enough; now they were ready to win.

So they went back out there and they began to press. Lo and behold, they saw it work. They saw how quickly Pittsburgh fell under the pressure they were applying. Finally, they understood the "why" behind all of the hard work, the drills, the early morning runs. *This* was why. They saw the fear in their opponents' eyes and they heard the roar of the crowd. At long last, what they'd put in was beginning to pay off.

The next day the freshmen stood in formation, ready to run suicides rather than ask questions to delay me. "If it's going to get done, it's going to have to be done by you," I had told them over and over. "That's the only way it's going to work." Sometimes, players have to get desperate before they understand what you've been saying. Now I didn't have to convince them anymore.

Once the 55 was in place, our opponents began to fall, and our team never looked back. When the girls were finally able to get past the idea that they were going to die from the effort, they gave me *everything.* They were working together and completely unified; nobody had another agenda. That run was something to see; sometimes, it seemed like the girls couldn't believe it themselves. In fact, I might even go so far as to say that the early part of the season had been an opportunity for these young women: it allowed them to see who they really were.

I always tell my teams that there are really three seasons: the regular season, the Big East Tournament, and then, if you're invited, the NCAA Tournament. Despite the turnaround we'd begun to make, we lost our last regular-season game at home against Connecticut, and by twenty-six points—another humiliating defeat. But we were off to the Big East Tournament, and I could feel how much the players wanted the chance to wipe the slate clean.

Our first game was against Marquette. We won that game, 63 to 55. We all noted the 55 in that score, and the players began flashing five fingers two times, a sign that we had the power of the 55 with us.

Next we went to play DePaul. Now, I had not had eighty-five

points scored against me in thirty years of coaching, but in 2006, *three* teams had scored more than eighty-five points; if that doesn't tell you that we weren't a defensive force, I don't know what does. DePaul had been one of those teams. But when we played them in the Big East Tournament, we beat them, and the score was 63–55—just as it had been against Marquette. "The fifty-five has arrived, just in time," I told the team, and I did a good job of convincing them that it would carry us through.

They needed convincing, because we were about to play Connecticut. Not only were they a formidable opponent—the number two team in the country—but they had beaten us less than a week before by twenty-six points. Now we were going to play them at the Hartford Civic Center Arena, which would be filled with sixteen thousand screaming fans wearing the UConn colors.

During our shooting practice before the game, we did a drill we've done many times. The objective is to score thirty-three points in two minutes. Right before the game, Rashidat Juniad, one of the quietest girls on the team, spoke up: "Uh, Coach? That last shooting drill? We scored fifty-five points." I was stunned. We'd never done that before, and there—again—was that *55*. The girls just started screaming.

We went out on the floor against Connecticut, believing with all of our hearts that the 55 would bring us to our victory. With less than a minute left to go, Connecticut called a time-out. As I pulled the girls into the huddle, I looked up at the clock, and I stopped right in the middle of what I was saying. The last time-out of the game, which had been called by Connecticut, was with fifty-five seconds left to go. All I did was point at the clock, with that big red *55*. We knew we were going to win that game, and we did.

Final score: 55–47.

How did we win the Big East Championship? Riding high on the 55. The same thing that had broken us down had allowed us to rise.

After our victory in the Big East Tournament, we had a couple of days off while the other teams finished playing their games and the NCAA determined the brackets. The best teams in the country are selected, ranked, and moved into a championship bracket. Champions from each Division I conference receive automatic placement; the remaining slots are determined by a selection committee. The NCAA wants the best teams to meet at the Final Four, so they try to put them in different brackets. To determine how your team will be seeded, or ranked, they consider a number of factors—your record, obviously, but also other things like the strength of the schedule you've played over the year, or an injured player who will affect the overall performance of the team. How you're seeded determines where you'll play, which affects how much traveling your team will have to do, and how many of your fans can come out to see you.

On Selection Sunday, the whole team and I waited to see how we would fare. We'd won seven games in a row—would they consider us hot? But when the brackets were announced, there was no good news. We were set to play not just the number one seed in our bracket but also the number one team in the *country*: Duke. At first I was very disappointed. But then I thought, *You know what? Bring it on. This team is strong enough.*

The 2007 NCAA Tournament felt like one of those myths in which the hero has to overcome a series of nearly impossible trials to win his prize. The teams we had to get past to get to the Final Four were all teams we had struggled mightily against during the regular season. It was as if someone had decreed that there would be no shortcuts. But I had always said, "In order to be the best, you have to play the best."

Well, we played East Carolina University and we won. We played Michigan State and we won. And in March, we played Duke again, this time in their arena in North Carolina. They'd had an unbelievable season, with only one loss all year. Given their record, as well as our previous history with them, the Scarlet Knights had a great deal of insecurity to overcome, but we were ready; nobody had come back from what we'd come back from.

That game was rough for us right from the beginning. A couple of times in the second half, Duke was up to a ten-point lead, and they were up by four as late as the final minute of the game. But we never stopped believing—even against the odds—that victory could be ours, and the 55 was what broke them. With twenty seconds left on the clock, down by one, one of the freshmen, Epiphanny Prince, stole the ball and shot the basket that won us the game.

And so we beat the top team in the country—the same team that had wiped up our own floor with us just a few months earlier—and in their house. We even found the 55: the score was 53–52—add 2 and 3 together, and you've got 5. That game took us to the Elite Eight.

I've never been so proud or seen young women so proud of themselves. You can make things easy for your players, allowing them to make excuses or helping them to find a shortcut. But challenge them at the highest level, tell them to get up when they get knocked down, and never let them stop believing in themselves, and they can accomplish the impossible. As parents and coaches, we need to inspire our children to be the best they can be, never forgetting that the kid who doesn't make the team is the one you should never stop encouraging. I've never seen a more powerful reminder of that than I did that season.

Our trials weren't over, however. We had been scheduled to play Arizona State early in the regular season, but we had canceled the game when one of the young ladies on their team suffered a family tragedy. If we had played them then, they would have blown us out of the water, and I had told the team so at the time. Now, in order to get to that next step, we would have to play them and prove ourselves.

After we won against Duke, Essence had lifted me up off my feet in a massive hug. In my ear, she said, "You told us that we weren't ready for Arizona. But we're ready now, Coach." She was right. It had been a longer race to run than they knew, but now this team was in total control.

And when we beat Arizona State, we knew something else: as much as these games did feel like trials, we also felt as though each challenge had been put before us exactly when we could handle it.

We didn't walk alone. When I called this a "team of destiny" to the press, I meant it. I was so overwhelmed with emotion during that run that it was only through the good Lord's intervention that I could still coach in a calm fashion.

With a young team like this, you have to work hard to maintain a balance: the girls must be motivated to play at their best for every single game, which means knowing what's at stake. At the same time, you can't let them be distracted or overwhelmed by that knowledge, which can easily happen as the games get more and more important. This team hadn't been here before; they'd had no time to get used to the spotlight. But I didn't have any of the nerves or the confusion that you might have expected. I felt a strength that wasn't mine, a peace and clarity that I couldn't explain, except to say that God was guiding me. I knew, at the very core of my soul, that there was a plan for us. Our steps were ordered, from the very start. And that was what I told the team through our run.

During the Final Four, I took away the team's cell phones and PDAs. It was vital that they focus on what they needed to do for themselves, and for one another; I didn't want other people's agendas to intrude. I know how the expectations of the outside world can affect me: people had come from all over to be there for me, including players from every school I'd ever coached. Knowing what they'd done to be there overwhelmed me with emotion, and the weight of their hope and pride was heavy on my shoulders. It might have seemed harsh, but I wanted to shelter my players from those pressures.

The night before the first game of the Final Four, a huge contingent of my former players came to a gathering at the hotel organized by Felicia Hall. Practically the whole Cheyney Final Four team was there as well as many of the girls from Iowa. There's a photograph on my desk, taken that night, with the forty-plus women who showed up to support me and this young team—players who spanned the decades. The truth is, the women who have played for me are like sisters, raised with the same rules. They know they can always count on one another, and if there's anything I'm proud of and grateful for, it's the way they take care of one another.

It's hard to explain to others how deep a bond we feel. Whether they graduated from Cheyney, Iowa, or Rutgers, *they understand.* Every year a new crop of freshmen come in and are shell-shocked. Sometimes they don't think they're going to make it; they think that what I'm asking them for is going to kill them. Ultimately, they do make it. They hang in there and they accomplish, and then they come back to tell the next generation of shell-shocked freshmen that they're going to be okay. "You'll live to tell the tale, too," they tell them. It means a lot to hear that from someone who has lived it.

At the reunion party, we ate hors d'oeuvres and caught up with one another, and then one person from each school stood up and spoke to the team about what it meant to play for me, and what it meant that this team would be playing for the championship. Each one of them urged the girls not to let this opportunity slip through their fingers. "Take what we didn't get," they told them.

It was a magical night. At one point, one of my players told me that the women who have played for me consider themselves to be in a sorority—one that happens to span thirty years and three different schools. I smiled to myself. Finally, a sorority I cared to belong to.

The first game of the Final Four was against LSU, the team I was most worried about. Like us, they were a strong defensive team, and I had real concerns about the ability of our team to get past them. No matter what, as the commentators pointed out, there weren't going to be a lot of points scored in that game.

But I was surprised: as soon as our team got out there, they made quick work of them. We played so hard and shot so well, it seemed like the jump shots were raining from the sky. At one point, I wished we could save some of those baskets for the game against Tennessee; I knew we were going to need them. But they came during the game against LSU, and with that victory, we were on our way to the championship game.

Truly, to be given the honor to play for that championship was like something out of a fairy tale. I had said they were the worst team I'd ever coached, and I had meant it. But the Cinderellas on that team proved everyone wrong, including myself.

Once again, nobody expected us to be there. When I had taken Cheyney to the championship, twenty-five years before, the joke was that nobody knew how to pronounce the name of our tiny, historically black school. In 2007, it was "Where's my bobblehead?" The vendors had made bobblehead dolls for every team in the Final Four except mine.

"When are they going to stop counting you out, Coach?" one of my former players joked. "Don't they know that's when you bring it?"

I genuinely don't think that it hit us that we were playing for the championship until we found ourselves standing for the national anthem in Cleveland's Quicken Loans Arena, with all twenty thousand seats sold out. The scoreboard shoots flames out of the four corners, and on the big board, they kept running pictures of our team with the electronic message AND THEN THERE WERE TWO.

I could not get that out of my head. Two. *Two.* Just two teams in the entire *nation,* facing off for this honor, and we were one of them. Five freshmen, three juniors, and two sophomores. Some of these girls had been sitting in high school bleachers nine months ago, and yet they had somehow managed to put away the little girl inside themselves so their sisters could play on the biggest stage in the world. For me, it had been twenty-five years since one of my teams had competed for the honor of being the best one in the nation. There was an air of unreality about it. I know that I will not be able to put that feeling in its place and give it its proper due for some time yet.

Ultimately, Tennessee took home the championship ring that day. To be honest, I knew I had reason to worry as soon as I walked into breakfast that morning. The room was eerily quiet, and the players had a dazed look in their eyes. It stayed that way throughout breakfast and during the shootaround prior to the game. One of my players was shooting with a tissue in her hand. The shootaround before the championship game and she's worried about blowing her nose?

I tried to shock them out of it by raising my voice: "I know you haven't come so far not to finish. I know you're not going to bring us to this game and not play it." But I wasn't able to shake them out of their stupor; the magnitude of the game had finally hit them.

Our strategy, throughout the postseason, had been to treat these games like any others: to play as hard and as well as we could, and to be the best team on that floor on that day. It worked—we found out later that our team had set *five* NCAA records during the tournament without even knowing it—but I couldn't shelter them from the enormity of this game.

"Don't go through these forty minutes and have regrets. This is not the time to hesitate—this is our time. This is our moment, right now. *This is it.*" And I reminded them of something I have told each one of my teams from the very beginning. "Tonight, lying in your bed, only you will know whether you gave it all, whether you risked everything for the chance to win, whether you did all you could. At the end of this day, let us all be at peace, with no regrets."

When I call the girls into a huddle when they're faced with a difficult situation, I often remind them of a similar challenge they've faced and conquered. But there wasn't another championship game that I could point to. I wonder if there's something I could have done to prepare them for that extraordinary place and time—something I could have said, or shown them—and in truth, I don't think there was. But if we ever meet that situation again, I think Essence will have to call to pick me up and tell me again: "We're ready now, Coach."

And I couldn't find the 55. As we'd been driving into Cleveland, I'd seen a building with a big red 55 on the roof, and I went so far as to call down to the hotel's front desk to determine whether or not the building I'd seen was part of a hotel. If it had been, and if Tennessee had been staying there, I swear I think we'd have won. But I never did find my 55, and neither did we find that victory.

Within twenty minutes of leaving the floor, I was addressing the team in the locker room. Without question, the most difficult thing a coach has to do is talk to her team after losing the last game of the season. There's something so *final* about that final game, and we all felt the loss so keenly. What do you say that can heal their pain and your own? But in 2007, one thing did make my heart a little lighter: none of them were seniors. They'd all be back next year, and we'd have another chance. It was the only saving grace.

I tried to communicate to them how proud I was of them, and how inspired I had been by them. I also told them something that not very many people know. After I lost my husband, I made up my mind to quit basketball if my Iowa team won the national championship. I was prepared to walk away from the sport without looking back. Of course, we didn't win that championship and I didn't quit; at the time, I felt there was unfinished business. Now I knew what had kept me coaching.

"I'm so glad that I didn't quit," I told them. "If I had, I would never have known what it was to coach you. I've never seen better evidence of the resilience of the human spirit. I've never coached a team that has accomplished so much in one year—ever. It seemed that there was no way for you to reach the levels you aspired to. But from you I've understood even more what it means to persevere in the face of adversity. I thank you from the bottom of my heart."

Championship or no championship, this had been the most rewarding year I'd ever had coaching basketball. The last few months had been a fairy tale. We were the team that had been written off by the world as nothings. There wasn't a single person in America who would have bet ten cents that we'd be the team to go to Cleveland. No one in the world would have thought that we'd be the ones looking up and seeing AND THEN THERE WERE TWO on that JumboTron—and that included me. But nobody knows better than me—a coal miner's daughter from Edenborn, Pennsylvania, a patch with no stop light—that it's not where you start but where you finish that counts. We might have started the season with a forty-point loss on our own floor, but we ended it by playing at the highest level, as one of the two best teams in the nation.

As I was talking to the team, I got a text message from Howard White, one of the top executives at Nike. He and I had spoken periodically over the previous four or five weeks about the incredible job the girls were doing, and I had shared my feeling with him that our team's steps had been ordered. "Somehow there's been a halo placed around this team that has allowed me and the other coaches to be free to make decisions, and the players free to play," I had told him. "I feel very strongly that we've been guided here. God has a plan for us."

The text he sent me, just minutes after that Tennessee game, read: "Viv, so sorry about your game. Perhaps the Lord has another plan for you—a greater plan than winning the basketball championship. I do believe your steps have been ordered."

Little did we know.

17

This Is Who We Are

The loss to Tennessee hurt, but we were pretty proud of our season when we came home to the arms of our fans and our state. I had put this young team out of their locker room and taken away their uniforms, and they had gone on to win the Big East Tournament title and then five straight NCAA games to play for the national championship. Unfortunately, there was no time for our achievement to even sink in.

On the morning of April 4, 2007, Don Imus made his now-infamous statement about the Rutgers women's basketball team. It was first reported that night on a media watchdog website called Media Matters for America. The next morning, my sports information director shared Imus's comments with the team, who were on the way to a bell-ringing ceremony at the school in honor of their extraordinary season.

Not one of them knew who he was.

The first thing that a number of the girls asked was "Why?" It was the same thing I asked when I was told, later. But there are a lot of different ways you can ask why, and I don't think that the players and I were asking the same question.

The girls, I think, were genuinely baffled. They were asking: "Why would someone say something like that about us?" They're young enough to be surprised by that kind of racism and sexism. My why was different—more of an expression of sickness, anger, and disgust. Let me say it like this: if you deny your three-year-old more ice cream, and he responds by throwing his bowl on the floor, you might ask in exasperation, "Why did you do that?" but you're not really looking for an answer. The best way I can put it is that there was a question mark at the end of their why and an exclamation mark at the end of mine.

Don't mistake me: I had questions, too. Why would a media personality go after student athletes—young people who give everything of themselves to represent their university, and without getting paid a dime? These weren't politicians or professionals with multimillion-dollar contracts. Why would he go out of his way to demoralize young women who represent exactly what we encourage our young people to be: disciplined role models working to get an education and to make a difference in the world? And why attack this group after our extraordinary season and all we'd been through?

I knew there would never be an answer to those questions that would satisfy me or that would give back to these young ladies what had been taken from them.

It was the first day of recruiting, so I spent most of it on the phone with high school students. I had my hands full and, to be perfectly honest, it wasn't until I saw a printout of the full text that the magnitude of what he'd said really sank in. He'd called my girls "nappy-headed hos." Even now I can hardly bear to repeat those vile, venomous, sexist, racist, and hurtful words; they still cause each one of us great anger and pain. He had also spoken about "wannabes," a reference to dark- and light-skinned black complexions—an issue that continues to cause pain in our community. This was more than a schoolyard taunt.

We needed to respond, so at about four o'clock that afternoon, the university and the NCAA issued a joint statement. Meanwhile, I refused to speak directly to the local papers—the only ones pursuing the story at the time—in the hopes that interest would die out.

That night, there was a celebration at the university, where the team was being honored. The governor of New Jersey was there, along with the president of Rutgers and our athletic director, Bob Mulcahey. The head football coach and the men's basketball coach were there, along with their teams and a number of other teams. Everyone was heading home for the Easter vacation right after the ceremony, so I knew that we wouldn't have a chance to talk as a team until we returned. But I wasn't about to send these young ladies home with a question in their mind about how we were going to deal with this, so I made sure to meet with them for a minute or two. I told them that I was fully aware of what had happened and that I would address it. I wanted to find out a lot more before speaking, but they needed to know that I wasn't going to stand by idly while someone hurt them. The girls left for home knowing that I had taken the situation in hand.

The truth was that I'd never felt so powerless in my life. When I was finally alone, my emotions were so strong and my hurt so deep that it took my breath away.

I called my brother and confidant Tim, who was as powerfully angry and outraged as I was. He felt that I should go out, guns blazing, to demand an apology on the team's behalf. I agreed with him in principle, but my first and strongest impulse was to do whatever I could to minimize the controversy and make it all go away as soon as possible. You see, I've never believed that any publicity is good publicity—in fact, quite the opposite. I have too many times in my life seen a lie become accepted truth simply through repetition. In my experience, the lie makes the front page, while the corrections and apologies are buried in the back with the classifieds.

Imus's comments had hurt us and I wanted to protect the players and the program from further damage. I felt sure that every time the slur was repeated, even in outrage, it would create a fresh wound for my girls. I might have been powerless to prevent it from happening the first time, but I wasn't going to let it happen again.

I called my dear friend Coach John Chaney. He warned me about the power of the media and the fruitlessness of fighting the wind. I asked him to help me get in touch with John Thompson, the great Georgetown coach, because I knew that he had protected his players from ugliness and handled some difficult things with grace; I thought he might be able to understand the position I was in. More than anything, I wanted to know what we risked by defending ourselves.

When I finally got home that night, I collapsed. I was just so devastated that Imus had demeaned us *in that way.* It felt like a personal blow, for a number of reasons. First of all, I felt guilty, almost. Pat Summitt had started four black players, just as I had. I couldn't help but wonder if the fact that I was black had made our team seem *blacker,* and therefore more open to ridicule and hatred.

But the real hurt was that I felt that a lifetime of working with young people—not to mention the twenty-five years I'd spent working my way back to another championship—had been wiped out in the fifty-four seconds it took to spew those words of careless hate. Since my very first day coaching, I have made it a policy to make sure that every one of my girls presents herself like a lady. When I was at Cheyney, I was always very conscious that we were representing a historically black school. I knew that, hearing that, some people might jump to a negative conclusion about those young women, something that had nothing to do with who they were. So I made sure that we never gave anyone anything to say, except, "What a classy group of young women."

I see other teams—both men's and women's—in airports and hotel lobbies. Often they're wearing gray sweatpants and untied sneakers, looking sloppy and slapped together like they just rolled out of their beds. Maybe it doesn't matter to them, or to their coaches, but there's never been any of that with my teams. My personal beautician was with us on the plane going to the championships! Even at Cheyney, when we had nothing at all, we represented ourselves honorably by looking and acting sharp. John Chaney used to tease me: "Come on! Why do those girls have to wear lipstick on the bus?" But his teams were always impeccable, too, and I believe that the girls felt good because they looked good.

I've preserved that standard with all the teams I've coached. Part of it is that I've always wanted to emphasize team unity the idea that we travel as a team, dress as a team, look and feel like a team. I like that uniformity. In Iowa, we always traveled in beautiful black blazers. (The weather was so bad in Iowa that I had to be a little more flexible about what the girls wore, especially in the footwear department, but even when it was thirty degrees below, you wouldn't catch a girl on one of my teams wearing Timberlands.)

It was no different when I got to Rutgers. My first day there I told them that I didn't want to see them in jeans. When we traveled, we'd wear the same-color sweater, the same-color turtleneck, the same pants. A girl could buy herself a khaki pant that had some style to it, but at the end of the day, she'd be wearing the same color as her teammates.

There's more to it than unity, of course. For me, the way you present yourself is a signal of self-respect, and of your respect for other people. Isn't it true that when you dress up—when a woman puts on heels and jewelry, or a man puts on a suit—you're telling yourself and the world that this is a special event? I believe that what you wear sends a distinct message. If I'm wearing the school colors, it *means* something—just as it does when I refuse to wear them, as I did this past season, when I wasn't proud of my team and their efforts.

The message that we sent was so important to me, it even affected the way my teams played. There were times when we could have scored more points by running and gunning, but I didn't ever want people thinking that my girls just ran around and shot at will. I was all too conscious of the stereotype of the black athlete who falls back on his talent and looks for the quick basket without using his mind. So we always sought to play with discipline and intelligence, because I never wanted anyone to have cause to say something like that about my girls.

Over the years, especially when I felt worn down from arguing with every new team about the shoes and the jeans and the sweatpants, I have wondered to myself, *Does it really matter? As long as they win, does it really matter how they carry themselves?* For me, the answer to that question has always been *yes*—yes, it does matter. So what Imus had said cut me to the core. All those battles over the past thirty years, all that work to present myself and the young ladies in the way that they *should* be presented—it felt as though none of it had made any difference at all.

There was a deeper hurt for me, too: I couldn't shake the feeling that I had fallen down in my responsibility to protect these girls. When a young lady comes to play for me, I make a pledge to her parents that I will take care of her. I tell them that I will nurture her heart and her mind, shelter her from the ugly forces in the world, and give her a place where she is safe to become the very best young woman that she can be. I promise these girls a future, whether that means going on to play basketball professionally or using the degree that they've earned in the service of another dream. And by and large, I've made good on those promises.

And yet I couldn't do a thing to protect the Rutgers 2006–2007 team from the ugliness that was raining down on their heads. *How could I have allowed this to happen to them?* I thought to myself all that night. *I'm supposed to make their dreams come true.*

Only as the sun came up did I finally shut my eyes. A few hours later, I woke up to a text message from Moses Malone, one of the greatest basketball centers of all time. He'd never called or texted me before, but we have a good friend in common. The message he sent was only five words long, but when I read it, tears sprung to my eyes.

His message read: "They hurt our girls, Coach."

They hurt our girls.

That short message encapsulated everything I had been feeling. I just put my head down and wept.

When I got myself together, I realized that if Moses knew about it, the rest of the world probably did, too. It was clear that my hope that the incident would quickly disappear from sight was misguided. Sure enough, there was an article in that morning's *New York Times,* and by the time I called in, my office had fielded hundreds of calls from newspaper and television reporters all over the world.

When I saw how hungry the media was, I felt that I needed some serious advice from another coach. The world was looking to me for a response, and I was afraid of coming across as angry or bitter. So I called Dr. Ann Griffith, my friend and my college coach. She had known me since I was seventeen, and she knew I was not a racist. She told me that my reputation and the accomplishments of this team would speak for themselves and would far outweigh anything that had been said on the radio. She advised me, as John Chaney had, to hold my tongue and rise above the fray.

It was good advice, but it pretty quickly became clear that the world wasn't going to let me do that. And in truth, I wasn't satisfied with the idea of remaining silent. I couldn't make the whole thing go away, as I had hoped, but I didn't have to allow the insult to stand, unchallenged.

I also spoke to Pat Summitt—not once, but several times—throughout this mess. Both of our teams had been mentioned, and I saw Imus's comments as a hurt to all women, not just the women on my team. Although what he'd said about Pat's team was less overtly offensive, it certainly wasn't an appropriate way to discuss an athletic competition, especially one at the national-championship level. When you talk about an athlete, you talk about her skills, her agility, her quickness, her athleticism, her tactics. Who calls an athlete cute? As I expected, Pat told me she'd support me and my team, whatever we decided to do.

My only course of action became clear to me. We hadn't asked to be thrust into this spotlight—but since we had been, it was time to step up.

In the aftermath of the media firestorm that followed, one of my Cheyney players, Yolanda Laney, reminded me of an incident from years before that I had completely forgotten. The team had been eating in a host school's cafeteria, and the students at that school threw food at our team. I was dealing with an administrative issue in the other coach's office and wasn't present, which is probably partly why it happened in the first place.

The girls didn't want to tell me what had happened, but someone did just as we were leaving. I stopped the bus, got off, went to the athletic director of the university, and made him come out to the bus to apologize to the team.

"Did anyone doubt for a minute that you were going to stand up for those girls, Coach?" Laney asked. "We knew, because that's what you did with us."

Over the Easter break, I went to church with Nina and Hyacinth. The press was there in force. Pastor Soaries, who has long been a personal friend and a friend of the team, spoke about the incident and called on the congregation to support us. It was an eye-opener to me how the media chose to portray the event. Like the rest of the congregation, I stood up to applaud a song the choir had sung, but the shot of me standing and clapping was spliced in after Pastor's speech, and it was filmed tight and close, so it looked like I was the only one standing.

We met as a team as soon as the girls were back from their break. Pastor Soaries joined us at that meeting and continued to play a crucial role in the days that followed. I didn't have an agenda when I walked into that room; I simply wanted to know what each of the girls had experienced while she was home. What I heard in that meeting made me angrier than I already was.

Most of them were still reeling from the shock and humiliation of what had been said. Others were angry and grew angrier each time those hateful words were repeated on television. They'd spent the vacation besieged with phone calls, text messages, e-mails, and visits to their homes by journalists. There had been no time to reflect on how far they'd come over the course of the season. What should have been one of the most triumphant and relaxing times of their lives had been ruined.

Many of them were confused by the reactions they'd gotten from their parents and relatives. "We had Easter dinner as usual, with a big group of friends and family, and no one mentioned the championship game," one girl said. Instead, the celebration had been eerily quiet, with everyone sidestepping the elephant in the room.

Others were taken aback by the depth of their parents' anger. They didn't understand that those words had stirred up a lot of old, unresolved feelings. One girl in particular said that her mother hadn't been able to meet her eyes the whole time she was home.

"Every time I looked, there were tears in her eyes," she said, and I understood that her mother hadn't been able to look at her because she hadn't wanted her daughter to see her weep.

I could understand why it had been so difficult. They had gone home and asked their parents, "Why?" It was a question that none of them had been prepared to answer, a question that every single one of us hopes we'll never have to address. I was glad I'd had a few days to pray and reflect, to think about the best way to protect them and help them heal.

I told them I understood why their parents were so hurt and furious. Every mother knows the feeling of looking down at her new baby and thinking that she would do anything—*anything*—to keep every hair on that child's head safe. Eventually you do come to grips with the fact that that child is going to fall and get up, but even when she's grown, when someone hurts her, you feel that pain as if it were your own. You don't send the child you've loved and nurtured off into the world to be abused.

I shared with them the story of my audition to be a cheerleader and explained that, without question, their parents had experienced something similar in their own youths. Imus's comment—made thirty-nine years to the day after the assassination of Dr. Martin Luther King, at thirty-nine years old—was simply the most recent chapter in an old, old story. I told them that I still remembered the day Dr. King died, just as I was sure their parents did, and how personally hurt I had felt by it. I had spoken out against inequality then. Had nothing changed?

But I knew something else too: nobody could rob them, without their permission, of the joy and pride they felt in their season. "You have to stand tall," I told them. "You know who you are and what you've accomplished. Let's remember those accomplishments and take pride in them. *We* define who we are."

We came out of that meeting knowing what we wanted to do. We took our next steps together, like a team, just as we had during the season. I promised them that anything I said publicly would be read and approved by them in advance. The last thing I wanted was to misrepresent their feelings or to speak for them in a way that anyone felt was inaccurate or inauthentic. They had been hurt enough.

Right from the beginning, I was clear on one point: I wasn't standing in judgment of Don Imus. That's God's work, not mine. We wouldn't call for his job or for anything else. I was concerned with one thing only, and that was clarifying, in the world's eyes, who we were. The world would see that these girls composed music, wrote poetry, went to church, told jokes, and did well in school. They aspired to be doctors, lawyers, psychologists, and journalists. The world would see these young ladies as children with families—or, in some cases, as people who had tragically and recently lost those closest to them. The world would understand the discipline and determination it took for this doormat team to turn around and go on the giant-killing run that brought them to the national championship game. If I had anything to do with it, the world would come to see these young women as *people.*

The media was ravenous and unstoppable; I'd never seen anything like it in my life. Reporters and television crews literally camped out outside the dormitories, the kids' apartments, the athletic center, my house. Reporters obtained copies of the players' class schedules and waited outside the buildings. Producers bombarded players with calls and text messages. (One of my players dryly commented that she didn't want a thing Don Imus could give her, unless he felt like reimbursing her the thirty-eight dollars and fifty-five cents that she'd spent receiving text messages she didn't want from journalists.) Even the players' brothers, sisters, and cousins were swamped with calls.

These girls weren't celebrities or politicians, used to wading through a crowd of people yelling questions and taking pictures. They were kids! They looked out the dorm window and saw the swarm and felt afraid to go outside. Everyone was demanding interviews, but these kids were in finals, and they'd already missed more school than they could afford. The meetings with the university administration and with our pastor took hours. It was a great deal to handle. I figured that if we held a press conference, we could appear and speak as a team and set the record straight.

So we did. My contract lawyer called me before I went down. "Be careful, Vivian—don't snap," he told me. I'm sure he was referring to the fact that I hadn't yet signed my contract with Rutgers. I told him I was just going to speak from my heart, as I had always done. "Anyone who knows me would be disappointed if I did anything differently," I told him. I had no idea the press conference was being carried live on CNN, and I'm glad I didn't. It allowed me to be relaxed and speak to the world as if I were just speaking to my team. Certainly, none of the reporters who have covered me over the years were surprised by what I said or how I said it.

I can tell you that I felt extreme pride, standing on that dais with those young women. Ours was not a scripted statement drafted by a public relations firm. Many people thought that was what we should have done, in order to protect the girls: open curtain, open mouth, read prepared statement, close curtain, never give another interview. But I knew these young ladies would rise to this challenge, just as they'd done all year.

And they did. They took questions, some of them tough ones, some coming from left field. They didn't hide; they spoke from the heart with dignity and compassion. I know that most adults in that situation, even professionals, would have crumbled. But there they were—children, practically; there were braces on some of their teeth—and their composure was incredible.

I cannot tell you how many people during that time told me, "I'm so sorry this happened to you—but I am so glad that it was you who it happened to." I can't help but think that they're right. I have been through a lot in my life, and if nothing else, it has made me strong. I wouldn't have wished it on the team for anything; if I could go back right now and steal those words out of his mouth, I would do it. But as I have spent a career telling the young women in my care, all you can do is focus on the things you control, and what we controlled in this instance was our response.

In my opinion, the young people sitting beside me that day epitomized everything that is right in this world. They were strong and they were proud. They looked injustice and adversity in the face and turned it into a teaching moment. At one point, Essence Carson looked down the line at her teammates and said, "We stand." When she said that, I felt my heart soar. You see, the two songs we listened to for inspiration in the locker room during the run-up to the championship were Christian songs. One was a song called "Victory Is Ours." The other was Rev. Donnie McClurkin's gospel song "Stand."

The latter had such significance to us during the season that it's the one we chose to play behind the final shot of our highlight reel: the girls, seconds after the buzzer announcing Tennessee's victory had sounded, confetti streaming down along with their tears. In it, Reverend McClurkin asks "What do you do when you've done all you can, and it seems like it's never enough? And what do you say when your friends turn away, and you're all alone? Tell me, what do you give when you've given your all, and it seems like you can't make it through?"

The answer was something that I knew all too well from my own life, and it was one that had brought this young team all the way through their difficult season. That lyric had always had significance to me, but it had never felt more relevant or powerful than it did that day. "After you've done all you can, *you just stand.*" And so we did.

The day after the press conference, the *New York Daily News* ran a photo of the team on its front page, under a one-word headline: DIGNITY.

I thought it was perfect.

The firestorm continued. The team and I appeared by satellite on the *Oprah Winfrey Show.* The players were absolutely giddy at the idea of speaking with Oprah, who is an icon to all of us. I think they were more nervous before the Oprah show than they'd been before the championship game!

I'll never forget what she said to the team at the end of our appearance: "I want to borrow a line from Maya Angelou, who is a personal mentor of mine and I know you all also feel the same way about her. And she has said this many times, and I say this to you, on behalf of myself and every woman that I know, you make me proud to spell my name W-O-M-A-N. "

No matter who we were talking to, our message remained consistent: look at who we are. We are not what he said we are. *This* is who we are. And as people began to see these young ladies as human beings, not just the butt of some supposedly humorous comment, what Imus had said began to feel very personal. People were forced to ask themselves, "How would I have felt if that comment had been directed at me? At my sister? At my wife? At my *daughter*?" Suddenly, the joke didn't seem so funny anymore.

Nike, which sponsors me and my team, placed a full-page ad in the sports section of the *New York Times.* "Thank you, ignorance," it read. "Thank you for starting the conversation. Thank you for making an entire nation listen to the Rutgers team story. And for making us wonder what other great stories we've missed. Thank you for reminding us to think before we speak. Thank you for showing us how strong and poised 18- and 20-year-old women can be. Thank you for reminding us that another basketball tournament goes on in March. Thank you for showing us that sport includes more than the time spent on the court. Thank you for unintentionally moving women's sport forward. And thank you for making all of us realize that we still have a long way to go. Next season starts 11.16.07."

Late in April, at a birthday dinner for the great civil rights activist Andrew Young, I met Maya Angelou, one of my heroes, who told me how proud she'd been of the girls. She was in a wheelchair when we met, and I bent down to have my picture taken with her. She said to me, "Bend down for no one, and bow only before the Lord." Those words still make the hairs rise on the back of my neck. She was telling me to stand tall—just as I had told my girls.

Male and female athletes from all sports reached out. We heard from high school runners and from Olympians. A number of coaches sent cards with personal messages from every member of their teams. Gwen Ifill, a journalist whose work I have admired for years, wrote an op-ed for the *New York Times;* she had been an Imus target as well. Perhaps most important, we were flooded with good wishes and beautiful messages of support from ordinary people, black and white, all over the world. Senator Hillary Clinton collected thousands of supportive comments and presented them to me when we met; even now, reading them is almost too much for me to bear. To everyone who took the time to pick up the phone, to write an e-mail, or to put pen to paper in order to let us know that you were behind us, we felt you there, we really did.

That outpouring of public support and love told me that we, as a country, are no longer willing to stand idly by when someone drags our best and brightest through the dirt. It told me that we as a nation would no longer tolerate complicity in casual, thoughtless degradation. It told me that the time had indeed come for someone to stand up for what was right.

And I am so proud of those girls for having the strength to do it. As hurtful as the comments may have been, these young women were given a chance to make an impact and to stand up for what was right, and they did. I believe that they were chosen; our steps had been ordered, all season long, and we were not deserted when Don Imus opened his mouth. Those girls were lifted and carried, that's the only way I can explain it.

As everyone knows, we met with Don Imus, and we accepted his apology.

It was Imus who initiated the meeting; he said that he wanted to hear what was really in our hearts and minds. I invited the families of the players because they had been affected as well. There was no hope of keeping the location of the meeting private, so the team met at the Rutgers Athletic Center and took a bus together to Governor Corzine's mansion. The press was there, but security prevented them from getting past the gates; we were grateful to have a neutral place to meet, as we weren't there to put on a show.

The governor is a sincere and straightforward person and had been a real supporter of ours throughout the ordeal. When he had told me he was sorry, there were tears in his eyes, and I appreciated that. Tragically, the governor was badly injured in an automobile accident on his way to the meeting, although we didn't know the real situation at the time. We heard only that he'd been involved in something minor, and we expected him to walk through the door the whole time we were there.

I can't talk about what happened in that room without violating the privacy of the people who were there, but I can tell you that it was a genuine—sometimes very emotional—dialogue. We were very grateful to have my pastor there; he proved to be an invaluable source of strength and counsel. Nobody felt rushed; over the course of several hours, every single person who wanted to speak stood up and said what he or she had to say.

As I had suspected, many of the coaches, parents, and grandparents had a story like the one from my own childhood of discrimination and hatred that had hurt them, and Imus's comments had reopened each one of those wounds. Some of those stories were so hard, you just had to drop your head into your hands and cry. Many things I hadn't known were revealed to me in that room, and I know that some of the players were hearing stories from people close to them for the first time as well.

It was truly a cathartic experience for me and for the players, and I want to believe that it was for Imus and his wife, Deirdre, as well. She embraced me and each and every one of the girls on the team. I think she was deeply hurt and that she was remorseful. I go by what I feel, and I felt her.

Imus might have started this whole thing, but by the time those stories were told, he was no longer the reason we were all there. In that room, the team, the moms and dads and grandparents and even the younger siblings of some of the players were able to share their souls with one another for the first time. And together, as a community, we helped one another to heal.

About a month or so after everything died down, the team and I were honored at Yankee Stadium.

That day was significant for me. When I was a little girl, I loved to listen to baseball on the radio; the announcers made the games so vivid that it felt almost like having a television. They told such wonderful stories about the players that the players on the baseball cards I collected came to seem like real people to me. But do you know something crazy? Although I think my field hockey team had done a demonstration at a baseball stadium in Philadelphia thirty years before, I had never actually gone to a game.

Yankee Stadium surprised me. It's right in the center of the thrill and excitement of New York City, smack dab in the middle of all the noise and lights and action. People were making a full-day event out of the game, and you could see the excitement and engagement on the fans' faces as they walked in. I kept thinking back to the old movies I'd seen as a child. It was so easy to imagine a bunch of scruffy little kids outside the stadium, just hoping that a ball would come over the wall, or waiting by the side door for one of their idols to come out and sign an autograph.

There we were, the Scarlet Knights, walking through the tunnel at Yankee Stadium—the same tunnel that so many greats had passed through on their way to make history. I got chills just looking at the photographs that lined the tunnel: Babe Ruth, Joe DiMaggio, Mickey Mantle, Lou Gehrig, Reggie Jackson—the Bronx Bombers. I couldn't help stopping, just to touch the frames. Baseball is America's sport, and the storied Yankees *are* baseball. Nothing less than the best is good enough for the New York fans.

When we walked out onto the field, Derek Jeter, who had been so supportive of us, was there, and the crowd made it clear what we meant to them. I would have been happy to sit in the highest bleachers, but there we were on the field, the envy of the entire nation. I looked up, and there on the JumboTron they were showing clips from our Final Four game and talking about the accomplishments of our team. I could not believe my eyes and ears. Were they really saying "Rutgers"? Were they really saying "women's basketball"? Were we really being honored at home plate in Yankee Stadium?

Later in Mr. Steinbrenner's box, I sat back and looked at my team—some of whom were chatting casually with former secretary of state and Nobel Prize winner Henry Kissinger—and realized that, in some ways, the season had encapsulated everything I've ever wanted for the young ladies I have coached. I wanted them to be winners at basketball—and the way this group of underclassmen came from nothing to turn themselves into a championship team demonstrated that they were. But the way they handled themselves in the face of the Imus situation proved without a doubt that they were champions in a bigger arena, too.

The 2006–2007 Rutgers women's basketball team demanded the respect that was owed to them, and in so doing, they stood up for the dignity of all people. It takes a great deal of confidence to hold your head high after you've been humiliated. It takes a great deal of fortitude to answer hate with compassion. It takes strength to keep your moral compass when faced with derision and contempt. But that is what this team did, and that is how they inspired the country.

EPILOGUE

We Stand

I'm very aware that our time on this earth is finite, and I remind myself every day to appreciate all that I've been given. Most important, I feel a level of peace with regard to my family that I haven't experienced in years. My sons are healthy and happy, and my mom has recovered very well from the stroke she had in April 2007. I push Nina through the fall leaves, knowing that she's gotten some fresh air, I've gotten some exercise, and that we've spent time together.

I wonder sometimes if I'll ever stop long enough to get caught up on all the feelings I have. I imagine myself in a beautiful glass house on a rocky cliff in an all-white room, listening to music while the waves beat against the rocks. There are so many books I want to read, so many things I want to study and understand, and I've always had the vision of a serene place where I could do that.

But I know the time has not yet come for me to bow out. I do believe that there is a national championship in my future, and I do believe that I still have some very important things to pass along to the young women I work with. As one of the very few black female coaches in the country, I consider it my mission to prepare them for the world.

When a girl comes to play for me, I make it clear that I will not tolerate anything that reflects negatively on her or on the program she represents. My standards are high, but I know that the burden I carry is not too great when my players understand it and carry it with me.

I was in a shoe store with the team this fall when I saw a little boy, about seven years old, with his mother and his sisters. His eyes were as big as dinner plates and he was hopping up and down in excitement; I could hear him saying to his mother, "Rutgers, Mom, that's the Rutgers team." I went over and asked him who his favorite player was; when he said Matee, I went to find her in line.

After the photos and the autographs, his mother told me, "He's going to remember this for the rest of his life." Someday, I knew, he'd tell his children about the day he met his idol. So how can you tell me it doesn't matter what Matee does?

I have far fewer years ahead of me than I do behind me in my coaching career, and it has become increasingly important to me that the young women I coach feel empowered to go out and make a difference in the world. Lee Iacocca famously asked, "Where have all the leaders gone?" The answer, of course, is that we're all leaders. Every one of us has the power to inspire the people around us and to change what has always been. I tell the young ladies I coach what my father told me: "This may not be about you, or for you, but for those who will come after you. You must stand."

I am not large in stature, but I have never doubted my ability to stand tall and to make a difference. That's what happened this year, and what a tremendously powerful thing it was! My young ladies stood up. They stood up for themselves and for what is right. And when they did, people all around the country stood up with us and for us.

And together, we stand.

Acknowledgments

I do not have words to fully express the depth of my gratitude and appreciation for Laura Tucker, my writer, without whom this book would not have been possible. She did more than faithfully collect my thoughts and words—she managed to assume my voice and leap straight into my soul. Writing this book was an extraordinary process—sometimes extraordinarily difficult—in part because I didn't really believe that any person who had not lived by my side for my entire life *could* succeed at this task. In this exceptional writer I found someone who truly was able to walk in my steps. She knows exactly what that means to me, as perhaps no one else can.

My agent, Laurie Bernstein, has been excited about this project from day one, more than three years ago. In fact, it was her boundless enthusiasm that convinced me of its value. I will never forget that she believed in me and in my story, and I am grateful for her zeal for bringing it to a wider audience. She is truly driven by excellence, and tireless in her pursuit of it. She will give you more hours than there are in the day, and I really appreciate her commitment and passion. If we were choosing teams, I'd want her on mine.

I continue to be astounded by Rachel Klayman, my editor at Crown, whose brilliance comes second only to her compassion. She *felt* this project, and her attention to detail and her perfectionism have inspired me to go to the next level. Like the best coaches, she makes me want to give more of myself, and I have played for her as hard as I could. I am grateful also to her incredible assistant, Mary Choteborsky; my amazing publicist, Penny Simon; the unflagging managing editor, Amy Boorstein; and to Jenny Frost, Tina Constable, Kristin Kiser, Katie Wainwright, Christine Aronson, Philip Patrick, Donna Passannante, Linnea Knollmueller, and Barbara Sturman. This is the best publishing team in America, and it's an honor to be a part of it.

In my life's journey, and in the path to make this book, there have been many angels. I do apologize for any names that I may have forgotten—charge the omissions to my head, not to my heart. Certainly, I am grateful for the staff at Rutgers, including Beth Schriefer, Mark Peterson, Corey Pegues, Tom Scott, Michelle Edwards, Celia Hill, Josh Reinitz, Chelsea Newton, Marla Rodriguez, and Heather Brocious, and Stacey Brann for her energy and organization.

I am grateful also to the Rutgers coaches: Jolette Law, Carlene Mitchell, Marianne Stanley, Tasha Pointer, Larry Lawler, Tom Lewis, and to the incomparable Betsy Yonkman, who repeatedly did the impossible with grace and good humor.

Thanks to my staff at Iowa: M. Dianne Murphy, Katie Slach, Cheryl Levick, Dr. John Powell, Faye Thompson, and my coaches, Marianna Freeman, Angie Lee, Linda Myers, Jen Bednarek, Larry Lawler, and Tim Eatman.

I must also thank my dear friend Ann Hill, who has been a believer since the beginning, as well as Bunny Shaeffer and my staff at Cheyney: Elaine Miller, Bill Morton, and Henry Hardy. And thanks to the managers of all my teams, over the years.

I want to thank everyone at Nike, especially Howard White and Jill Pizotti, for making me feel like a member of the family. I'd like to thank Dennis Coleman of Robeson Gray.

We are only as good as the players we get, and so I would like to thank Edward Black, Vanessa Watson, Dorothy Gaithers, and Apache.

A special acknowledgment goes to the university administrators who believed in me over the years: the late Dr. Wade Wilson, president of Cheyney, who gave a twenty-two-year-old a coaching job; and Ed Lawrence, my athletic director there; Dr. Christine Grant, the athletic director at Iowa, who convinced me to come out to the cold; Fred Grunninger, former athletic director at Rutgers, and Dr. Fran Lawrence, the president, who promised me that Rutgers women's basketball belonged on the national map; and Bob Mulcahey and Dr. Richard McCormick, my current athletic director and president, who made it happen.

Special thanks to our governor, Jon Corzine, for his commitment to the women's program throughout my tenure, and to the president of the NCAA, Myles Brand, whose words told the world what this team meant to you.

My mother, Thelma Stoner, and my late father, Charles Stoner, always insisted that our family be extremely close. On behalf of all my brothers and sisters, I thank them for teaching us what true family is all about. And I thank each and every one of my brothers and sisters—Verna Frazier, Tim Stoner, Madeline Williams, Richelle Davis, and Jack Stoner, and their children, Keonte and Teonta Williams; Erica and Leslie Davis; Tesha and Brendan Stoner; Natalie and Felicia Frazier; and Kena Stoner—for their help in my life and in the writing of this book. I pray that we will always be together, and that our children will always treat one another like siblings.

I have many relatives, but I'd like to personally thank my aunt Mildred Stith, Linda Stith Threadgill, and my late aunt Celeste, the true keepers of the family history, for their love, as well as the many photos they provided for this book. And I'd like to thank Mrs. Stringer, for sharing Bill with us, and with whom I have shared so many tears; you've always understood me.

I could not go about my work each day with any level of peace if I did not know that my family was loved and cared for. This would not be possible without Hyacinth Gray, who truly is a member of our family. And for all the little things that make a big difference, I thank Lisa Blackman and Rhona Stewart.

Anyone fortunate enough to enjoy any level of success can point to key people in their life who make it possible. My mom has always been a beacon of light for me when I'm down and don't think I can go on. She has been the backbone of our family, and I appreciate her faith and her daily strength.

My brother Tim has been by my side since childhood: my best friend, confidant, and lawyer. I have always respected your brilliance, and your commitment to equality for everyone. All of this is a dream that could not have come true without you. I love you, and thank you every day for your belief in me.

After my husband died, my sisters Madeline and Ricky gave of themselves, wholly and unconditionally. Thank you for helping me as I healed. You held my head and my heart, you shielded me, and you let me borrow your strength when I had none of my own. Thank you for taking care of my family—and of me. Madeline, know that I do appreciate your help with this book, especially your heroic efforts in the homestretch.

John Chaney is my mentor, and my best friend. All of what I know about basketball and about people I know from you. You have never swayed in your faith in the human spirit, or about the ethical principles upon which we should all guide our lives. Thank you for always taking the time to laugh with me and to support me. I would not be the coach that I am without your guidance, and only hope that I have proven a worthy student.

George Raveling's shoulders are broad enough to carry the burdens of the world, and I was one of those that he carried along when I thought I couldn't make it. You have been a guardian angel in my life, looking after me and showing me the way.

I always know that Coach John Thompson is just a phone call away, and I know that he has quietly been there, all along. I appreciate your friendship; thanks for extending your hand to help me, in basketball and in life.

I'd like to thank Pastor Soaries for serving as my spiritual guide and a personal friend to me and my family, as well as my extended basketball family. You and your wife, Donna, have been a source of strength and encouragement for all of us.

Barb Yenchik and Linda Argall are college friends who have

proven that a college friendship can last for life. By the way, thank you for buying my college graduation ring.

Janice Fitzgerald, thank you for being my soul sister and confidant, the person I cried to and told my deepest, darkest secrets to. Thank you for accepting me, even with all of my many flaws.

Margaret Alston, you were there during one of the darkest moments; I do not think I could have gotten through my illness or Nina's hospitalizations without you. Thank you for your many sacrifices and for your support and love. Jada Alston, your future is bright.

Dr. Griffith and Dr. Zimmerman, my college coaches, left an indelible impression on my young mind. You brought out the best in me always; thanks for continuing to be my friends.

Ongoing thanks to my many coaching colleagues and friends, who have always been there with a kind word. You bring honor to our profession. My special thanks to Pat Summitt. Our late-night talks enlighten and inspire me; I'm grateful to you for demonstrating that we can compete and still love each other.

Thanks to Debra Walker and Yolanda Laney, who shared their memories of a very important time for this book. They continue to remind me that it's not for four years, but forty-plus.

I owe a real debt of gratitude to the parents who have entrusted their daughters to me over the years. In your eyes I searched for the true meaning of what it is to coach, and through you I learned that it's not about the wins and the losses, but growing your daughter so that she's comfortable and confident as she takes on the world's challenges. For any of this to happen, you had to believe in me first.

Finally, I would like to thank each and every player whom I have had the privilege to coach. Thank you for having the confidence in me to allow me to be a part of your life. Your names are too numerous to mention, but your faces are the ones that I see when I think back on the tears and on the joy. Thank you.

About the Authors

C. VIVIAN STRINGER is the head coach of the Rutgers University women's basketball team. Stringer is a member of the Women's Basketball Hall of Fame, has been named National Coach of the Year three times by her peers, and is one of only three women's coaches to have celebrated 750 victories.

Stringer was the first coach, men's or women's, to lead three different teams to the Final Four (Cheyney University in 1982, the University of Iowa in 1993, Rutgers University in 2000 and again in 2007). She also served as an assistant coach of the U.S. national women's team when they won a gold medal at the 2004 Olympics. The U.S. Sports Academy's award for women's coaching is named in her honor.

A native of Edenborn, Pennsylvania, she is a member of the Alumni Hall of Fame at her alma mater, Slippery Rock University. She has two sons, David and Justin, and a daughter, Nina, and lives in New Jersey.

LAURA TUCKER has coauthored books on a wide range of topics. She lives in Brooklyn, New York, with her husband and daughter.